George Washington Curtis

Horses, Cattle, Sheep and Swine

Origin, history, improvement, description, characteristics, merits, objections, adaptability, etc., of each of the different breeds, with hints on selection, care and management, including methods of practical breeder. Vol. 2

George Washington Curtis

Horses, Cattle, Sheep and Swine
Origin, history, improvement, description, characteristics, merits, objections, adaptability, etc., of each of the different breeds, with hints on selection, care and management, including methods of practical breeder. Vol. 2

ISBN/EAN: 9783337328474

Printed in Europe, USA, Canada, Australia, Japan

Cover: Foto ©Andreas Hilbeck / pixelio.de

More available books at **www.hansebooks.com**

HORSES, CATTLE, SHEEP AND SWINE.

Origin, History, Improvement, Description, Characteristics, Merits, Objections, Adaptability, Etc., of Each of the Different Breeds,

WITH

Hints on Selection, Care and Management, Including Methods of Practical Breeders in the United States and Canada.

Illustrated.

BY

GEO. W. CURTIS, M. S. A.,
Director Texas Experiment Station, and Professor of Agriculture
in the Agricultural and Mechanical College of Texas.

Second Edition—Revised and Enlarged.

1893.
THE RURAL PUBLISHING COMPANY,
NEW YORK.

PREFACE.

IN THE PREPARATION of the second edition I have aimed to use to best advantage the valuable suggestions of my co-workers in other states, who so warmly endorsed the first edition by promptly adopting it for text use, and the no less valuable hints from farmers and stockmen who so kindly judged my work from their own standpoint of practical value on the farm.

From the few who harshly criticised I have also learned, and the critics may be, therefore, thanked for giving aid, although not so intended.

To the personal friends who have given their encouragement and aid in the prosecution of my work, I can only offer my sincere appreciation, and express the hope that what I have accomplished may, in measure, meet their honest approbation.

COLLEGE-STATION, TEXAS,
JANUARY 1, 1893. GEO. W. CURTIS.

PREFACE TO FIRST EDITION.

From early boyhood I have been a lover of good stock, familiar with the everyday, practical work in handling and feeding; and when, as a student in one of our agricultural colleges, my attention was first drawn to the need for a suitable text-book on domestic animals, I began a more extended study, with the purpose in view which I have since striven to accomplish.

In presenting this volume to the public, I desire especially to acknowledge the kindly encouragement received from my co-workers in the line of agricultural instruction. Many, like myself, have been giving lectures to their students on the subjects treated in these pages, and, from very lack of time, the lectures have been incomplete and unsatisfactory. The urgent requests which have reached me, especially during the past year, have greatly encouraged me to push forward the work. From another class—the general stockman and farmer—has come a still more urgent demand for information of this character. I have received many inquiries which these pages will answer, and, while the successful stockman is one who understands his work, I trust all will find much of interest and something of profit in their perusal.

The statements of actual methods pursued by successful breeders in different parts of the country will be found of great value. There are many young farmers, and perhaps some older ones, who are in need of information of a practical kind regarding the "points" in handling stock, and for all such, the letters from practical men given in the Chapters on Care and Management are worthy most careful study.

In all assertions as to average weights for the different breeds, it must be remembered that animals are frequently found which exceed the weights given, and others, just as frequently, which fall below them. It is very difficult to make statements of this kind which will not be subject, perhaps justly, to criticism from partisans of the several breeds; but it has been my aim to give what I believe to be the truth, regardless of whose shoulders it may strike most heavily.

The statements regarding ease of acclimation in the fever belt are made after a very careful study of the subject for the last five years, and an extensive correspondence with breeders and importers of northern bred stock—especially cattle—in the states bordering the Gulf of Mexico.

It is believed that full credit has been given for every quotation; but

I desire to make especial mention of the Agricultural Press. From many papers I have quoted—from all, derived something of value which has aided me in my work. The following list, while it does not include all, represents most of the periodicals devoted wholly or in part to live stock to which I am in any way indebted: *Turf, Field and Farm*, New York; *Breeder's Gazette*, Chicago; *National Live-Stock Journal*, Chicago; *American Agriculturist*, New York; *Western Agriculturist*, Quincy, Ills.; *Canadian Live-Stock Journal*, Hamilton, Ont., Canada; *American Sheep Breeder*, Chicago; *Herds and Flocks*, Chicago; *Hoard's Dairyman*, Fort Atkinson, Wis.; *Spirit of the Times*, New York; *Country Gentleman*, Albany, N. Y.; *Rural New-Yorker*, New York; *Southern Cultivator*, Atlanta, Ga.; *American Farmer*, Fort Wayne, Ind.; *Farm and Home*, Springfield, Mass.; *Breeder's Journal*, Beecher, Ill.; *Texas Farm and Ranch*, Dallas; *Texas Live-Stock Journal*, Fort Worth; and the *Texas Stockman and Farmer*, of San Antonio.

To many breeders I am indebted for information respecting various matters of interest, and to each I would express my appreciation of the aid thus kindly given. Among others to whom I am indebted in a personal way, I can not fail to mention my father, Lyman J. Curtis; to the early training on the farm, under his—at times severely strict—direction, I owe much of whatever I have since been able to accomplish; the later instruction of my valued friend, Professor S. A. Knapp, is remembered with pleasure and profit. Of more immediate importance has been the faithful assistance of my wife; without her aid, relieving me from all details of correspondence and clerical work, it would have been impossible to publish this volume for at least another year. To my co-worker, Professor F. A. Gulley, I am indebted for valuable suggestions; to Professor Louis L. McInnis, Chairman of our Faculty, for various courtesies; and to my assistant, Mr. J. F. Duggar, and Foreman of Farm, Mr. J. H. Alsworth, I return thanks for relief from routine work which would otherwise have required my personal attention.

THE AUTHOR.

STATE AGRL. AND MECHL. COLLEGE,
COLLEGE STATION, TEX.,
August, 1888.

CONTENTS.

PART FIRST.

THE DIFFERENT BREEDS OF HORSES.

CHAPTER I.	PAGE
PERCHERONS	10

CHAPTER II.	
FRENCH DRAFT	15

CHAPTER III.	
BELGIANS	19

CHAPTER IV.	
CLYDESDALES	22

CHAPTER V.	
ENGLISH SHIRES	27

CHAPTER VI.	
SUFFOLK PUNCH	31

CHAPTER VII.	
CLEVELAND BAYS	34

CHAPTER VIII.	
FRENCH COACH	37

CHAPTER IX.	
OLDENBURG COACH	40

CHAPTER X.	
GERMAN COACH	42

CHAPTER XI.	PAGE
HACKNEYS	44

CHAPTER XII.	
THOROUGHBREDS	47

CHAPTER XIII.	
AMERICAN SADDLERS	58

CHAPTER XIV.	
AMERICAN TROTTERS	61

CHAPTER XV.	
ORLOFF TROTTERS	90

CHAPTER XVI.	
SHETLAND PONIES	90

CHAPTER XVII.	
WELSH PONIES	93

CHAPTER XVIII.	
EXMOOR PONIES	93

CHAPTER XIX.	
MEXICAN PONIES	94

CHAPTER XX.	
INDIAN PONIES	96

CHAPTER XXI.	
HINTS ON SELECTION, CARE AND MANAGEMENT	99

PART SECOND.

THE DIFFERENT BREEDS OF CATTLE.

CHAPTER XXII.	PAGE
HOLSTEIN-FRIESIANS	116

CHAPTER XXIII.	
JERSEYS	125

CHAPTER XXIV.	
GUERNSEYS	131

CHAPTER XXV.	
AYRSHIRES	135

CHAPTER XXVI.	
DUTCH BELTED	140

CHAPTER XXVII.	
AMERICAN HOLDERNESS	144

CHAPTER XXVIII.	
BROWN SWISS	146

CHAPTER XXIX.	
BRITTANIES	152

CHAPTER XXX.	PAGE
KERRIES	154

CHAPTER XXXI.	
SHORTHORNS	157

CHAPTER XXXII.	
RED POLLED	163

CHAPTER XXXIII.	
DEVONS	167

CHAPTER XXXIV.	
LONGHORNS	173

CHAPTER XXXV.	
NORMANDIES	176

CHAPTER XXXVI.	
NORTH WALES BLACK	180

CHAPTER XXXVII.	
PEMBROKES	184

CONTENTS. vii

CHAPTER XXXVIII.	PAGE	CHAPTER XLIII.	PAGE
HEREFORDS	185	SIMMENTHAL	207
CHAPTER XXXIX.		CHAPTER XLIV.	
GALLOWAYS	191	BRAHMINS (ZEBU)	210
CHAPTER XL.		CHAPTER XLV.	
ABERDEEN-ANGUS	196	WEST HIGHLANDS	215
CHAPTER XLI.		CHAPTER XLVI.	
POLLED DURHAMS	201	TEXANS	220
CHAPTER XLII.			
SUSSEX	204		
		CHAPTER XLVII.	
		HINTS ON SELECTION, CARE AND MANAGEMENT	223

PART THIRD.
THE DIFFERENT BREEDS OF SHEEP.

CHAPTER XLVIII.	PAGE	CHAPTER LII.	PAGE
MERINOS	236	SHROPSHIRES	264
Atwoods	241		
Paulars	243	CHAPTER LIII.	
Dickinsons	246	HAMPSHIRES	267
Black Tops	249	CHAPTER LIV.	
Delaines	250	OXFORDSHIRES	271
CHAPTER XLIX.		CHAPTER LV.	
HORNED DORSETS	255	COTSWOLDS	274
CHAPTER L.		CHAPTER LVI.	
CHEVIOTS	257	LEICESTERS	278
CHAPTER LI.		CHAPTER LVII.	
SOUTHDOWNS	260	LINCOLNS	282
		CHAPTER LVIII.	
		HINTS ON SELECTION, CARE AND MANAGEMENT	286

PART FOURTH.
THE DIFFERENT BREEDS OF SWINE.

CHAPTER LIX.	PAGE	CHAPTER LXVI.	PAGE
BERKSHIRES	294	DAVIS VICTORIAS	312
CHAPTER LX.		CHAPTER LXVII.	
POLAND-CHINAS	298	CHESHIRES	314
CHAPTER LXI.		CHAPTER LXVIII.	
DUROC-JERSEYS	301	SMALL YORKSHIRES	317
CHAPTER LXII.		CHAPTER LXIX.	
CHESTER-WHITES	305	ESSEX	320
CHAPTER LXIII.		CHAPTER LXX.	
TODD'S IMPROVED CHESTER-WHITES	307	NEAPOLITANS	322
CHAPTER LXIV.		CHAPTER LXXI.	
GOTHLANDS	309	ENGLISH, or BLACK SUFFOLKS	323
CHAPTER LXV.		CHAPTER LXXII.	
CURTIS VICTORIAS	310	AMERICAN, or WHITE SUFFOLKS	324
		CHAPTER LXXIII.	
		HINTS ON SELECTION, CARE AND MANAGEMENT	325

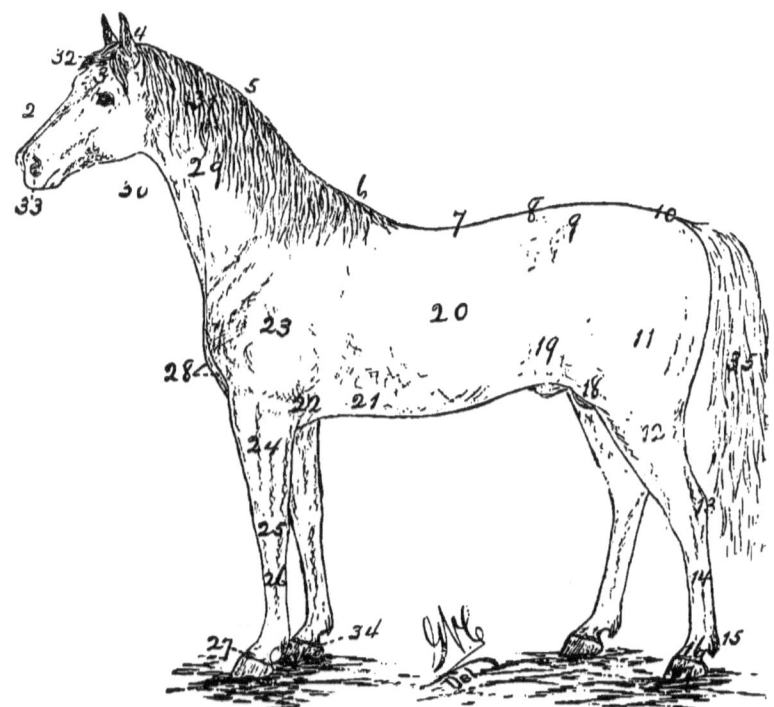

1, Muzzle; 2, Race, Nose-bone, or Face; 3, Forehead; 4, Poll; 5, Crest; 6, Withers or Shoulder-points; 7, Back; 8, Loins; 9, Hook, Hip or Haunch-bone; 10, Croup-bone, or Upper-rump; 11, Upper-thigh, or Quarter; 12, Lower-thigh, or Leg; 13, Hock; 14, Hind Cannon, or Shank-bone; 15, Fetlock-joint, sometimes covered with long hair called the "Feather"; 16, Pastern; 17, Hoof; 18, Stifle; 19, Flank; 20, Side, or Ribs; 21, Girth; 22, Elbow; 23, Shoulder; 24, Fore-arm; 25, Knee; 26, Front Cannon; 27, Coronet; 28, Breast; 29, Neck; 30, Throat, or Throttle; 31, Mane; 32, Foretop; 33, Nostril; 34, Bulbs of the Heel; 35, Tail.

PART FIRST.

HORSES.

DRAFT BREEDS.

		PAGE
PERCHERONS	Chapter I.	10
FRENCH DRAFT	" II.	15
BELGIANS	" III.	19
CLYDESDALES	" IV.	22
ENGLISH SHIRES	" V.	27
SUFFOLK PUNCH	" VI.	31

HEAVY CARRIAGE BREEDS.

CLEVELAND BAYS	Chapter VII.	34
FRENCH COACH	" VIII.	37
OLDENBURG COACH	" IX.	40
GERMAN COACH	" X.	42
HACKNEYS	" XI.	44

RUNNING AND SADDLE BREEDS.

THOROUGHBREDS	Chapter XII.	47
AMERICAN SADDLERS	" XIII.	58

TROTTING BREEDS.

AMERICAN TROTTERS	Chapter XIV.	61
ORLOFF TROTTERS	" XV.	90

SMALL, OR PONY BREEDS.

SHETLAND PONIES	Chapter XVI.	90
WELSH PONIES	" XVII.	93
EXMOOR PONIES	XVIII	93
MEXICAN PONIES	" XIX.	94
INDIAN PONIES	" XX.	96

HINTS ON SELECTION, CARE AND MANAGEMENT.

CHAPTER XXI. 99

Chapter I.

PERCHERONS.

The Percheron is an old French breed, long noted for rapid and effective draft work, and always supposed to owe much of its excellence to Eastern blood. When steps were taken to compile the Percheron Stud Book of France, careful inquiry revealed a much greater predominance of Arabian blood than had been previously claimed.

It was then found that—as Mr. Sanders, in his treatise on Horse Breeding puts it—

"What the Darley Arabian was to the English Thoroughbred, and the gray Arabian Smetanxa to the Orloff, the gray Arabian Gallipoli has been to the Percheron horse of France"

Du Hays (American Translation of the Percheron Horse), after expressing his belief in its descent from Arabian blood, says:

"We cannot, however, find in history the written positive proof that the Percheron is an Arab, but we believe it easy, by fair historical deduction, to prove what he is in fact."

The same author, speaking of the improvement of the breed, states that:

"The Percherons must have been especially modified by contact with the breed of Brittany, where their striking characteristics are now met with in a large number of individuals."

In Volume I. of the American Percheron Stud Book we find this statement:

"Aside from the history and traditions of the country, the Percheron horse himself furnishes unmistakable evidence in his form, disposition, color and general characteristics that he is closely allied to the Arab."

Again, from the same source, we quote:

"As the immense draft horses of the North (Flemish) were closely allied to, if not identical with, the large breed that prevailed in Normandy and La Perche, prior to the modification produced by the introduction of the blood of the Arabian and the Barb, heretofore alluded to, it was very natural that, when the Percheron breeders found it desirable to increase the size of their horses, their eyes should be turned towards this kindred race, from which other countries had already drawn so heavily for the same purpose. Accordingly we find that mares in large numbers were taken from these northern departments, and from Belgium, under the various names of Belgians, Boulonnais, Mares of Picardy, etc., and were bred to the stallions of La Perche. Stallions from the same country were also extensively introduced, under various names and of slightly differing types. But, notwithstanding the multiplicity of names arising from the different departments in which they had been bred, and the slight variation in form that existed, they were, after all, nothing more nor less than the Flanders Draft Horse—the same blood that had already exercised so potent an influence upon the horse stock of Great Britain."

PERCHERONS.

PERCHERON STALLION, JOSEPH, 6471.
Property of J. W. Akin, Scipio. N Y

To sum up, then, briefly, there is ample proof of the use of the celebrated Arabian stallions (both gray) Godolphin and Gallipoli in the formation of the Percheron breed; and there is little doubt that—like the heavy British breeds—it owes its superior size to crosses with the large horse of Flanders.

Importations to the United States of what are now claimed to have been Percherons were made as early as 1851, but they were called simply French Horses. In 1866 Mr. W. S. Ficklin, of Charlottesville, Va., imported several Percheron horses under their proper name; and in 1868 William T. Walters, of Baltimore, returning from France, after a sojourn of several years, brought with him a considerable number of these horses; he also caused to be translated and published that interesting little work, the "Percheron Horse," by Du Hays, from which we have quoted.

And now a word in regard to the Perchero-Norman controversy. In 1854 one of the stallions imported in 1851, under the name of French Horses, was sold to Messrs. Dillon & Co., of Normal, Ill. This horse was exhibited, with many colts of his get, at county and state fairs, under the name "Norman," and soon obtained a high degree of favor among horsemen of Illinois and neighboring states. In this way began the confusion of names which has continued more or less unabated until within the past few years, and is, even now, a matter of considerable uncertainty and vexation. When the first steps were taken to form an American Stud Book, in 1876, it was proposed to adopt the name "Norman." For reasons which he considered satisfactory, Mr. Sanders, secretary of the association, changed the name to "Percheron Norman Stud Book," the association afterward ratifying the change. Many breeders of French horses, however, were in favor of the term Norman, and accordingly withdrew from the offending society and began the publication of the National Register of Norman Horses, all draft horses imported from France being eligible for record. There was, if such were possible, greater confusion than before, the names Norman, Norman-Percheron, Percheron-Norman, Percheron and French Draft obtaining equal prominence, and, indeed, were used interchangeably as synonymous terms for the same breed.

In 1883, the *Societe Hippique Perchonne* was organized in France, and the Percheron-Norman Society immediately, and wisely, adopted the name by which the breed is recognized in its native country. The name was thus changed to the Percheron Society, and their record the Percheron Stud Book of America. Thus the matter of nomenclature rests for the present; each breed has its partisans; both are valuable. While we do not propose to decide between them, yet we cannot forbear noticing this fact: the Norman Register admits all draft horses imported from France. The Percheron Society requires that all animals

Louis 6337 (2430)
PERCHERON STALLION.
Property of H. A. Briggs, Elkhorn, Wis.

imported after January 1st, 1884, must be recorded in the Percheron Stud Book of France. The value of this restriction, in preserving the purity of the Percheron breed, is at once apparent, and cannot fail to attract favorable notice from all lovers of thoroughbred stock.

Secretary S. D. Thompson, Chicago, Ill., writes under date of December 20, 1892:

"The Percheron Association is in a flourishing condition, the number of entries up to date being greater than those of all the other draft horse associations combined. The fifth volume of the Percheron Stud Book is now in press, and will be issued at an early date."

DESCRIPTION AND CHARACTERISTICS.

Color varies, gray—mostly dappled—predominating, while there are many pure blacks and bays, and all shades of gray, from the darkest iron to almost pure white. The body is low, square and full in all points, with magnificent head, and a neck which, for beauty, would not disgrace the proudest of Barbs. Legs are short in proportion, and while very massive, are yet fine and close knit. Percheron breeders claim almost perfect immunity from bone and leg diseases, such as ringbone, splint, wind-galls, etc. Our own experience with the breed, particularly with the half-blood colts from native mares, has not justified an admission of this claim, and we feel compelled to state that some breeders, and many who have used the Percheron grades for heavy farm or other work, have expressed a belief that the Percherons are even more subject to these troubles than some of the other breeds.

The Percheron is a draft breed, mature stallions weighing from 1,600 to 2,100 or 2,200 pounds, and their get from ordinary mares weighing from 1,200 to 1,700 or 1,800 pounds, when grown. They are quick, active and intelligent. Some have thought them vicious, and we have known a number of **ill-tempered** representatives of the breed; but it is more than likely that the troublesome temper was caused by unskillful or "vicious" grooms. Quite a number have been brought to Texas from Northern states, and some imported direct from France. While they stand the climate as well as any of the large breeds, yet we cannot say—as do some of their partisan breeders—that they acclimate with perfect safety.

Chapter II.

FRENCH DRAFT (NORMAN).

From the chapter on Percherons will be gathered somewhat of the author's ideas as to the name and present status of the Norman or French Draft. As there stated, the term French Draft includes not only the Percheron, but also the other heavy families or breeds of French horses. We can see much good sense and considerable necessity in perpetuating the registry of French Draft horses; many have been and are still being imported to the United States which are not eligible to record in the Percheron Stud Book by reason only of nativity in another province than Perche; and many of these horses stand as individuals, and produce a progeny, second to none of the modern draft breeds. The National Register of Norman Horses admits all draft horses of thorough French blood, no matter to what breed or family they may belong. We can see no just cause for the apparently interminable wrangle between those who set themselves up as champions of, and authority on, respectively, the French Draft and Percheron breeds. The former includes the latter, and the latter is now undoubtedly more closely bred and limited as to registry than the former. There is no foundation that we can see for claiming that any breed should have exclusive credit for improvement in American draft horses, and there is no doubt that very many of the French Draft horses now in the United States have no superior among even the most select Percherons.

The precise origin of the French Draft horse would be hard to trace. So many strains or families, all bred out from a common center, and improved in whatever direction best suited the demands of any peculiar locality, would naturally tend to break somewhat the line of descent. According to Youatt, who wrote in 1831, the Province of Normandy was the one most noted at that time for its horses, the French government buying annually from the Norman stock for use in the other provinces.

Prof. Low, in his great work on the Domestic Animals of Great Britain, published in 1842, noted the same facts, and attributed it to the better grass and food conditions found in this province. All the heavy horses of the continent, and through these, of the British Islands, may be traced to the low, rich regions of middle and southwest Europe. The old Black Horse of Flanders doubtless owed his great size to these natural conditions of vegetation, and may very properly be considered a sort of mile-post—a stepping stone—between the horses left in that

FRENCH DRAFT STALLION, SUPRENANT, 5355 (721).

Color, black; foaled 1883; winner of Diploma, 1885, and Medal, 1886, at National Concours of France; imported by Messrs. SPRINGER & WILLARD, Oskaloosa, Iowa.

FRENCH DRAFT (NORMAN). 17

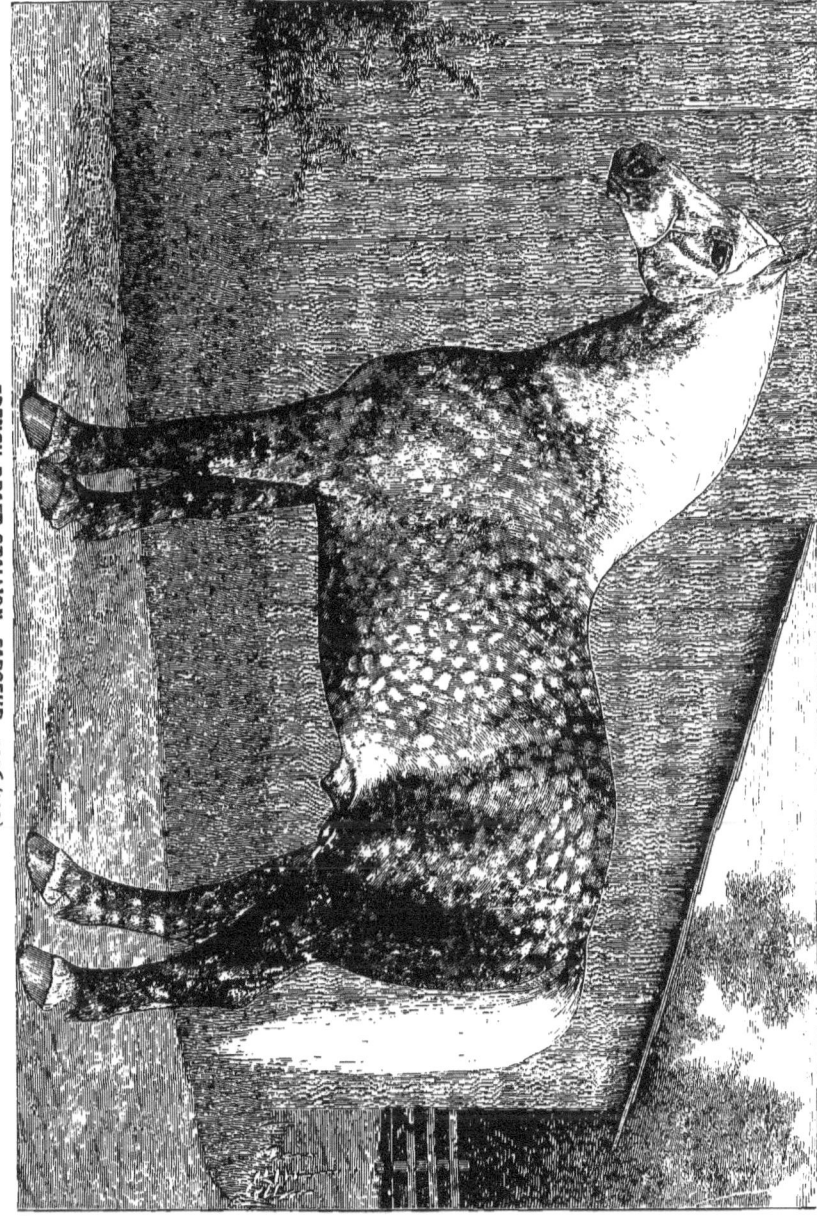

FRENCH DRAFT STALLION, FARCEUR, 5356 (140).

Color, dapple gray; foaled 1882; weight, 2,000 lbs.; winter First Prize at National Concours of France, 1886; imported by Messrs. SPRINGER & WILLARD, Oskaloosa, Iowa.

country by the warlike nations of northeast Europe in the frequent invasions west and southward, and the modern draft horses of France.

The first importation of Norman horses to the United States was made about 1839, but not until 1850-60 were many imported to the Western states. Since that time, however, they have become widely and favorably known. In the South they are better known than the Percherons, and do as well in all respects.

The National Norman Horse Association, organized in 1876, was, in 1884, changed to and incorporated as the National French Draft Horse Association. C. E. Stubbs, of Fairfield, Ia., is the present secretary.

DESCRIPTION AND CHARACTERISTICS.

As bred and known in the United States, there is so little difference between the French Draft and the Percheron as to preclude any necessity for statement, other than has been already given in the preceding chapter (which see). The only point to which attention may be called is that there appears to be a wider diversity in color and a greater variation from type among French Draft than among Percheron horses. In this connection, compare also the illustrations of French Draft and Percheron horses, all of which have been carefully selected as representative animals of the breeds in question.

Chapter III.

BELGIAN DRAFT.

A comparatively new breed to America, but one which is earning marked distinction on merit alone. The Belgian Draft is a direct descendant of the original Black Horse of Flanders, and has been developed in unison with his neighbor breed, the Boulonnais; indeed, the latter bids fair to become a member, part and parcel, of the former. There has been more or less activity among Belgian importers to the United States since about 1870. Dr. A. G. Van Hoorebeke, of Monmouth, Ill., was probably the first to import, and his early importations in 1866 and next succeeding years were called Boulonnais. Of late years, however, Belgium has insisted, and rightly, on giving her name to her peculiar horse stock, and the Doctor's later importations, as well as those of Messers. Massion & Son, of Minonk, Ill., and other reliable importers, have been under the name by which they are now recognized.

The American Association of Importers and Breeders of Belgian Draft Horses was organized in 1877, with J. D. Conner, Jr., of Wabash, Ind., secretary. All draft horses imported from Belgium prior to January 1st, 1888, on satisfactory proof of same, are eligible to registry. Any horse imported from Belgium after January 1st, 1888, is not eligible to registry unless previously registered in the Government Register of Belgium, known as the Society of Belgian Stock Farmers. Animals bred in the United States from registered sires and dams are eligible to registry under the rather peculiar caption: "Native Full-Bloods."

DESCRIPTION AND CHARACTERISTICS.

Color generally bay or brown-black, but sorrel, roan and other colors are occasionally found. In size they are about equal to the Percheron, perhaps somewhat larger, say an average of from 1,650 to 2,200 lbs. for mature stallions. The head is small and close fleshed; the neck, short and very powerful; chest, wide and deep; back short and broad, full over kidneys; hips long; legs short, with wide, flat bone, heavy muscle, and feet of proverbial soundness. As compared with the Percheron, they are more compact—"blocky"—and more nearly round in the body, but withal, resemble them so closely in many points as to warrant a second look, even from an expert, before passing judgment as to breed of the animal in question.

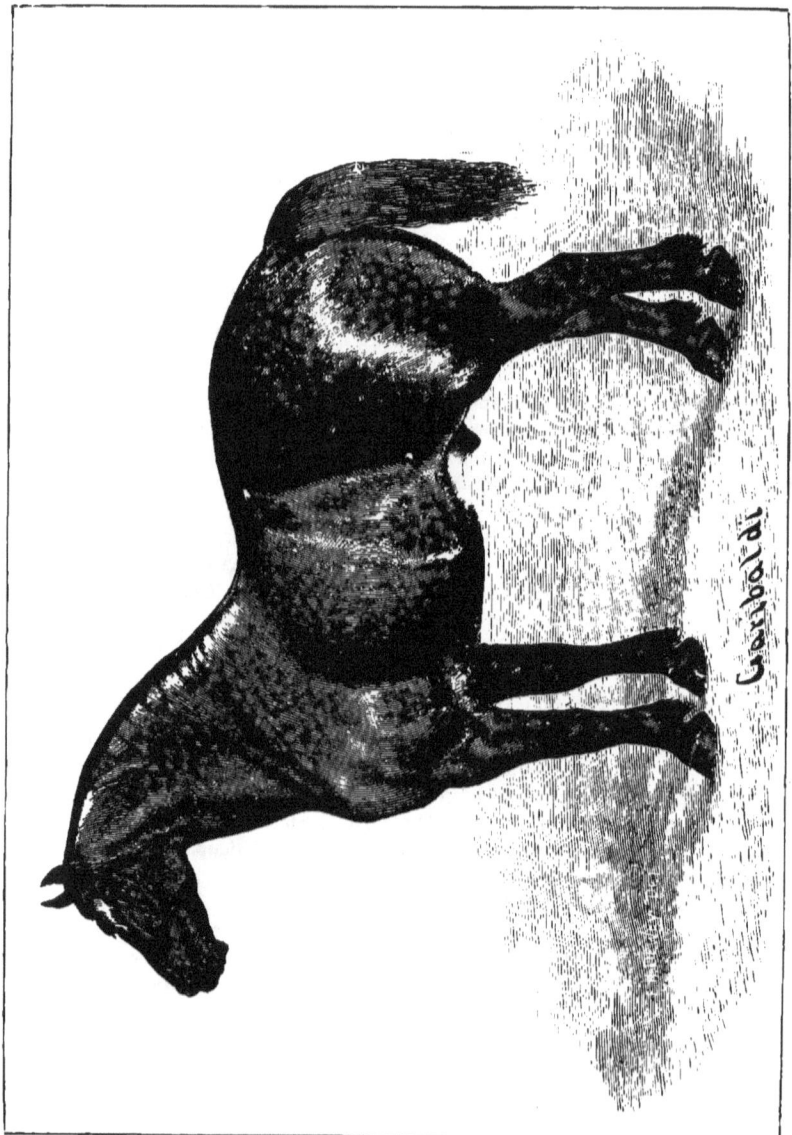

BELGIAN DRAFT STALLION, GARIBALDI.
Property of Nikolas Massion, Minonk, Ill.

BELGIAN DRAFT.

BELGIAN DRAFT MARE, BRUNETTE.

Chapter IV.

CLYDESDALES.

Like the Percheron, the French Draft, and in fact all of the other Draft Breeds, the Clydesdale owes its original merit to the Black Horse of Flanders—a lineal descendant of the great Black Horse of Northern Europe, which, according to Professor Low, inhabited "in the wild state the vast regions of marsh and forest which stretched all through Europe to the Euxine [Black] sea." The first mention we have of large horses in Scotland is found in a particular edict of "Safe Conduct" from King Edward I., issued in 1352, and referring to "ten large horses," which were to be taken to Teviotdale. Although it is not definitely stated whence these horses came, yet from the fact that the edict was obtained by the Earl of Douglas, it may be reasonably inferred that the horses were taken from Douglas Castle, in the upper portion of Lanarkshire, otherwise termed Clydesdale; and from the additional fact that the Earl of Douglas was an ancestor of that famous breeder of Clydesdales, the Duke of Hamilton, we may reasonably suppose that these "ten large horses" were an important factor in laying the foundation of the original Lanarkshire breed.

And now, in relation to the use of the Black Horse of Flanders, we have the following from the retrospective Volume of the Clydesdale Stud Book:

"Some time between 1715 and 1720, John Paterson, of Lochlyoch, on the estate and in the Parish of Carmichael, grandson of one John Paterson, who died at Lochlyoch in 1682, went to England, and brought from thence a Flemish stallion, which is said to have so greatly improved the breed in the Upper Ward as to have made them noted all over Scotland."

From the same authority we quote:

"The Lochlyoch mares were generally browns and blacks, with white faces and a little white on their legs; they had gray hairs in their tails, occasionally gray hairs over their bodies, and invariably a white spot on their belly, this later being recognized as a mark of distinct purity of blood."

There can be little doubt of the presence of Flemish blood in the present Clydesdale race. But we are strongly inclined to give credit, not so much to the heavy, clumsy Black Horse, as to the infusion of some lighter but stronger blood, which has given to the breed its well known courage and action, in marked contrast to the sluggish movements of the old Cart or Lincoln horse of England. The colors of the Lochlyoch mares—the last of which died out some thirty-five years ago—considered in connection with the predominant bay color of modern Clydesdales,

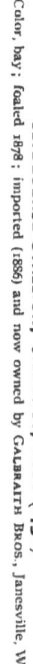

CLYDESDALE STALLION, GILDEROY, 2826 (1438).
Color, bay; foaled 1878; imported (1886) and now owned by GALBRAITH BROS., Janesville, Wis.

would point toward the old Cleveland horse as a probable factor in improvement, and this view is strengthened by many characteristics common to both breeds.

The name of the breed, Clydesdale, would indicate its restriction to that particular locality, but these horses were very generally bred in other portions of Scotland, and obtained their name solely from the fact that in Clydesdale they were earlier brought to a high degree of merit and pushed into more prominent notice.

Importation to America, both Canada and the United States, has been active and long continued. Through the kindness of Mr. C. F. Mills, Springfield, Ill., the present secretary of the association, we are enabled to give the following list comprising all the early importations of Clydes:

"In 1842, Gray Clyde 78 was imported by Archibald Ward, of Markham, Ontario.

"1845, Sovereign 181 was imported by R. Johnson, Scarboro, Ontario.

"1847, Marquis of Clyde 101 was imported by Thomas Summerville, Whitby, Ontario.

"1850, Cumberland 106 was imported by David Roundtree, Jr., Weston, Ontario.

"1855, Bay Wallace 5 was imported by William Cochrane, Claremont, Ontario.

"1855, Clydesdale Jock 33 was imported by John R. Torrence, of Markham, Ontario, and Jock of the Side 760 by Simon Connor, Markham, Ontario.

"1855, Merry Farmer 20 was imported by Mrs. A. Ward, of Markham, Ontario, and Byron 197 by James Dalziel, of Chesterfield, Ontario.

"1857, Rob Roy 90, by Thomas Irving, Montreal, Quebec; and Black Douglas 27 by William Miller, Pickering, Ontario. Prior to 1860 a number of very choice Clydesdale stallions were imported into Ohio by Fullington & Co., none of which have been recorded."

Since 1860 their introduction has been very rapid, and the number bred in America has more than kept pace with imported stock.

The Clydesdale Society of America was organized in 1877, and the first volume of the American Clydesdale Stud Book was issued in 1882; imported animals, to be eligible, must be recorded in the Clydesdale Stud Book of Great Britain and Ireland; and American-bred stallions or mares must trace to recorded sires or dams, or have four or five recorded top crosses.

DESCRIPTION AND CHARACTERISTICS OF MODERN CLYDESDALE:

Color, either bay, brown or black, with usually a white strip in the face—"blaze"—and more or less white on the feet and lower parts of the legs; occasionally there is found a dun, chestnut, or even sorrel. The color which may be called peculiar to the breed is a light bay, fading to still lighter bay at the flanks, between the thighs, and forward on the belly line. In size they are classed with the large breeds, stallions ranging from 1,700 to 2,100 pounds, and mares from 1,200 to 1,600 pounds. In appearance the Clydesdale horse is a large, tall, rangy animal, with a long head, medium neck, strong legs, heavily fringed with hair below

CLYDESDALE STALLION, TINWALD CHIEFTAIN.
Property of Galbraith Bros., Janesville, Wis.

the knee, and long slanting shoulders—the latter a point well worth noticing as inclining toward greater activity than is usual with the large breeds.

As compared with the Percheron or the French Draft, the Clydesdale horse is longer legged, longer bodied, and of more quiet temperament. Our observation and experience with the half blood colts from native mares fully bear out the assertion that they are, almost without exception, kind, quiet, intelligent and easily broken. One very prominent characteristic is their naturally fast walk. The American farmer is not slow to appreciate the superior value of a team that will plow three acres of ground in a day, as against one that with the same plow, will turn but two acres; and this fact has done much to advance the interests of the Clydesdale in America. The tendency of late to widen the breach between Clydesdales and English Shires has induced breeders of the former to look more to appearance and action, and gradually lower the average in weight—thus leaving to breeders of the latter a market demand for great weight and appearance, with action somewhat in the background.

A point to which many object is the fringe of long hair at the fetlock, already referred to; the objection, however well founded, has caused certain breeders to attempt a reduction of the characteristic—with what success remains to be seen. In the South the Clydes are perhaps not so well known as the French Draft; but the few shipments made are said to have done remarkably well. It is claimed, indeed, that no other horse of the heavy breeds can so well endure the Southern climate.

The engravings give an accurate idea of representative Clydesdales, and illustrate, at the same time, the superior character of Galbraith Brothers' stud.

Chapter V.

ENGLISH SHIRES.

From the preceding chapter on Clydesdales, we have seen that all of the modern draft breeds are descended from the great Black Horse of northern Europe, with such modifications as different soils, vegetation, climate and care would induce. Referring to this breed, Prof. Low, of Edinburgh (already quoted), writing in 1842, after speaking of its occupying the entire west and southwest portions of the mainland, says:

"The same widely-spread race extends into England, where it presents itself with the same general characters as in the ancient countries of the Belgic Gauls, the Batavi, the Frisiandones, and others. It is found in numbers from the Humber to the Cam, occupying the rich fens of Lincoln and Cambridge, and extending westward through the counties of Huntingdon, Northampton, Leicester, Nottingham, Derby, Warwick and Stafford to the Severn. Although most abundant in districts of rich pastures, it has extended northward, and very widely southward into the counties of the Chalk, retaining the typical characters, but varied with the climate, food, and other circumstances affecting its culture and condition. In the commons and poorer grounds it presents the coarse pack-horse form, distinctive of the greater part of the older horses of England. But in the fens and richer cultivated country, it attains the strength and stature of the largest horses which the world produces."

From these early horses, then, have descended the modern Shires of England; but we must look further, under the head of improvement, to find how the unwieldy giant Lincolnshire or Black Cart-horse was finally moulded into the handsome, large but fairly active horse now known as English Shire. Of the first improvement, we get a good idea from Youatt (on the Horse), 1861, who says:

"All our heavy draft horses, and some even of the lighter kind, have been lately much crossed by the Flanders breed, and with evident improvement. Little has been lost in depth and bulk of carcase; but the fore hand has been raised, the legs have been flattened and deepened, and very much has been gained in activity. The slow, heavy black, with his 2½ miles an hour, has been changed into a lighter but yet exceedingly powerful horse, that will step four miles in the same time, and with perfect ease, and has considerably more endurance. * * * As the Racer is principally or purely of Eastern origin, so has the English Draft horse sprung chiefly from Flemish blood, and to that blood the agriculturist has recourse for the perfection of the breed."

During late years, the improvement of the Shire has been very great, breeders struggling successfully to secure less bulk with equal weight and added muscle. Probably the lighter horses of England, as well as the famous medium-sized "Dutch Mares," have had something to do in bringing about this very desirable change; certain it is, that the English Shire of to-day is a horse fit to walk in the front rank of any breed of modern draft horses.

ENGLISH SHIRE STALLION, BUCKDEN (Vol. 8), 3.

Color, chestnut; foaled 1883; imported (1886) and now owned by GALBRAITH BROS., Janesville, Wis.

ENGLISH SHIRE STALLION, GOTH, AT FARM WORK.
Property of Galbraith Bros., Janesville, Wis.

Importation to America has been slow. No very large importations had been made up to eight or ten years ago; but since that time, western farmers have found out their peculiar worth, and the demand thus created has led to great activity in importing circles. The American Shire Horse Association has been lately organized, with C. Burgess, of Wenona, Ill., secretary. The first volume of the English Stud Book for Shire or Cart Horses was published in 1880, since which time some seven volumes have appeared—a fact which in itself illustrates the remarkable demand upon English breeders to supply registered Shire stock for American shipment.

DESCRIPTION AND CHARACTERISTICS.

The full description given of the Clydesdale in preceding chapter, with some few changes, may be accepted as a correct description of the English Shire. Colors are about the same, with, perhaps, a predominance of blacks, browns and bays; but the darker shades of gray, both dappled and steel or iron gray, are more frequently met with. The "blaze," or bald face, and white feet and stockings, are marks common to both Shire and Clyde, and the same is true of the long hair at and above the fetlocks, commonly known as the "feather." English breeders adhere with rigid tenacity to their faith in purity of blood, as shown by the feather; while American importers and breeders are as surely convinced that the feather is not only worthless but positively injurious, by reason of keeping the feet in foul condition unless carefully cleaned and attended to. We can honestly admire the silken fringe of soft feather, but we must express our belief that its absence would detract nothing from the value of either Shire or Clyde. In point of size, the English Shire is larger of the two, and has, perhaps, less of that American objection—daylight—underneath. Importers, however, as a rule, have brought over the more compact and stylish Shires, and it is commonly no little trouble to decide by simple judgment of the individual, whether the animal is Clyde or Shire. (Compare, also, illustrations of the two breeds.)

In the South the Shires are little known, and we can say nothing as to their relative merits in our warm climate; but in the West they are becoming more popular with each succeeding year, and have an assured future along with the other draft breeds.

Chapter VI.

THE SUFFOLK PUNCH.

This breed of horses, which has for many years enjoyed such merited popularity in England, has of late years found substantial and growing favor with American breeders. The origin of the Suffolk Breed is somewhat obscure, but the best evidence obtainable indicates the use of Norman stallions on the best native Suffolkshire mares. That this is true is strongly evidenced by the Suffolk color—sorrel, or light chestnut—which has so often been found a compromise color between bay and gray; the former being represented in the native mares, the latter being the predominating color of the Norman stock.

As far back as 1745 the Suffolk was famed for its still prominent characteristic—draft; and notices of the breed at the drawing matches of that period may be unearthed among the old files of some of the English newspapers.

Improvement of the Suffolk has been very great, especially within the last quarter century. Formerly there was said to be a tendency to foot troubles, but in the modern breed this tendency has disappeared. Among the later breeders and improvers, we may mention Mr. Alfred I. Smith, of Woodbridge, Suffolkshire, England. Mr. Smith has been especially active in stimulating American demand for his sorrel favorites, and since 1861, when his stud was established, has furnished many of the noted prize winners at English fairs. In the United States, many of our most prominent importers of Shires and Percherons have lately been importing Suffolks, and, we understand, the demand is fast increasing. The incorporation of the American Suffolk Punch Horse Association—A. R. Galbraith, Janesville, Wis., secretary—places the breed in popular light, and insures the steady advance of Suffolk interests in the United States.

DESCRIPTION AND CHARACTERISTICS.

Color, almost invariably chestnut or sorrel; size, somewhat less than Shire or Clydesdale, having an average height of 15¾ to 16½ hands, and weighing at maturity from 1,400 to 1,800 lbs. The body is round, close and compact, with short, clean legs, and pasterns, free from the troublesome long hair of the Shire and Clyde. The shoulders are long, and lie well forward for draft; the bone is small but firm; the hind quarters long, heavy and well coupled to a short, close-knit back. The

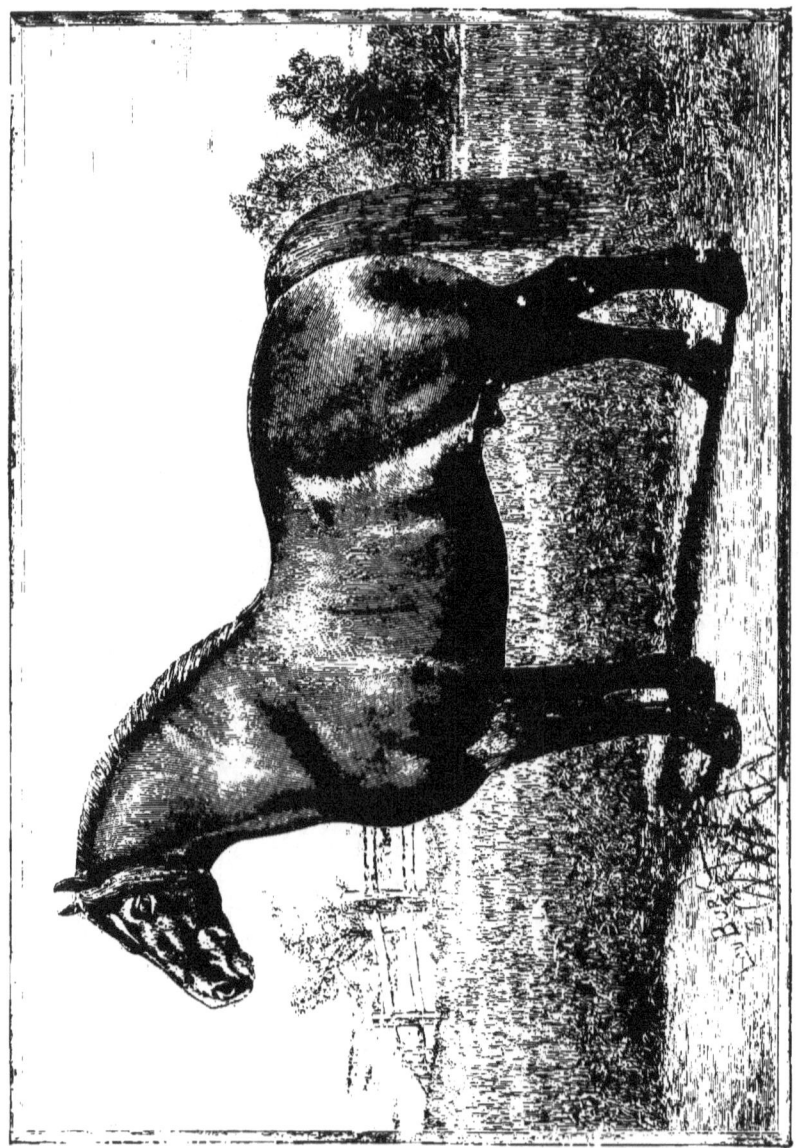

SUFFOLK PUNCH STALLION, LEISTON (1415).

Color, chestnut; foaled 1878; imported (1887) and now owned by GALBRAITH BROS., Janesville, Wis.

general appearance indicates a rather over medium-sized sorrel horse with heavy, round body and short legs. The Suffolk is emphatically a draft animal, valuable for remarkable steadiness and great faithfulness in the collar. He will pull every pound which is possible, and no whip is needed or should be used to urge his natural freedom in work. As a horse for the general farmer, it would be hard to find one more suitable —having a good, fast walk, an even "all-around" trot, and sufficient weight to save muscle work before plow or harrow.

Chapter VII.

CLEVELAND BAYS.

We have no authentic data regarding the origin of the Cleveland breed, but give what seems to be the most probable of the many theories advanced. Professor Low says:

"It has been formed by the same means as the Hunter, namely, by the progressive mixture of the blood of the Race Horse with the original breeds of the country."

A later writer regards it as an offshoot from the old Scandinavian horse, improved by careful breeding under the different climatic conditions of England. By others he is thought to be a lineal descendant of the old war horse in ages past. We think it probable that a gradual use of horses of higher breeding on heavy mares of the larger English breeds, combined with marked skill and care in handling, has finally resulted in the formation of this excellent breed. Certain it is, that about the beginning of the present century, the horses of Cleveland were in great demand, and their breeding was carried on with system and success; for a time they gradually declined in public favor, and indeed were threatened with total extinction, but during later years the breed has again advanced in favor, and, thanks to the efforts of the American Cleveland Bay Society (R. P. Stericker, of Springfield, Ill., secretary), is once more widely and favorably known. The name of the breed is taken from the district of Cleveland, in Yorkshire, England, where it was first known, and the term bay was added to indicate the prevailing color.

DESCRIPTION AND CHARACTERISTICS.

Color, invariably a bright bay, either light or dark, with black mane and tail, black points, and usually a small white spot between "bulbs" of the heel. In size they are medium, individuals standing from sixteen hands to sixteen hands three inches in height, and weighing from 1,100 to 1,300 lbs. The head is of fair size, with a face of kindly expression and intelligent cast; neck finely arched and well set on to long, sloping shoulders; back short; loins even and powerful; hips of good length and legs straight, close knit, and free from long hairs at the fetlock.

The Cleveland Bay is a general purpose horse, heavy enough for all ordinary farm work, and active, stylish and with ample speed for either wagon or carriage use. In breeding he transmits color, bone, style, kind and docile disposition, and general characteristics to a marked degree; he is easy to handle, and for use in grading on the pony mares of the great Southwest, we doubt if his superior can be found, or indeed his equal. Royalty and Lord Derby (see illustrations), both prize winners are excellent representatives of the breed, and fully bear out the proverbial good judgment of their respective importers

CLEVELAND BAYS.

Royalty.
Imported and Owned by Fields Bros. Cedar Falls, Ia.

CLEVELAND BAY STALLION, LORD DERBY, 231 (740).
Foaled, 1884; imported (1887) and now owned by GALBRAITH BROS., Janesville, Wis.

Chapter VIII.

FRENCH COACH HORSES.
(Demi-Sang.)

These horses are the direct result of the wisdom and foresight of the French government. Some time during the latter part of the 18th century the government began the establishment of studs and breeding stables, in anticipation of an approaching scarcity of good horses for the cavalry service. Thoroughbred stallions from England were introduced and their services offered to breeders at remarkably low rates, the policy of the government being to buy back the get of these horses, and eventually establish a breed of the peculiar type desired. The practice led to a great deal of trickery in the way of selling good-looking individuals on appearance solely, the fraud only appearing when the animal was used for breeding purposes. To obviate this trouble, the French government adopted the plan of buying up superior stallion colts and rearing them in the public studs. In addition to this, the owners of very superior stallions are granted a bonus by the government, on condition that the stallion in question shall remain in the country for service; a second class—the owners of stallions good but not fine—are allowed to offer their stallions for service, but receive no subsidy; no stallions except these two classes, and those belonging to the government, are allowed to stand. In certain departments of France only—as notably in Orne, Calvados and Seine-Inférieure—is government attention directed to the production of Coachers; in other departments the Thoroughbred, the Breton and the celebrated Norman and Percheron horses receive in turn particular attention. The American French Coach Horse Association has been organized, and a Stud Book started. S. D. Thompson, of Wayne, Ill., is the present secretary.

DESCRIPTION AND CHARACTERISTICS.

The color of the French Coach is usually bay, but chestnuts are abundant and blacks quite common; the fashion in America calls for bays, and most of our importers have selected with a view of supplying this fashionable demand. In size they rank with the Cleveland—an average weight falling between 1,000 and 1,200 lbs. for stallions. The head is small, with full forehead, expressive eyes, fine muzzle, and medium, quick-playing ears The neck is long, well arched and firmly set on long, sloping shoulders. The back is short; hips long and well up; legs of good length, firmly knit, and with tough, well-made feet. In general appearance—as will be seen by a glance at the engravings—the French Coach Horse is just what the name indicates, a stylish, well-made carriage horse of good action and fine appearance.

FRENCH COACH STALLION, ESBLY.
Owned by J. W. Ramsey, Springfield, Ill.

FRENCH COACH. 39

FRENCH COACH STALLION, FRANCONI, 189-
Winner of Gold Medal at New York State Fair four years in succession; property of SMITHS & POWELL, Syracuse, N. Y.

Chapter IX.

OLDENBURG COACH HORSES.

Concerning the origin of the Oldenburg Coacher, we learn from Hoffmeister's "History of the Oldenburg Horse," published in 1884, that Oldenburg has long been noted for its fine horses. As far back as the 16th century, careful steps were taken to advance the horse-breeding interests. Hoffmeister, in the work above mentioned, says:

"From 1552 to 1557 Count Johann was on intimate terms with the sons of Christian III. of Denmark, then being educated at Copenhagen, afterwards aiding each other in the wars of Sweden and Denmark. These kings took an active interest in the horse culture, and imported horses from Turkey, Italy and Spain. The pride that Johann XVI. took in horse culture, without doubt, was taken up by his relatives and carried to Oldenburg."

Unlike the French Coacher—admittedly of recent formation—the Oldenburg horse is supposed to be the product of steady breeding in blood lines for many generations, with a basis of Oriental blood—Turk, Barb and Arabian—on the best common or native mares of the Duchy. C. E. Stubbs, one of the leading breeders of Oldenburgs in America, says concerning their origin:

"Without a doubt the blood of the Arabian and Barb was more than 300 years ago carried to Oldenburg and infused into the native blood of the country, which has developed the present large, high-gaited, symmetrical horses of the Duchy."

Their importation to America has been only within the last few years, but there are already a goodly number of breeders and very many excellent individual animals credited to this side of the Atlantic. The American "Oldenburg Coach Horse Association" has been recently organized (C. E. Stubbs, Fairfield, Iowa, secretary), and after some trials and tribulations in the way of suits and restraining injunctions, is now fairly launched before the public.

DESCRIPTION AND CHARACTERISTICS.

Uniformly blacks, bays or browns, with or without dapples, and invariably with mealy nose. In size they are about equal to the Cleveland Bay—stallions weighing from 1,100 to 1.300 or 1,400 lbs., and standing from 16 to 16½ hands in height. They are spirited, high headed, high-knee acting, intelligent looking carriage horses, with neat, clean legs, and firm, well made feet. Although spirited, they are uniformly kind in disposition, and are known to be easily broken and handled for carriage uses.

OLDENBURG COACH STALLION, LANDESSOHN.
Owned by C. E. Stubbs, Fairfield, Iowa.

Chapter X.

GERMAN COACH HORSES.

("*German, Hanoverian and Oldenburg Coach Horses.*")

As the name of the breed indicates, it is of immediate German origin, and as the name of the American Association appearing in parentheses at the head of this chapter further indicates, there are admitted to entry horses from several different sections of the German empire.

As near as we can learn, the status of the two Coach breeds from Germany furnishes a parallel to that of the two Draft breeds from France —Percheron and French Draft. Beyond all question there is much if not all the same foundation stock in both Oldenburg and German Coach, the main difference being that, while with the Oldenburg registration is limited to horses produced in Oldenburg, or descendants of horses so produced, with the German Coach Horse Stud Book, not only Oldenburg Coachers, but also Coach Horses from other portions of the empire and their descendants are admitted to registration. It is doubtless true that many equally good horses are to be found in Germany outside of the Duchy of Oldenburg, and that, therefore, there is some wisdom in having a Stud Book Association which admits to entry good horses not strictly Oldenburg bred. At the same time we cannot fail to notice the value of the restriction to certain set blood lines which the Oldenburg Stud Book requires. The Oldenburg is to the German Coacher what the Percheron is to the French Draft—the more carefully guarded blood element, which has been and is still being preserved in restricted registration, and which must, therefore, prove of greatest value for breeding purposes.

The first importation of German Coachers to the United States was made by the well-known firm of Oltmann Bros., Watseka, Ill., in 1885, since which time they have been imported and bred in large numbers.

DESCRIPTION AND CHARACTERISTICS.

Color, black, bay, brown or chestnut, with or without dapples—sometimes with a small white star, and occasionally with white feet and ankles. In size they also vary somewhat more than the Oldenburg, stallions standing from $15\frac{1}{2}$ to $16\frac{1}{2}$ hands, and weighing from 1,000 to 1,400 lbs. As above indicated, they differ from the Oldenburg chiefly in showing greater variation in all things—color, size and action; but the really good specimens of either breed are identical to all intents and purposes.

GERMAN COACH. 43

GERMAN COACH MARES, ELSE AND ANNA.

Chapter XI.

HACKNEYS.

The origin of the Hackney cannot be stated in definite terms; indeed, it has been only within the last decade that it has been strictly considered a breed. The late change in rules of the English Association, permitting entry to the English Hackney Stud Book on a basis of inspection of individual animals, and infusion of blood other than Hackneys proper; and which was immediately followed by one of the Hackney Associations in America, if persisted in, should not fail to draw disfavor upon the breed, and cause a real degeneration in fixedness of character among Hackneys on both sides of the Atlantic. There are over 10,000 horses now recorded in the English Hackney Stud Book, and with this number as a basis, it is surely time to draw the lines closely regarding the admission of more outside blood.

The foundation of the Hackney must be sought in the blood of the Hunter, combined with that of the English Thoroughbred, and with sufficient infusion of blood of the common middle-sized horse—generally known in England as the "Farmer's Horse"—to insure harness gaits and tractability. The strains of blood which are just now most popular among Hackneys are those of "Confidence" and "Fireaway"—individuals, especially of the latter breeding, commanding ready sale at good figures. The Fireaways were especially noted as the best saddle strain which England has ever seen, and their blood, handed down through imported Bellfounder, as will be seen in Chapter on American Trotters, has proved desirable in more than one direction.

It cannot be stated that the Hackney is yet a finished product so far as breeding is concerned. He is, rather, a horse of education, style and fashion; the breeders of Hackneys formerly selecting individual animals which were nearest the type demanded by the fashion of the day, regardless of the blood lines which they represented. In later breeding, however, a great deal of this uncertainty has been eliminated, and with a proper system of registration the Hackneys would soon become an established fixture in blood.

Concerning the origin of the name, the *Horse-Breeder*, London, England, says:

"We cannot altogether say whether the Hackney derives its name from the London Suburb of that name, or from the verb *to hack*, derived from the French, to chop small or to cut to pieces; most likely the latter, as hacks of all sorts come in for a good deal of chopping and cutting to pieces. It is from the same word we have the Scotch word

HACKNEY STALLION, LORD KINGSBURY.
Owned by Galbraith Bros., Janesville, Wis.

"haggis," a very healthy national dish, most indigestible to most Englishmen. There seems a disposition on the part of some of our northern friends to go back to the original verb, and make the Hackney Stud Book a sort of "haggis" Stud Book; at any rate, a Stud Book for hacks. Now, hacks and hackneys are very different animals."

From the above it will be seen that the *Horse-Breeder* is disposed to exercise what in America we call "good horse sense," in that it emphatically objects to the introduction of any more outside blood, and consequent production of a "haggis," or in American parlance "hash," Stud Book. The American Hackney Horse Society of New York City is the one recognized by the English Association as the "Hackney Association of the United States," and as such should be the one to pay close attention to the real improvement of the Hackney breed. A proposition has been made offering to compromise on a set of rules for entry, and it is hoped that the two American Associations will agree upon some of the disputed points, and work together for Hackney interests.

DESCRIPTION AND CHARACTERISTICS.

The colors found are bays, blacks, browns and chestnuts, often with white star and sometimes with white feet and ankles. In size they are about equal to the French Coacher, standing 15 to 16 hands high and weighing from 1,000 to 1,300 pounds. The Hackney is especially high at the withers; shoulders strongly slanted; neck well crested, and carrying the head very high; back short; legs of medium length, close knit; cannons broad and flat; pasterns shorter than with Thoroughbreds and Trotters, but longer than with draft breeds; feet firm and of moderate size; forearm especially short, giving an unusually high knee action, and quarters well muscled and compact.

The fashion has made it imperative to practice "docking," which consists in shortening the tail to a length of about 10 to 14 inches, and cutting the cords so as to force its carriage at a certain angle. The illustration will give a better idea of the appearance of the tail after this operation than can be given by word description.

The Hackney's disposition is usually kind, and his speed in harness, while by no means comparing with that of the trotting horse, is still amply sufficient for all heavy carriage use. The Hackney really approaches closer to the standard of the Trotter than any of the other carriage breeds. They are uniformly hardy, strongly built, have an abundance of "style," and the best specimens can be relied on for endurance at long distance.

The Hackney has become the English gentleman's favorite horse-of-all-work—being largely used for park-riding as well as light road driving; and in our eastern cities, where the tendency is so often to pattern after English custom and style, the Hackney finds his most congenial American home.

Chapter XII.

THOROUGHBREDS.

(*Running Horses.*)

We have thought best to commence this chapter by a brief notice of the term "Thoroughbred," and the confusion which has existed—indeed, confusion still exists—regarding its use in America. In England, the home of the Thoroughbred, the term is naturally well understood. In America all animals, whether horses, cattle, sheep or swine, if eligible to entry in the register of their peculiar breed, are spoken of as "thoroughbred," as, for example, thoroughbred Shorthorns, thoroughbred Herefords, thoroughbred Southdowns, thoroughbred Berkshires, and so on through the list of recognized breeds of domestic animals.

The term "thoroughbred," as thus used, is, it will be noted, an adjective, and is employed merely to express the fact that such an animal is eligible to entry in the Herd Book or Register of the breed to which he belongs. It is convenient and expressive, if not strictly accurate, and, as it will doubtless always be retained by American stock breeders, we may as well acquiesce in its acceptance, and try to thoroughly understand the difference between its use as an adjective and as a noun. It must be remembered that at the time the name first came into use as a synonym for the English race horse, it did so by reason of the acknowledged purity or "thorough" breeding of the animal in question. No horse without the blood of some celebrated runner of the English turf, or the blood of the Arabian, Turk or Barb in his pedigree, could at that time be even thought of as a horse of any breeding at all. The race horse was the especial horse of the nobility, and was the only animal at that time whose ancestral blood was known and recorded. The runner was commonly spoken of as "thoroughbred," and the word has naturally been adopted by all breeders as the proper name of the breed of running or racing horses, whose origin is found in Oriental blood transmitted through the veins of the early English race horse.

Let us understand, then, that the noun "Thoroughbred" is simply the name of a breed of horses, just as Cleveland Bay and Percheron are the names, respectively, of other breeds of horses; and with this understanding we may proceed to a brief review of the origin and early history of the breed.

As already intimated, the English Thoroughbred is the undoubted scion of Eastern blood—Turk, Barb and Arabian—improved and perfected by the influence of skillful handling and natural conditions peculiar to English soil and climate. The horses now generally regarded as of most value among the early invoices of Oriental blood may be named as follows, in order of their importation: The White Turk, owned by Mr. Place, stud groom of the Lord Protector Cromwell; the Byerly Turk, owned by Captain Byerly, and used by him as his charger in the wars of William in Ireland, about 1689; the Darley Arabian, owned by Mr. Darley, of Yorkshire; and last in point of time, but by no means least in the number and great excellence of his descendants, the Godolphin Barb, called also "Godolphin Arabian," but erroneously, since he was universally admitted to be a Barb.

Many other noted parents of racing stock might be named as illustrating the extent to which the blood of the desert has been used in forming the modern Thoroughbred, but space forbids. The Darley Arabian, bred in the desert of Palmyra, may be said to be the parent of our best racing stock. From Youatt, in reference to this horse and his descendants, we quote:

"His figure contained every point, without much show, that could be desired in a turf horse. The immediate descendants of this invaluable horse were the Devonshire or Flying Childers; the Bleeding or Bartlett's Childers, who was never trained; Almanzor, and others. The two Childers were the means through which the blood and fame of their sire were widely circulated; and from them descended another Childers, Blaze, Snap, Sampson, Eclipse, and a host of excellent horses. The Devonshire or Flying Childers, so called from the name of his breeder, Mr. Childers, of Carr House, and the sale of him to the Duke of Devonshire, was the fleetest horse of his day."

Probably the most noted of the descendants of Flying Childers was King Herod, the founder of the old Herod line of English Thoroughbreds. He was the sire of 497 winners, who gained for their owners some £200,000.

Of Sampson more extended mention will be found in the chapter on American Trotters. His reputed and recorded sire was Blaze, but his actual sire has been commonly supposed to be of heavier, coarser extraction; be that as it may, in the horse Sampson, regardless of his pedigree, was combined the exact elements necessary to plant the germ of the trotting instinct, which has been so highly developed in the long list of trotting horses descended from his great-grandson, imported Messenger.

Eclipse was, by acknowledged right, the most wonderful horse ever produced on English turf. His career was so brilliant both on the turf and in the stud, and his exploits so remarkable, that the following quotation from Prof. Low's great work may prove of interest:

"Eclipse was got by Marske, a grandson of Bartlett's Childers, out of Spiletta. He was foaled in the year 1764, during the eclipse of that year, from which circumstance he took his name. He was bred by the Duke of Cumberland, and on the death of that prince sold to Mr. Wildman, a salesman at Smithfield, and afterwards he became the property of Mr. O'Kelly. Eclipse had not the grandeur of form of the Flying Childers, and might have escaped notice but for the accidental trial of his stupendous powers. He was about fifteen hands and one inch high. His shoulders were very low, and so thick above that, according to the observation of the times, a firkin of butter might have rested upon them. He stood very high behind, a compilation suited to his great power of progression; he was so thick winded as to be heard blowing at considerable distance. In the language of the honest John Lawrence, 'He puffed and blowed like an otter, and galloped as wide as a barn door.' No sooner were his powers exhibited on the turf, than every eye was set to scrutinize his form, and he was then admitted to possess in perfection the external characters indicative of great speed. A volume was written on his proportions by M. Saint Bel, a veterinary surgeon, whose investigations showed that his figure differed greatly from the conventional form which speculative writers had assigned as the standard of perfection. He was of an indomitable temper, and his jockeys found it in vain to attempt to hold him, but contented themselves with remaining still on the saddle while he swept along, his nose almost touching the ground. His full speed was not determined, since he never met with an opponent sufficiently fleet to put it to the proof. He not only was never beaten, but he was able to distance some of the best horses of his time, and the fleetest could not keep by his side for fifty yards together. This remarkable horse first appeared on the turf at the age of five, in 1769. In the first heat he set off of his own accord, and easily gained the race, his rider pulling in vain with all his force for the last mile. O'Kelly observing this, and aware of his horse's powers, offered in the second heat to place the horses, and he took heavy bets that he did so. When called upon to declare, he said, 'Eclipse first, and the rest no place.' He gained his wagers; Eclipse was first, and all the others were distanced, or, in the language of the turf, had no place. From this time Eclipse was continually on the turf, and gained every race; no horse daring to contend with him, he closed his career of 17 months by walking over the Newmarket Course for the King's Plate, in October, 1770. During this brief period, it is said that he gained £25,000 for his owner. He was then employed with prodigious profit as a stallion. He got 334 winners at our numerous race courses, who are computed to have gained about £160,000 to their owners, besides cups and plates. He died in 1789, at the age of 25."

The later English racers have been horses of great speed and endurance—great in those things that go to make up a great horse; but many seem to think that the modern English Thoroughbred is not the equal of his former self. Sharper races, more of them, and especially coming at an earlier age—very frequently at the age of two or three years—have, it is claimed, decreased somewhat the stamina and wonderful endurance found in the earlier horses of note.

The American Thoroughbred is, of course, a lineal descendant of the parent stock (English); in other words, all American horses eligible to entry in the American Stud Book for Thoroughbred Horses—edited and published by Col. S. D. Bruce, of New York—are either imported from England, or are the descendants of horses so imported.

In the United States, it has been found advisable to permit a certain relaxation of the rigid rules adhered to in the English Stud Book, and to admit animals that show an unmixed descent for five generations of pure blood. This necessarily admits animals which are not strictly Thoroughbred, but if for five generations nothing but Thoroughbred stallions are used, the resulting animal is so nearly Thoroughbred as to answer all requirements. Indeed, we are inclined to think that the American system of breeding and recognized rules for entry have done much toward making the American Thoroughbred the successful rival of his English cousin, which he has proved himself to be.

Of the American Thoroughbreds which have earned distinction on the turf, we may mention: American Eclipse, by Duroc, out of Miller's Damsel, by Imp. Messenger; Lexington, by Boston, out of Alice Carneal, by Imp. Sarpedon; Prioress, by Imp. Sovereign, out of Reel, by Glencoe; Leamington, by Faugh-a-Ballagh, out of a mare by Pantaloon; Springbok, by Australian, out of Hester, by Lexington; Nettie Norton, by Imp. Leamington, out of Long Nine, by Lightning; Ten Broeck, by Imp. Phaeton, out of Fanny Holton, by Lexington; Tom Ochiltree, by Lexington, out of Katona, by Voucher; Parole, by Imp. Leamington, out of Maiden, by Glencoe; and Iroquois, by Imp. Leamington.

Iroquois, in 1881, played havoc with English ideas of the supremacy of English horses, winning both the English Derby and the St. Leger against the pick of English Thoroughbreds. Concerning his victory in the St. Leger, Mr. Curzon, in his interesting chronicle of the Derby— "The Blue Ribbon of the Turf"—after telling of the intense but fortunately futile opposition to the American contestant, says:

"At the last moment the betting settled down and Iroquois started for the St. Leger as first favorite, the price offered being 2 to 1. The story of the struggle need not be retold. An exciting race between Geologist and the American resulted in the victory of the latter, well ridden by England's greatest jockey [F. Archer], by a length. The win was a popular one. As Iroquois was seen to have the race in hand, the excited shouts of 100,000 persons rent the air, the cheers resounding again and again as Archer brought his horse into the enclosure. All present seemed highly gratified at the result of the race and the defeat of those birds of evil omen which had croaked a few short hours before, as if the disgrace of the gallant American steed was a certainty.

"Some backers of the colt never faltered in their loyalty. The more Iroquois was decried, and his chance made light of, all the readier they seemed to back their opinion with their money. When the horse was seen stripped for the race, all men who could judge saw in a moment that he was as fit as hands could render him, and many of those who had hedged their money at a loss, because of the evil reports which had been so industriously circulated, would have been glad enough to have again backed him could they have the opportunity; but, alas! it was too late. They were wedged in the dense mass of people who filled the stand, and had no alternative but to patiently wait and see Iroquois credit Brother Johnathan with his first St. Leger.

"During all that took place the quiet confidence of Jacob Pincus [Iroquois' trainer] never faltered. Some persons were so bold as to suggest that he might have been bought by the "enemy," but Jacob went on with his training duties, heeding not the idle rumors. And who will say that his reward was not a great one, as he proudly led the steed into the paddock, after the supreme excitement of witnessing the race had been endured."

Among the later celebrities of the turf, not one, perhaps, has stood higher in public favor than the Bard (see illustration), a bay stallion, foaled 1883, owned by A. J. Cassatt. As a recognition of his remarkable career on the turf, we give place to the following tabulated pedigree:

THOROUGHBREDS. 51

AMERICAN THOROUGHBRED.

THE BARD	LONGFELLOW { Leamington	Faugh-a-Ballagh	Sir Hercules. Guiccolli.
		Daughter	Pantaloon. Daphne.
	Nantura	Brawner's Eclipse	American Eclipse. Daughter.
		Queen Mary	Bertrand. Lady Fortune.
	BRADEMANTE { War Dance	Lexington	Boston. Alice Carneal.
		Reel	Glencoe. Gallopade.
	Brenna	Imp. Knight of St. George	Irish Birdcatcher. Maltese.
		Levity	Imp. Trustee. Vandal's Dam.

Concerning the race for Freehold Stakes at Monmouth Park, N. J., August 2d, 1888, in which the Bard suffered defeat for the first time, the *Turf, Field and Farm*, of New York (issue August 10th, 1888), says:

"Since our last issue, sudden checks have been given to the victorious careers of several public idols. The Bard has succumbed to Firenzi, Raceland lowered his colors to Badge, Kingston and Terra Cotta suffered defeat by Elkwood, Little Minch was out-speeded by Yum-Yum, and even in England, the crack two-year-old Donovan has met with a reverse. But the case of the Bard is the most serious of all, for not only has he been beaten after winning seven straight stakes, but, in all probability, he has appeared for the last time in public.

"The race in which he met with his mishap was the Freehold, at Monmouth, on Thursday of last week. Firenzi was his only opponent. The Bard made the running, setting a fast pace, but at no time did Garrison permit the filly to be more than three lengths behind. He closed in the stretch, forced Hayward to the whip at the last sixteenth pole, and then coming away, won by two lengths in 2:34, which equals the record, Luke Blackburn having made the same time at Monmouth as a three-year-old on August 17th, 1880, with 102 pounds up, and Jim Guest, when four years old, and carrying 98 pounds, having made a like record at Washington Park, Chicago, July 24th, 1886. The first quarter was run in 0:27, the half in 0:52, the three-quarters in 1:18, the mile in 1:42½, and the mile and a quarter in 2:08½. It was a splendid performance for both.

"While The Bard did not pull up lame, as far as could be noticed at the close of the race, it was but a short time before he began to favor his off hind leg, which began to swell. Dr. Shepherd was called to examine the horse, but inflammation was so great, the swelling being midway between the hock and fetlock joint, that it was impossible to diagnose the case, and the extent of the injury had not been definitely determined on Tuesday last, although it was generally deemed to be permanent. After the race, Hayward said that for the first time this season, The Bard had not tried to get away from him when he had mounted, not taking hold of the bit in his accustomed style. Like his illustrious sire, he has gone down in battle, covered with glory, both finishing their races in the gamest manner on three legs. That there would have been a still greater contest and in faster time had The Bard been right, there is no question in our mind, for we have long been of the opinion that, under favorable conditions, he could lower almost any record."

The Emperor of Norfolk (see illustration from sketch immediately after winning the American Derby) is another one of the successful winners of 1888. At Chicago, June 23rd, he won the American Derby,

THOROUGHBREDS.

53

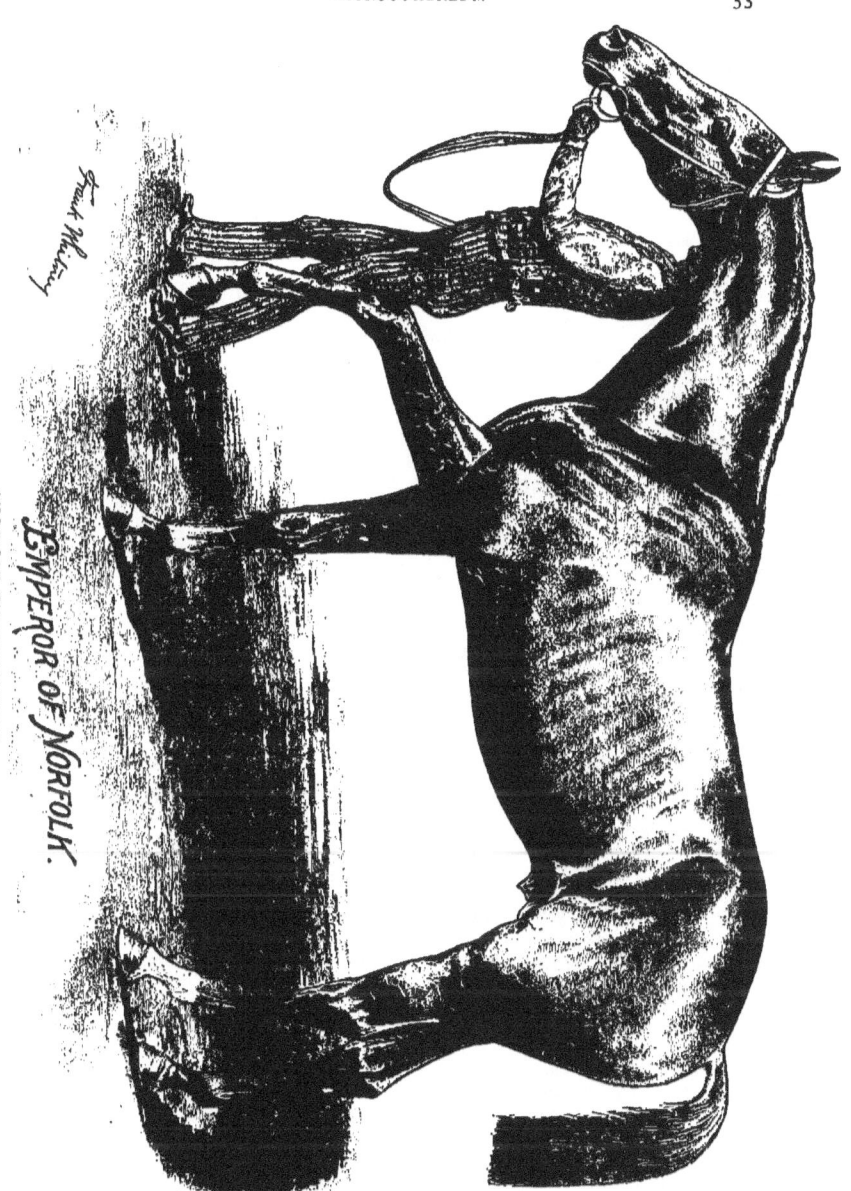

EMPEROR OF NORFOLK.
AMERICAN THOROUGHBRED.

netting in this one race $14,590, and making a total amount thus far won for his owner of $28,530, said to the largest winnings credited to any living horse. There is a little "cold" blood in the remote pedigree of the Emperor, coming through the Potomac mare—dam of Betsy Malone—but it is so far back that it affects neither his speed nor his breeding value. His abridged pedigree may be given as follows:

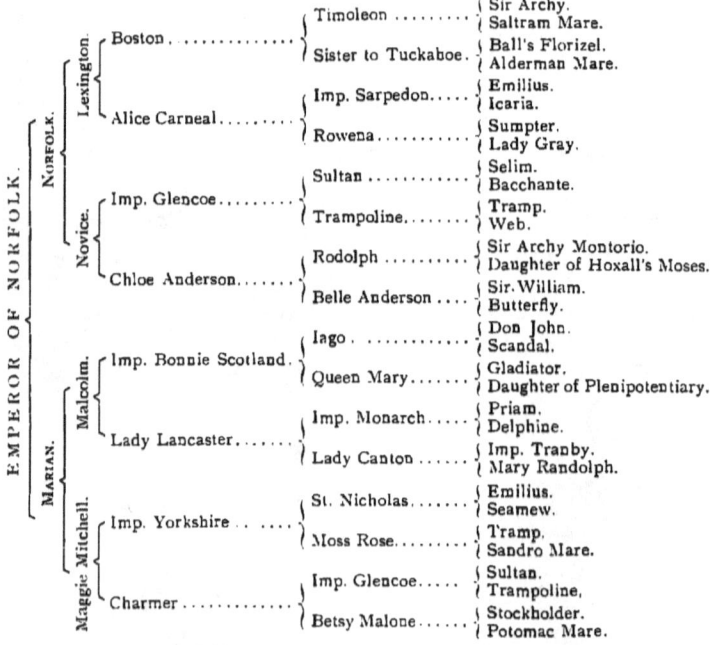

The *Chicago Horseman*, in a notice of the Emperor, says:

"He is a grandly proportioned horse, and is so constructed that he can carry all the penalties that are piled upon him without materially interfering with his speed. He has defeated all the best three-year-olds of the year so easily that it is impossible to accurately gauge his powers. Should he meet The Bard at weight for age, we shall expect to see a grand struggle, and one which will be fully described in the annals of the turf. Both in his two and three-year-old career, he has proved himself to be a race-horse of the very highest quality, and one of those exceptionally great horses which only appear once in a decade.

"The Emperor of Norfolk was bred by Theodore Winters. He was foaled on January 12, 1885, and was purchased at the Winters sale on December 20, 1886, by E. J. Baldwin for $2,550. He is by that mighty son of Lexington, Norfolk, out of Marian by Malcolm. In the veins of the Emperor flows the rich red tide which came from those grand fountains of speed—Lexington, Glencoe, Bonnie Scotland and Yorkshire. When as a racing star of the first magnitude the Emperor has run his allotted course, his splendid individuality, grand speed powers and patrician lineage will combine to enthrone him as the first lord of the harem."

AMERICAN THOROUGHBRED STALLION, TAMMANY.
(Courtesy of *Turf, Field and Farm*, New York.)

One of the best of the winners of 1892 is the chestnut colt Tammany, son of Iroquois and Tullahoma, whose likeness we present through the courtesy of *Turf, Field and Farm*, New York. Tammany was bred by General W. H. Jackson, Nashville, Tenn., and was foaled March 23, 1889. He was purchased as a yearling by Mr. Marcus Daly for $2,500, and as he has already credited back to his owner, in stake earnings alone, something over $100,000, the price paid can hardly be considered a high one. Tammany's best victory was won from Yorkville Belle in the rich Jerome stakes at Morris Park, Saturday October, 8, 1892, concerning which the *Turf, Field and Farm*, issue of October 14, 1892, says:

"Although the race had five other starters, scarcely a person cared to invest on any one of them, and 40 to 1 bar two was freely offered. At the start Silver Fox and Julian started out to make the running, each for his stable companion, and so well did they perform their mission that they were soon many lengths in advance of their field, while Yorkville Belle was lying fifth and Tammany yet further behind; this was about the order until three-eights from home, when Yorkville Belle went to the front, but no sooner did she make this move than Garrison was after her with Tammany, and the two raced together until within a sixteenth of home when Tammany with a little shaking up, drew away and won by a good length."

As a fitting refutation of the absurd theory of degeneration among Thoroughbreds, and as expressing at the same time the improvement of the running course and nearer approach to perfection in the trainer's art, we give herewith a brief statement showing the running records at the close of the racing season of 1892, with name of horse, age, weight carried, record and time at which made, for each of the main divisions of distance from one-half to four miles:

One-half mile, 0:46, Geraldine (4), 122 lbs., made August 30, 1889.

Three-fourths mile, 1:10¼, Fides (4), 116 lbs., made May 31, 1890

One mile, 1:35½, Salvator (4), 110 lbs., made August 28, 1890. The world's mile running race record is 1:37¼, and is held by the Rancocas filly Kildeer, made August 13, 1892.

One and one-eighth miles, 1:51½, Tristan (6), 114 lbs., made June 2, 1891.

One and one-fourth miles, 2:03¾, Banquet (3), 108 lbs., made July 17, 1890.

One and one-half miles, 2:32¾, Lamplighter (3), 109 lbs., made August 9, 1892. This distance had been previously covered by Firenzi as a six-year-old, and carrying 117 lbs., in exactly 2:33.

Two miles, 3:27½, Ten Broeck (5), 110 lbs., made May 29, 1877.

Three miles, 5:24, Drake Carter (4), 115 lbs., made September 6, 1884.

Four miles, 7:15¾, Ten Broeck (4), 104 lbs., made September 27, 1876. The four mile running race record is 7:19½, held by Fellowcraft, who covered the distance as a four-year-old, carrying 108 lbs, on August 20, 1874.

The Coney Island Jockey Club this year (1892) offered a purse for a four mile race, and it was won by Demuth from Tea Tray in 7:20, but one-half second slower than the race record of Fellowcraft, and this, too, without any attempt at, or idea of, lowering a record. It is fairly probable that almost any one of the best performers of 1892, if fitted for the four mile distance, could lower the record made in 1874, and some of them at least, could approximate, if not defeat, the time record of Ten

Broeck, which has stood unchallenged since 1879. Drake Carter's granddam is by Lexington, and is a half-sister to Fellowcraft, who ran four miles in 7:19½, while Demuth's sire, Ten Broeck, is out of Fanny Holton by Lexington—his dam being by Longfellow, a son of imported Leamingington, and a half-brother to Fanny Holton—dam of Ten Broeck.

Ten Broeck's mile record of 1:39¾, made against time, May 24, 1877, was the first time record at that distance, and stood untouched until 1890, when first lowered by Senator Stanford's Racine to 1:39½. Racine's record was made as a three-year-old, carrying 107 lbs. in a race, and on a regulation track, Washington Park, Chicago, June 28, 1890. August 28th the same year Salvator set the mark so low (1:35½) that it will likely remain for some time. It must be remembered, however, that Salvator's great mile was made against time and over the straight course at Monmouth Park. Since Racine first lowered Ten Broeck's mile record it has been beaten not only by Salvator as above noted, but by Raveloe, 1:39¼, July 31, 1890; La Tosca, 1:39½, 1891; Kirsch, 1:38, August 4, 1892, and Kildeer, 1:37¼, in a race August 13, 1892.

While no two famous winners have ever been exactly alike in conformation, there are yet many points of similarity, and we have thought best to give the following short

DESCRIPTION OF A TYPICAL THOROUGHBRED.

The head is fine; neck slender but well set on at the shoulders; chest deep, wide and bounded by shoulders long and slanting; hind quarters high and well muscled; legs flat, with short cannons, long, elastic pasterns, and rounded, well-made feet. Not a pound of surplus fat is carried when in racing trim; the cords and muscles stand out clearly, and play in action like the sensitive strings of some delicate instrument. The Racer is essentially nervous in temperament; many have been made vicious by careless handling, and not a few have failed to show extreme speed on the turf because of failure to understand and appreciate their nerve peculiarities.

Many regard the Thoroughbred as a mere fancy animal—the especial horse of the sporting fraternity—but we do not agree with such expression. His indomitable will and wonderful endurance, combined with his beauty of form and usually good size, make him a horse of much value to use on native mares of mixed breeding, and the colts thus produced are among our most stylish saddle and harness horses. The South has always been rich in the blood of the Thoroughbred; and since there has been little call for horses of the heavier breeds until recent times, mules being employed almost exclusively for heavy draft and farm work, the Racer has served a most valuable purpose. As heavier stallions are now being introduced extensively, we shall find the mares of racing stock a valuable foundation for producing an excellent general purpose horse.

Chapter XIII.

AMERICAN SADDLE HORSES.

The saddle horse is a modern production—based on a growing demand for something not only handsome, but comfortable as well, for saddle use. The English style of riding, as aped by "riding masters" in the eastern cities, is so essentially uncomfortable and really inelegant as to seem ridiculous to any one who knows what a good saddle animal is. The trot, of all gaits, is the one least suited to ease and elegance in the saddle, and the bent-knee, sit-down-on-a-tack-and-jump-up-again action of the would-be stylish, short-stirrup rider of the park hack should be very stylish, indeed, to compensate for the utter absence of all things elegant.

The American Saddle Horse is now recognized among the newly formed breeds. The National Saddle Horse Breeders' Association was organized in June, 1891, and under the guidance of Secretary I. B. Nall, Louisville, Ky., has already issued Vol. I. of the Stud Book. Rules for entry to the second volume are as follows:

"1. Stallions that trace on either sire's or dam's side direct to foundation, registered stock, or to stock eligible to registry, and go the following gaits: (1) walk, (2) trot, (3) rack, (4) canter, (5) running walk, fox trot or slow pace. Mares or geldings that go the gaits specified above.

"2. Any stallion whose sire, grand sire, dam and grand dam are of strains of blood recognized by this association.

"3. Any stallion that has sired five or more performers under rule 1.

"4. Any mare that has produced two or more performers under rule 1.

"5. Progeny of a standard horse out of a standard mare.

"6. The female progeny of a standard horse, when out of a mare by a standard horse."

The origin of the Saddler is, of course, found in Thoroughbred blood, supplemented by the blood of easy pacers which have proved potent in imparting saddle gaits. As stated by Secretary Nall, the association recognizes as "foundation stock," under rules above, the following individual sources of saddle blood:

Denmark, Thoroughbred, by Imp. Hedgeford; Brinker's Drennon, by Davy Crockett; Sam Booker, by Boyd McNary, Thoroughbred; John Dillard, by Indian Chief; Tom Hal, imp. from Canada; Coleman's Eureka; Vanmeter's Waxy; Cabell's Lexington, by Blood's Black Hawk; Copperbottom, pacer; Stump-the-Dealer; Texas, by Comanche; Prince Albert, by Frank Wolford; Peter's Halcorn, and Varnon's Roebuck, a Missouri horse.

AMERICAN SADDLE STALLION, STAR EAGLE, 289.
Owned by J. D. and L. B. Smith, New Berlin, Ill.

The gaits recognized by the association, as stated in rule 1, are walk, trot, rack, canter, running walk, fox trot and slow pace. Of these gaits, the running walk—more commonly known as the "single-foot"—is by odds the most elegant saddle gait, combining the style and speed of the trot and rack, or pace, with the comfort and stability in the saddle of the easiest "lope" or canter. In the southern portion of the United States, and especially in Texas, are the finest single-footing saddlers of the world; and a goodly percentage of the number are able to go a better than three-minute rate. The fox trot is as easy, but has not the style or speed of the fleeter single-foot. The fox trot, the slow pace and the fast walk will always remain the standard long-distance gaits of the educated saddler, making five to seven miles per hour, and doing it with ease to both horse and rider.

DESCRIPTION AND CHARACTERISTICS.

In appearance the typical Saddler is a combination of Thoroughbred and Trotter, having the size, gameness, and easy, clean-going action of the former, with the quiet, intelligent appreciation of education at the trainer's hands, which we find so marked among the Trotters. All colors are found—bays, browns, blacks, chestnuts and grays, about in the order named. Stallions weigh from 1,000 to 1,200 pounds, mares proportionately less. The head is fine; neck slender, but well arched and muscular; shoulders and girth deep and ample; back short; rump close and generally sloping; quarters long and well muscled, and legs fine-boned, neat, close-fleshed, and without feather.

Our illustration represents one of the most noted of modern American saddle stallions.

Chapter XIV.

AMERICAN TROTTERS.

While not yet recognized as a separate breed, the American Trotter is fast approaching that distinction, and the long lines of fast moving offspring from the famous stallions that founded the several strains of modern Trotters point unmistakably to that constant transmission of characteristic qualities which alone determines a breed.

ORIGIN AND IMPROVEMENT.

The history of the origin and improvement of American Trotters furnishes one of the most, if not the most, remarkable examples of human skill in developing and training to desired lines qualities which before had remained partially developed or entirely latent. The courage and stamina of the Trotting Horse, in brief, are found in the use of oriental blood in and through the royal blood of the Thoroughbred; but to those remarkable individual animals hereinafter mentioned—in which the trotting gait seems to have been a spontaneous development of the trotting instinct combined with the energy and speed of the Racer—belongs the credit for his immediate origin.

Among the horses which may be thus considered original sources of trotting blood, and first in the list, by acknowledged right, stands

IMPORTED MESSENGER,

himself a Thoroughbred, and embracing some of the choicest blood of the desert in his make-up, as will be seen by a simple statement of his paternal ancestry: Imported Messenger was a gray horse, foaled in 1780; imported to United States in 1788, and died on Long Island in 1808. His first sire was Mambrino, second sire Engineer, third sire Sampson, fourth sire Blaze (?), fifth sire Flying Childers, sixth sire Darley Arabian. His dam was sired by Turf, by Matchem, by Cade (who was a son of Godolphin Arabian), and his second dam was by Regulus, also a son of Godolphin Arabian. His great grandsire, Sampson, was a black horse out of all keeping with the ideal Thoroughbred in appearance, being large, coarse and heavy boned, but with a wonderful power of speed and bottom. Sampson's reputed and recorded sire was Blaze, a bay Thoroughbred, but his conformation and the inclination to trot which he transmitted to his offspring have led students of equine history to doubt the record of his paternity, and assert that his dam was covered by a coach horse. If this were true—and it seems at least reasonable—it was the most fortunate accident that could have occurred, since it furnished the exact combination to insure a change of gait and still retain the fire and instinctive speed of the Racer.

The peculiar conformation of Imported Messenger—low, round, almost flat withers—has been faithfully handed down to his lineal descendants; and it is a matter of common note, that all true Messenger-bred Trotters have always enjoyed a remarkable freedom from all kinds of foot, leg and bone diseases. Messenger blood is found in nearly every family of American Trotters; and through his great grandson, Rysdyk's Hambletonian, we have a family pre-eminent above all others in steady reproduction of the trotting gait, through a long line of noted descendants, of which we shall write later.

Another original source of trotting blood was found in

IMPORTED BELLFOUNDER,

a blood bay, with white diamond on nose, and white left hind foot. His breeding has always been a matter of question, but by the best evidence obtainable his pedigree is as follows: Sire, Old Bellfounder, out of Velocity by Haphazard, by Sir Peter, out of Miss Hervey by Eclipse. Grand dam of good blood but not Thorougbred. This stamps him as a true descendant of the Fireaways—a strain which has never been excelled for the saddle. Bellfounder, the "Norfolk Trotter," was foaled about 1815, imported to America in 1822, and died on Long Island in 1843. He was a natural trotter, of remarkable honesty, and his truest descendants have since been known as "field trotters," showing their best speed when free from all restraint of reins. The peculiar value of the Bellfounder blood is found, like that of Duroc, in its happy combination with the blood of Messenger.

DUROC

was not an imported horse, but was foaled (1806) and bred in Virginia. He was a chestnut in color, of remarkable frame and muscle, got by imported Diomed—a small chestnut horse, winner of the first English Derby—and from him (Diomed) he derived many serious blood defects —such as a tendency to foot and leg troubles, as well as those high qualities of nerve and spirit which are found in all of Diomed's descendants. On his dam's side he traces to imported Medley, a gray by Gimcrack, also a gray, and from this quarter comes the peculiar conformation of his descendants—wide hips, long powerful thighs, and hocks placed low down over short hind cannons—which is always accompanied by an open, loose "straddling" action, by many regarded a sure indication of trotting promise. As already noted, his greatest value was found in combination with Messenger blood, and in such horses as Alhambra, Messenger-Duroc and American Star was found its happiest combination.

ST. LAWRENCE

must not be omitted in our mention of the early sources of trotting blood. He was a small, bay, Canada-bred horse, standing about 15½ hands ; was foaled about 1841, brought over to New York about 1848, and died in Michigan 1858. His breeding is not known, but he was a trotter and a sire of trotters. The peculiar motion which proclaims St. Lawrence blood is seen among all of his descendants : The hind quarters gently swing from side to side, as the hind feet successively advance, trotting with an even but rolling and far-reaching action, that gives an idea of almost irresistible power and momentum.

In this connection we quote the opinion of Mr. H. T. Helm—an acknowledged authority in matters concerning trotting stock—as given in his valuable work on "American Roadsters and Trotting Horses":

"The fact has become so clear that in some parts of our country the Messenger blood has been bred too closely, and the need of a suitable out-cross of high trotting quality having become apparent in many instances, such a blood as that of St. Lawrence affords, for all such, one of the most valuable strains with which to inter-breed. Many valuable mares now exist that are so closely and strongly in-bred in the Messenger blood that their value as breeding stock mainly depends on the obtaining of a suitable out-cross to invigorate the blood, and maintain the trotting excellence for which it has been noted. For all such the male descendants of St. Lawrence will afford the desired cross, and the union will in all probability result, as did that of Bellfounder in the Hambletonian, in the further advancement of the American Trotter."

Next on the list comes the Canadian pacer,

PILOT.

His breeding, like that of St. Lawrence, is not known, except that his ancestry came originally from France to Acadia, and thence to Canada, forming a class of tough and valuable horses, since known as French Canadians, or Kanucks. He was foaled about 1826, but was first known at New Orleans, 1832, when he was said to be six years old, and was purchased of a peddler for $1,000; he died in Kentucky in 1855. Pilot, in brief, was a black stallion, standing less than 15 hands, with short neck, rather thick and heavy about the throat ; a long, coarse mane, showing the handsome, wavy curl which characterizes the French Canadian wherever found ; a close-knit, muscular body; a sloping rump ; a heavy tail of same quality as mane, and long quarters, with hocks placed low down. His whole make-up was one of utility, and his descendants —chiefly through the blood of his greatest son, Pilot Jr., combined with the blood of established trotting strains—have among them the fastest trotters in the world.

The dam of Maud S.—2:08¾—the fastest trotter known before the advent of the kite track and the bicycle sulky, was by Pilot Jr., as was also the dam of the famous gelding Jay Eye See—2:10—whose 1892 pacing record of 2:06¼ makes him the fastest double-gaited horse in the world. True, these famous movers are descended on the other side in direct line from Hambletonian, but this fact does not detract from the great value of the Pilot blood when used in such mighty combination.

GRAND BASHAW,

a Barb of the purest lineage, was imported from Tripoli in 1820, and died in Pennsylvania in 1845. His color was black, with small white star, and he was said to be of very great beauty. In 1821 he produced Young Bashaw—from Pearl, by Bond's First Consul, out of a mare by Imp. Messenger—and through this son has come the credit to Grand Bashaw as an original source of trotting blood. In view of the fact that the grand dam of Young Bashaw was by Imp. Messenger, and the further fact that Young Bashaw was a coarse-looking gray horse, in many respects resembling the Messenger strain, it has been claimed that the Bashaws and their noted descendants—the Clays—are really nothing but branches of the great Messenger stem, and that, therefore, the claims of Grand Bashaw are naught, and his name, assumed by the family, an usurpation of Messenger right.

In part, at least, this may be considered sound reasoning; but we think it more just to admit that the blood of the imperial Barb, Grand Bashaw, was the one element needed in combination to develop the strain of trotters that bears his name.

Last on the list, but by no means least in importance, stands old

JUSTIN MORGAN,

a clear, bright bay, foaled in 1793 near Springfield, Mass.; died near Chelsea, Vt., in 1821. His parentage cannot be definitely ascertained, but from the best circumstantial evidence it would appear that his sire was a horse called True Briton, or Beautiful Bay, and in all probability a Thoroughbred. His dam was said to be of the "Wildair" breed, and to have a share, be it more or less, of the blood of the Lindsey Arabian in her veins. There is some reason, also, for the belief in certain quarters that he had a trace of Canadian blood in his make-up; although the remarkable impressiveness of Morgan and his descendants in matters of color, form, gait and disposition mark a predominance of Oriental, rather than Canadian blood. Justin Morgan left several sons, only three of which occupy places of any real importance—Bulrush, Woodbury and Sherman. Through Sherman—the best of the three sons of old Morgan —we have Vermont Black Hawk, and, passing down the list, General Knox, Ethan Allen and Daniel Lambert; through Bulrush we have the Morrills; and through Woodbury, Hale's Green Mountain Morgan, Magna Charta and (probably) Gold Dust.

From this short summary of the horses classed as sources of trotting blood, we may pass to brief mention of a few of the numerous strains or

DICTATOR.
Brown stallion; foaled 1863; property of H. C. McDowell, Lexington, Ky.
(Sire of Jay Eye See, 2:10—2:06¼.)

families now holding more or less of public favor. First, by acknowledged right, are

The Hambletonians: The family takes its name from Rysdyk's Hambletonian, descended on the paternal side from Imp. Messenger, through his Thoroughbred son Mambrino (American) and Mambrino's son, Abdallah, sire of Hambletonian. The dam of Hambletonian was by Bellfounder. Through Hambletonian we have the Volunteers, Edward Everetts, Alexander's Abdallahs, Almonts, Messenger-Durocs, Happy Mediums, Wilkeses, Dictators, Wood's Hambletonians, Electioneers, and many others of acknowledged eminence laying claim to the general title of Hambletonian.

The Mambrinos, another great family—descended on the paternal side from Imp. Messenger—take the name from Mambrino Chief. His sire was Mambrino Paymaster, a son of Manibrino, who was also the grandsire of Hambletonian. All the Mambrinos, Champions, and many others are grouped under this head.

The Bashaws take their name from Young Bashaw, a son of the Imp. Barb, Grand Bashaw. Young Bashaw was the sire of Andrew Jackson, who in turn got Long Island Black Hawk; and through the latter we have Green's Bashaw, the Mohawks, and others of note.

Closely related to the Bashaws are

The Clays, who take the family name from Henry Clay, a son of Andrew Jackson, above mentioned. From this horse we have the numerous strains of Clays; and through his famous grandson, George M. Patchen, we have the branch which bears his name.

The Morgans we have already mentioned as taking the name and excellence of old Justin Morgan. Under this head we have the Black Hawks (exclusive of Long Island Black Hawk, who was by Andrew Jackson, with no trace of Morgan blood), Ethan Allens, Knoxes, Daniel Lamberts, Fearnaughts, Morrills, and others.

Pacing blood is represented chiefly by the *Pilots*, who take their name from Pilot Jr., already noted, and the *Blue Bulls*, from the celebrated pacer of that name; with the *Royal Georges*, *Hiatogas*, *Bald Stockings* (descended from Tom Hal, lately deceased), *Copper Bottoms*, and others, as seconds of no mean value. Right here we cannot fail to notice the peculiar force of pacing blood, especially on the side of the dam, when joined with paternal blood of established trotting excellence. The mares by Pilot Jr., St. Clair, and other noted pacers, have given us the fastest flyers of the age, and no amount of self-confident reference to "Thoroughbred grand dams," in the cases of Maud S. and Jay Eye See, can now breast the tide of popular favor which the pacing element enjoys. Old Blue Bull, a horse of great speed at the pacing gait alone, stands now, at the close of the racing season 1892, sixth on the list as a sire of trotters; having to his credit 56 horses with a trotting record of 2:30 or better.

PHALLAS, 2:13¾.
Bay stallion; property of J. I. CASE, Racine, Wis.

It is now well known and admitted that the trot and the pace are interchangeable, and that a horse may be taught to go at either gait. The idea of 20 years ago, that pacing blood was of no value in a trotting pedigree, has gone, and gone to stay.

SOME OF THE FASTEST—1888.

An examination of the list of fast records brings up matters of such interest as to warrant at least notice in these pages. In every case, through the list of stallions, mares and geldings, the really fast movers have been the result of steady breeding in blood lines to attain the desired ends. It is this fact which points conclusively toward the inevitable recognition of the claims of the American Trotter to be classed as a breed.

The fastest stallions at close of the racing season 1888, were: Maxey Cobb, 2:13¼; Phallas, 2:13¾, and Patron, 2:14¼. Maxey Cobb has the best record, but it is admitted that Phallas—next by a difference of one-half second—is really the better horse, since he met and defeated the former in an easy victory. The 2:13¾ of Phallas was, at that time, the fastest time ever made by a stallion in a race, and the fastest time ever made in a fourth heat by any horse; and cannot at least be considered inferior to the 2:13¼ of Maxey Cobb, made in a trial against time.

Phallas (see pedigree in full) is a bay son of Dictator, out of Betsy Trotwood by Clark Chief. Dictator was by Rysdyk's Hambletonian, out of Clara, by Seely's American Star, and was a full brother to Dexter.

Maxey Cobb, a bay, is by Happy Medium—a trotting-bred trotter, standing third on the list as a sire of 2:30 horses; he by Rysdyk's Hambletonian, out of the trotting mare Princess, the famous California long-distance mare, whose history is so intimately connected with that of Flora Temple, through their struggles on the track. Princess was by a grandson of Bishop's Hambletonian—the son of Messenger, supposed to be Thoroughbred, and whose name was at first spelled H-a-m-i-l-t-o-n-i-a-n.

Patron, a bay, is a great grandson of Mambrino Chief, through his sire Pancoast. On the other side, he runs again to Mambrino Chief family, his dam being by Cuyler out of a mare by Mambrino Patchen. When we consider the age of Patron (five years) at the time his record of 2:14¼ was made, he may fairly be called the equal of the two preceding: indeed, taking the trio together, a horseman could hardly choose one without an innate fear that a better judgment would have chosen another.

The fastest mares at close of the racing season 1888, were: Maud S., 2:08¾; Belle Hamlin, 2:13¾; Goldsmith Maid, 2:14, and Trinkett, 2:14.

Maud S., a chestnut, the then queen of the trotting turf by virtue of

AMERICAN TROTTERS. 69

JAY EYE SEE.

Jay Eye See, 5 Yrs Old.—2-10¼

Trotting record 2:10 (1884), pacing record 2:06¾ (1892). Black gelding, owned by J. I. Case, Racine, Wis.

her 2:08¾, is by Harold—a son of Rysdyk's Hambletonian, out of a mare by Hambletonian's sire Abdallah. The dam of Maud S. is Miss Russell, whose sire was the now famous Pilot Jr. Probably no other trotter ever enjoyed such high public favor as this famous mare. She was foaled in 1874, and is now owned by Robert Bonner, of New York.

Belle Hamlin, a bay, next on the list, is by Hamlin's Almont, a son of Alexander's Abdallah—out of a mare by Vermont Black Hawk. The dam of old Almont was by Mambrino Chief.

Goldsmith Maid and Trinkett, who are tied as to record, each standing at 2:14, are distinctly trotting bred. Goldsmith Maid, a bay, was sired by Alexander's Abdallah, a son of Rysdyk's Hambletonian, and one whose early death was not the least disaster of the late civil war. The dam of Goldsmith Maid was a daughter of the original Abdallah, by Mambrino by Messenger.

Trinkett, a bay, was a trotter at an early age, having a record of 2:19¾ as a four-year-old, at a time when such a record was considered wonderful. Her sire was Princeps, a son of Woodford Mambrino, out of a mare by Alexander's Abdallah. The dam of Trinkett was by Rysdyk's Hambletonian.

The fastest geldings at close of racing season 1888, were: Jay Eye See, 2:10; St. Julien, 2:11¼, and Guy, 2:12¾. Jay Eye See, a black, is by Dictator, out of the mare Midnight, whose sire was Pilot Jr. The parentage of Dictator has been already mentioned under the notice of Phallas.

Jay Eye See is one of the most remarkable little horses that ever wore harness. On account of an accident which injured his leg, he was thrown out of training not long after making his record of 2:10—for a few days the best trotting record of the world—and was not again actively trained until the past season, 1892, when it was found that the lateral gait seemed to favor his leg trouble, and he was therefore trained for pacing. Although now fourteen years old, and for long years not able to trot fast because of his injured leg, he improved so rapidly at the side-wheel gait as to astonish even his friends. During the summer meeting at Rush Park, Independence, Iowa, on the 26th day of August, 1892, driven by his owner, Jackson I. Case, he paced a beautifully even mile under official rules for time records, in 2:06¼ — making him the fastest double-gaited horse in the world, and demonstrating the wonderful strength and speed of the blood which courses through his veins.

St. Julien, a bay, is by Volunteer, a son of Rysdyk's Hambletonian, out of Flora, by Sayre's Harry Clay. Harry Clay was also the sire of the famous brown mare, Green Mountain Maid, whose fame as the dam of Electioneer and other noted horses is only exceeded by the universal regret among breeders of trotting stock at her death, which occurred June 6th, 1888. The dam of Harry Clay was by Imp. Bellfounder.

Guy, a black, third on the list in 1888, is by Kentucky Prince, and out of Flora Gardner. His record, placing him third on the list of geldings, was not made until near the close of the racing season, September 19, 1888; so that prior to that date the third place had been held by Rarus, 2:13¼, a bay, with blazed face and white hind ankles, sired by Conklin's Abdallah, and out of a mare by Telegraph. Guy, although an erratic performer, is a horse of great gameness and spirit, and shows bursts of speed at a rate far beyond his official record. August 1, 1889, at Cleveland, Ohio, he again lowered his mark to 2:10¾, where it now rests.

The holders of the records for age in 1888 were: Manzanita, Sable Wilkes, Sunol and Norlaine.

Manzanita, a bay mare, bred at Palo Alto, Cal., the then best four-year-old, has a record at that age of 2:16. Her dam is Mayflower, by the pacer St. Clair, and her sire is Electioneer, the famous son of Green Mountain Maid and Hambletonian. (Manzanita was severely injured by fire at Palo Alto, April 17th, 1888.)

Sable Wilkes, a black stallion, the then best three-year-old, has a record at that age of 2:18. His dam is Sable, who combines the blood of Pilot Jr., Young Copper Bottom, Hambletonian and Mambrino Chief. His sire is Guy Wilkes, a grandson of Hambletonian, and tracing on the maternal side to Mambrino Chief and Seely's American Star.

Sunol, the best two-year-old to close of 1888, has a record at that age of 2:18. It was late in the season when Sunol made the record which placed her first among two-year-olds. Earlier in the season this honor had been gracefully borne by Wildflower, 2:21, a bay mare by Electioneer, out of Mayflower; but on October 19, 1888, at the Bay District Track, San Francisco, Sunol passed the Wildflower mark and established the slightly better one of 2:20½. Eight days later (Oct. 27, 1888), at the same place, she reduced her own record to 2:18, exactly equaling the three-year-old record of Sable Wilkes, above noted.

Sunol is a bay mare, foaled in 1886, got by Electioneer out of Waxana. Waxana, a chestnut, is by General Benton, out of the Thoroughbred mare Waxy, whose breeding has been the subject of so much, and so ill-natured, criticism. Mr. Bonner, the owner of Sunol, writes under date December 5, 1891:

" * * * Sunol's second dam is by Lexington [Thoroughbred]; that has been established beyond the shadow of a doubt. * * * "

Sunol's career has been a series of triumphs, holding in succession the two-year-old, three-year-old, four-year-old, five-year-old and aged trotting records of the world; being the first to lower the long-time standard, 2:08¾, of Maud S., and establish the newer world's record, 2:08¼, as a five-year-old in 1891. Her career the past season (1892) has disappointed her admirers to some extent, as she has done practically nothing but jog, her best mile rating a little slower than 2:11 ; but she is said to be in good condition, and some fast work may reasonably be expected in 1893.

Norlaine, a brown filly, the then best yearling, whose record of 2:31½ at that age astonished the world, was by Norval, a son of Electioneer, out of Elaine, the famous trotting daughter of Messenger-Duroc and Green Mountain Maid. (Norlaine was fatally injured by fire at Palo Alto, April 17th, 1888, and died on Thursday, April 19th, following.)

All of the young Champions of 1888 were from California; three of them trace in direct descent to Electioneer—the greatest sire of trotters the world has yet known—and all are from mares speedy both in blood and performance. Another point of interest in these cases, is found in the element of pacing blood, which has so kindly mingled with that of high performing trotters in their royal ancestry.

We have thought best to insert the above outline statement of records to close of 1888—when first edition of this work was written—that the student, and the general reader as well, may form some idea of the wonderful progress made in speed development during recent years. A comparison with the following list of present champions may be of interest:

SOME OF THE FASTEST—1892.

The fastest stallions at the close of the racing season 1892 are: Stamboul, 2:07½ ; Kremlin, 2:07¾ ; Palo Alto, 2:08¾, and Allerton, 2:09¼.

Stamboul, a brown bay, is by Sultan, 2:24, out of Fleetwing—a daughter of Hambletonian 10. He was foaled in 1883, and was recently sold at auction to Mr. E. H. Harriman, of New York, for $41,000. There has been started an attempt to overthrow the honestly made 2:07½ on technical grounds—a few claiming that the start (Stockton, California, kite track, November 23, 1892) was made a few minutes prior to 10 o'clock, A. M., which is contrary to the rules of the Register Association. Whether technically barred as a "record" or not, the distance was never more honestly covered, and we shall most emphatically place his name at the head of the stallion list by virtue of the time officially reported. Stamboul's blood lines are those of the trotting-bred trotter, there being no running blood closer than the fifth generation.

Kremlin, a bay, foaled 1887, is by Lord Russell—a full brother to Maud S.—out of Eventide, a triple speed-producing grand-daughter of Hambletonian 10. His record of 2:07¾ was made on the regulation track at Nashville, Tenn., November 12, 1892, and no shadow of technical error has been charged against it. He is owned by W. R. Allen, of Allen Farm, Pittsfield, Massachusetts.

Kremlin and Stamboul have had a veritable game of see-saw for the stallion championship. Stamboul on the kite track at Stockton, Cal., Kremlin on the regulation track at Nashville, Tenn., the former driven by Walter Maben, the latter by Ed. Bither, each hooked to a bicycle sulky with pneumatic tires, began their struggles early in the fall, when Stamboul wrested the crown from Palo Alto by trotting in 2:08½. Almost immediately after, Kremlin placed it at 2:08¼ and a few days later Stamboul again reduced it to 2:08 flat. Saturday, November 12th, Kremlin again took the crown with his present record, 2:07¾, only to lose it again to Stamboul on Wednesday, November 23rd, when the present stallion record, 2:07½, was made.

Palo Alto, a bay, bred by Senator Stanford, and worthily carrying the name of the Senator's famous breeding farm, was got by Electioneer out of a strictly Thoroughbred mare—Dame Winnie. Dame Winnie, now dead, has the distinction of being the only strictly Thoroughbred mare that has produced three trotters in the 2:30 list—one of the three being better than 2:10. She was sired by Planet, out of a mare by imported Glencoe. Palo Alto was the one brilliant example of the "Thoroughbred-blood-in-the-trotter" advocates, and nobly did the game old horse support their theories. He was foaled February 15, 1882, and died July 21, 1892, of pneumonia from the effects of a cold contracted in shipment east. On Tuesday, November 17, 1891, Palo Alto wrested the stallion championship from Allerton, 2:09¼, by trotting a mile to an old-style sulky in spite of lameness in 2:08¾, equaling the ex-world's record of Maud S, and carrying the stallion crown safely into winter quarters.

Allerton, a bright brown bay, with white spots on front coronets and white hind ankles, was foaled in 1886, bred, and is still owned by C. W. Williams, Independence, Iowa. Allerton is by Jay Bird, out of Gussie Wilkes. Jay Bird is a son of George Wilkes, and Gussie Wilkes is out of Dora Wilkes, a daughter of George Wilkes. Mambrino Boy, the sire of Gussie Wilkes, is a grandson of Mambrino Chief, and Lady Frank, the dam of Jay Bird, is a granddaughter of Mambrino Chief. George Wilkes is by Hambletonian 10, and both Hambletonian and Mambrino Chief are grandsons of Mambrino (American), a son of imported Messenger. The blood which Allerton boasts carries with it speed and bottom, yet even this is second to his splendid individuality. Win or lose, that element of tenacity, which has earned for him the title of the "bull-dog trotter," never leaves him, and his warmest admirers are those who have witnessed his very few defeats. His record of 2:09¼ was made on Saturday, September 19, 1891, on the kite-shaped track at Rush Park, Independence, Ia., and the crown was held until lost to Palo Alto on the 17th of November following. As a three-year-old his performances, while overshadowed in the popular mind by the wonderful speed of his stable companion and close relative, Axtell, were, in the minds of close observers, nothing short of wonderful, and in some respects showed marked superiority to the son of Lou and William L.

C. W. Williams, who bred, owned and drove to fastest records both Axtell and Allerton, says in Rush Park catalogue for 1890:

"I was proud of Axtell on the day that he carried me a mile in 2:12 at Terre Haute, but I am free to confess that I felt a keener thrill of admiration for the young race horse Allerton when he landed a winner of the Brewster stakes at the Northwestern Breeders' Meeting, after having fought out two races of eight heats within four days, both against large fields of aged and seasoned campaigners, either one a better race than has ever been trotted by a three-year-old, and the last quarter of the last mile done at a 2:12 gait in a head-and-head contest with other horses. Axtell lowered the three-year-old record that afternoon, but the cheers which greeted his performance were feeble and tame beside the storm of applause that followed the suspense of the fight to the wire between Bassenger Boy and Allerton. When the great colt flashed past the post in that heat with Bassenger at his saddle, still trying to win, I think he placed to his credit the gamest and greatest, if not the most brilliant, record ever made by a three-year-old. And this opinion I find is shared by many breeders, particularly in Kentucky, where a popular horse must be a race horse as well as a trotter. The men who still love to talk of old Dexter and Director are the ones who fancy Allerton."

Allerton's best record of 2:09¼ was obtained as a five-year-old, hooked to an old-style sulky and against time, but after a brilliant racing campaign, in which he met and defeated the handsome bay stallion Nelson, 2:10, and Delmarch, 2:11½, and was himself defeated by the present queen of the trotting world—Nancy Hanks, 2:04.

Nelson, by the way, has been peculiarly unfortunate in having to suffer expulsion from the American Association tracks through the machinations of his owner, whose name he bears. By formal action of the Board he has lately been reinstated, and we should like to see him placed in the hands of some such man as Doble, Marvin or Splan for the campaign of 1893. The breeding of Nelson is peculiarly strong—his sire, Young Rolfe, tracing back to the famous old white-faced, white-legged pacing mare Pocahontas, 2:17½, and his dam Gretchen—a granddaughter of old Hambletonian—being out of the Morgan mare Kate, whose sire was the famous Morgan representative, Vermont Blackhawk. If Nelson does not reduce his record in 1893 it will be through no fault of his breeding or his individuality.

The stallion crown has had a numerous succession in the last few years. Allerton took the championship from Nelson, who had held it prior to September 4, 1891, with his record of 2:10¾, made October 21, 1890, and who had in turn received it from Axtell, whose record of 2:12 was made as a three-year-old earlier in the same year. Axtell received the crown from Maxey Cobb, 2:13¼, who was first by record at the close of 1888. Axtell, a dark bay, was bred by C. W. Williams, of Independence, Iowa, who also drove him to his wonderful three-year-old record. His sire is William L., a son of George Wilkes, and his dam is Lou by Mambrino Boy—a grandson of Mambrino Chief. The contest

AMERICAN TROTTERS. 75

NANCY HANKS, 2:04.
The present Queen of Trotters.

between Axtell and Sunol for the three-year-old championship in 1889 is still fresh in the minds of horsemen; and, although at length beaten as to record by the fleety daughter of Electioneer, the sturdy son of William L. was sold to Col. John W. Conley, W. P. Ijams and others, for $105,000 net cash—a sum he has much more than paid back in his three years' stud service at a fee of $1,000.

The fastest mares at the close of the racing season 1892, are: Nancy Hanks, 2:04; Martha Wilkes, 2:08; Sunol, 2:08¼; Maud S., 2:08¾, and Belle Vara, 2:08¾.

Nancy Hanks, the reigning queen, is a beautifully built bright bay mare, owned by J. Malcolm Forbes, Boston, Mass., and was foaled in 1886. Her sire (see pedigree in full) is Happy Medium—a son of Hambletonian—and her dam is Nancy Lee, by Dictator—also a son of Hambletonian. Her record at the close of 1891 was 2:09, but in 1892 it was rapidly lowered at least a half dozen times until Wednesday, September 29th, when she made her present mark, 2:04, on the regulation track at Terre Haute, Indiana, hooked to a bicycle sulky, and driven by Doble. The gait of Nancy Hanks when going at full speed is about as near the perfection of trotting motion as the writer ever expects to see. There is absolutely no friction, and almost no body motion; indeed, when at full speed she would prove as comfortable a saddler as any of the modern "single-footers" that delight the rider's heart. She is still in the hands of Mr. Doble, who has driven her to all her fast records, and may very possibly lower her present mark the coming season.

We present her portrait through the courtesy of the *American Trotter*, Independence, Iowa.

Martha Wilkes (foaled 1883), a large, rangy, rather coarse-looking bay mare, is by Alcyone, a son of George Wilkes, and out of Ella by Clark Chief. Her record of 2:08 was made with a bicycle sulky, on Thursday, September 1, 1892, at Independence, Iowa. It is possible that on account of a technicality this record will not be allowed by the Register Association, in which event her best technical "record" will be the mark 2:08¼ made at Evansville, Indiana, in the second heat of a race, September 29th, following. She was bred by Mrs. Carrie M. Marders, Pine Grove, Kentucky, who sold the mare to Mr. E. D. Wiggin, of Boston, her present owner. In the opinion of some, Martha Wilkes is a dangerous rival to Nancy Hanks, but we cannot concur in such opinion. That she is both game and fast there can be no question, but on neither count does she equal the present queen.

Sunol, third on the list by virtue of her 2:08¼ (Stockton, California, kite, November 20, 1891, old-style sulky), we have already mentioned in detail. She is in the hands of Charles Marvin, and if no further misfortune occurs we expect to see her reduce her record in 1893. Whether she may reach the record set by Nancy Hanks is a question to be settled by trial; she undoubtedly is capable of trotting in very fast time, and we hope to see her fulfill Mr. Bonner's expectations during the coming season.

Maud S. and Belle Vara are tied as to record, 2:08¾, for fourth place. Of the former we need say little. The chestnut daughter of Harold and Miss Russell is now in her nineteenth year, and, although possible, it is hardly probable that she will ever again trot to as low a record as her own 2:08¾, made with an old-style sulky, July 30, 1885, and so many years untouched as the fastest trotting record of the world. Maud S. has been a queen indeed; and, while we doff our hat to Sunol, Martha Wilkes and Nancy Hanks, we cannot fail to record our loving admiration for the great mare whose name is yet a household word throughout her native land.

Belle Vara (foaled 1887) is a black mare by Vatican, out of Nell by Estille's Eric—a son of Ericsson. Her 2:08¾ was made September 30, 1892, in the first heat of a race against Walter E. and three other horses, at Terre Haute, Indiana. Although Belle Vara had the advantage of Maud S. in being hooked to a bicycle sulky, the fact that her record was made in a neck and neck race with other horses should place her on a fairly equal footing as to actual merit with the ex-queen, whose 2:08¾ was made against time. Vatican is by Belmont, out of Vara, by Rysdyk's Hambletonian—a statement which explains sufficiently well the wonderful speed of Vatican's daughter, Belle Vara.

The fastest geldings at the close of racing season 1892, are: Jay Eye See, 2:10; Lord Clinton and Little Albert, each 2:10¼; Guy, 2:10¾, and St. Julien, 2:11¼.

Jay Eye See was first on the gelding list in 1888, and no gelding has yet supplanted him. His breeding, description, and wonderful pacing record of 2:06¼ made this season, have already been given.

Lord Clinton and Little Albert, tied for second place at 2:10¼, are both newcomers, and as their records show, are phenomenally fast. Lord Clinton is a handsome, mouse-black gelding, carrying a large per cent. of Morgan blood—his sire being Denning's Allen, he by Honest Allen—a son of Ethan Allen. Clinton's dam is a speedy-looking little running mare of unknown breeding, but supposably bearing Thoroughbred blood. His record of 2:10¼ was made with a bicycle sulky at Independence, Iowa, September 1, 1892, and was one of the most remarkable performances it has ever been the writer's good fortune to witness. His main competitors in the race were Lobasco—a bay stallion driven by McHenry—and Little Albert, who were made even favorites in the pools. Little Albert was really believed to be the better horse, but the fact that the stallion was to be driven by McHenry brought him up to even money with the chestnut gelding. Clinton was practically overlooked by the "talent," and his backers secured long odds and made heavy winnings. In the first heat Clinton finished third, Lobasco and Little Albert fighting neck and neck from start to finish. The judges gave the heat to Lobasco in 2:11½, but the blaze face of Little Albert was plainly a few inches in front of Lobasco's nose, as was afterwards proved by the instantaneous photograph of the finish. In the second heat, Raybould held Clinton well back until the turn into the stretch, when he set sail for the leaders. McHenry, behind Lobasco, and Kelly with Little Albert, were busily watching each other, and hardly realized the danger that threatened until Clinton was fully abreast and going at a 2:08 clip. Lobasco could not carry the speed, and Clinton won by a length from Little Albert, who gamely drove the winner out in 2:10¼. After this heat Little Albert was never better than third.

In the scoring for the third heat, McHenry, who had laid up the stallion after his break at the stretch in the second heat, looked smilingly confident and determined to win. Lobasco was still the favorite; but the speed which Clinton had shown in the stretch, and the really easy manner in which he stepped away from Little Albert, after passing the distance, found him plenty of buyers, and the mutuals showed nearly even betting when the word was given. McHenry drove like a demon, and to his credit be it said, Lobasco never made a gamer fight against greater odds. Clinton kept the pole in spite of McHenry's driving, and down the stretch the two came neck and neck. The stallion was trotting a magnificent race, and his friends were never more confident of success. But the scene soon changed: Lobasco had done his best; Clinton had plenty to spare, and in the last fifty yards stepped easily away from the stallion, winning by an open length in 2:11 flat. The concluding heat was won by Clinton in slow time, Lobasco winning place from Little Albert.

Little Albert is a light chestnut gelding with blaze face, campaigned by Mr. Saulisbury, of Pleasanton, California. His sire is Albert W., a son of Electioneer, and his dam is a daughter of Roach's American Star. His record of 2:10¼ was made with a bicycle sulky, September 22, 1892, at Columbus, Indiana, in the third heat of a five heat race, which he won.

Guy, third on the list by record, we have already mentioned. His record of 2:10¾ was made with an old-style sulky, at Cleveland, Ohio, August 1, 1889.

St. Julien, who was second on the list in 1888, has fallen back to fourth place, and his record, 2:11¼, has been beaten by so many trotters as to seem comparatively slow.

The present holders of the mile records for age are: One-year-old, Frou Frou, 2:25¼; two-year-old, Arion, 2:10¾; three-year-old, Sunol, 2:10½, and Arion, 2:10½; four-year-old, Moquette, 2:10; five-year-old, Kremlin, 2:07¾.

Frou Frou, the best yearling, is a bay filly foaled 1890, got by Sidney, a trotting bred pacer, out of Flirt by Buccaneer. Her record of 2:25¼ was made on the Stockton, California, kite, November 28, 1891. She was hooked to an old-style sulky, and driven by Millard Saunders.

It will be remembered that in 1888 the yearling record was held by Norlaine, 2:31½. Since that time Norlaine's mantle has successively fallen on Freedom, a bay colt by Sable Wilkes, who made a yearling record of 2:29¾, October 18, 1890; Bell Bird, a brown filly by Electioneer, who made a yearling record of 2:26¼, October 21, 1891; and on Frou Frou, where it now so gracefully rests.

Arion, the best two-year-old, is a bay colt, foaled 1889, got by Electioneer out of Manette by Nutwood. His record of 2:10¾ was made on the Stockton kite, November 10, 1891. He was driven by Charles Marvin to an old-style sulky, and the performance may be justly considered the most remarkable record for age ever made. Arion was bred by Senator Stanford, at Palo Alto, California, and by him sold to Mr. Forbes, of Boston, Massachusetts, at the reported figure $125,000. The 2:10¾ of Arion, by the way, is the seventh fastest stallion record of the world, an honor which he divides with Lobasco, who made an equal record during the fall of 1892. In his three-year-old form, Arion, at Nashville, Tennessee, November 12, 1892, reduced his two-year-old record to 2:10½—equaling the three-year-old record of Sunol, and placing him sixth on the stallion list—but there are so many good ones in the field that it would be pure conjecture to attempt to name the winning four-year-old of 1893.

Sunol, in her three-year-old form, easily reduced the three-year-old record of Sable Wilkes, by trotting the regulation track at San Francisco, California, on November 9, 1889, in 2:10½. She pulled an old-style sulky, with Marvin up. The fight between Sunol and Axtell for the three-year-old championship in 1889 is a notable companion piece to the struggles of Stamboul and Kremlin this year for the stallion crown. Axtell began the fight August 25, 1889, when he trotted in 2:14 at Chicago, Illinois. Sunol followed October 2, by trotting in 2:13¾, at Fresno, California. On October 11, 1889, Williams drove Axtell to his present record, 2:12, at Terre Haute, Indiana; and the Iowa colt was thought to be secure in his well earned laurels. His victory, however, was short lived, as Marvin was able to drive the California filly a mile in 2:10½, at San Francisco, November 9th, following, and leave her in possession of the three-year-old record, which she still holds, but jointly with Arion since November 12, 1892.

Moquette, the best four-year-old, is a bay horse, foaled in 1888, got by Wilton, 2:19¼, out of Betsy and I, by Ericsson. His record of 2:10 was made on the regulation track at Richmond, Ind., September 16, 1892. He was hooked to a bicycle sulky, and driven by Mike Bowerman.

At the close of 1888, the four-year-old record was held by Manzanita, 2:16. The year following (1889) her record was equaled by Edgemark, and on August 23, 1890, it was reduced by Sunol, who trotted at Washington Park, Chicago, in 2:10½, and carried the four-year-old record for over two years, until lost to the stallion Moquette.

Kremlin, the best five-year-old, we have mentioned as second on the stallion list. His record was made to a bicycle sulky, with Bither up, on the regulation track at Nashville, Tenn. Prior to this, the five-year-old record had been held by Sunol, at 2:08¼, made before an old-style sulky, and driven by Marvin, on the Stockton kite, November 20, 1891.

The advance in speed since 1888, and especially since 1891, has been phenomenal, and marks the rapid evolution of the forces joined to push the interests of the trotting horse. Track improvement was the first step—closely followed by the advent of the modern bicycle sulky, with ball bearings and pneumatic tires. Beyond all queston the bicycle sulky cuts from 2 or 3 to 6 or 8 seconds from a horse's record made with old-style sulky, and this fact must be borne in mind when records are compared. With the old-style sulky it was conceded by all horsemen that the kite-shaped track was faster than the regulation track by from 1 to 3 seconds, but since the bicycle sulky has come into general use the records have apparently suffered more on ovals than on kites.

What the outcome of the present record reduction may be, we shall not attempt to predict. Many think the mile in two minutes a probability of the coming season, but it must be remembered that the drop of four seconds from the present fastest record, 2:04, to the supposable 2:00 flat, means a wonderful increase in the rate at which the horse must travel. Sixty yards in a race is a long distance between first and second horses, yet this is what four seconds, at the rate of speed supposed, would cover. It is certainly possible, but the horse that accomplishes the result must be favored in everything—including driver, sulky, track and weather.

As a fitting recognition of the value of pacing blood in the American trotting horse, we give the following list of pacers that have made 2:10 or better:

Mascot, 2:04; Hal Pointer, 2:04½; Direct, 2:05½; Flying Jib, 2:05¾; Johnston, 2:06¼; Jay Eye See, 2:06¼; Guy, 2:06¾; W. Wood, 2:07; Vinette, 2:07¼; Roy Wilkes, 2:07¾; Silkwood, 2:08¾; Blue Sign, 2:08¾; Robert J., Manager and Winslow Wilkes, each, 2:09¾; Cricket, 2:10.

When it is remembered that only one horse (Johnston, 2:06¼) had a record better than 2:10 in 1888, we can understand how great has been the progress in pacing speed development. Mascot's 2:04—exactly equaling the world's trotting record of Nancy Hanks—was made to a bicycle sulky, on the regulation track at Terre Haute, Ind., in the first heat of the fastest and most remarkable pacing race on record, September 29, 1892.

MASCOT, 2:04.
Bay gelding; the present King of Pacers.

Concerning this race, the *American Trotter*, Independence, Ia., issue of October 6, 1892, has this to say:

"For the second time in history the 2:05 mark has been beaten in harness, the pacer Mascot putting in a heat at Terre Haute last week in the same notch that Nancy Hanks touched when she trotted in 2:04. As the gelding did this in a race, starting from the outside, the performance surpasses that of the Kentucky mare in point of merit, and one of the quarters was a trifle faster, when Mascot stepped from the half to the third of the gold-tipped posts in 29½ seconds. The effort told on him so much that he did not get another heat of the free.for-all pace, and Flying Jib, who carried the new champion along, was also defeated for the same reason. The pair went lapped to the quarter in 32¼ seconds, and were at the half in 1:03½, where Mascot drew away a little. The Californian closed from there, and the clip became terrific. The three-quarters were covered in 1:33, or a 1:58 clip, and Flying Jib was at Mascot's shoulder when he finished in 2:04. The second heat was also sensational, but rated differently, Flying Jib carrying Mascot to the quarter in 30¼ seconds, and the half in 1:00¾. To come up the hill at a two-minute gait tired the pair, but Jib had enough speed left to out-finish the other gelding in 2:05¾. Meanwhile McHenry had been laying Guy up to the flag, and cutting him loose in the third heat had the faster pair at his mercy. Flying Jib made the gray stallion pace the third heat in 2:06¼, and the fourth in 2:08¾. Mascot then tried to redeem himself, and was closing on Guy in the last quarter of the fifth heat, when he rushed to the pole, so that Andrews could not pull him out in time to overhaul the leader. Guy was under the whip, but came home resolutely in 2:08¼, making five heats that paralyzed all previous averages in a race, the rate being 2:06⅗. There is little doubt if the judges had forced McHenry to drive for every heat, he would have been unable to win the race."

Mascot, whose pedigree we give in full on another page, is a bay, foaled in 1885, and is now owned by W. P. Taylor, Buffalo, N. Y. We present his portrait through the courtesy of *Breeder's Gazette*, Chicago, Illinois.

For the benefit of those who wish to know the leading blood lines in the stud, we give the following list of sires in order of merit at the close of 1892, kindly prepared at our request by Mr. S. S. Toman, the genial editor of the *American Trotter*, Independence, Iowa:

SIRE.	NUMBER IN 2:30 LIST.	
	Trotters.	Pacers.
1st, Electioneer	131	1
2nd, Nutwood	82	12
3rd, Happy Medium	80	4
4th, Red Wilkes	69	14
5th, Geo. Wilkes	71	7
6th, Onward	53	11
7th, Blue Bull	56	5

Before leaving this chapter it may be well to explain what is meant by the term "Standard Bred," as applied to trotting stock, and this we do by inserting in full

THE STANDARD OF REGISTRATION,

as revised and adopted by the American Trotting Register Association, May 19, 1891:

"In order to define what constitutes a standard-bred horse, and to establish a breed of trotters and pacers on a more intelligent basis, the following rules are adopted to control admission to the records of pedigrees. When an animal meets the requirements of admission and is duly registered, it shall be accepted as a standard-bred animal :

"First. Any trotting stallion that has a record of two minutes and thirty seconds (2:30), or pacing stallion that has a record of two minutes and twenty-five seconds (2:25) or better, provided any of his get has a record of 2:35 trotting, or 2:30 pacing, or better, or provided his sire or dam is already a standard animal.

"Second. Any mare or gelding that has a trotting record of 2:30, or pacing record of 2:25, or better.

"Third. Any horse that is the sire of two trotters with records of 2:30, or two pacers with records of 2:25, or one trotter with a record of 2:30, and one pacer with a record of 2:25, or better.

"Fourth. Any horse that is the sire of one trotter with a record of 2:30, or one pacer with a record of 2:25, or better, providing he has either of the following additional qualifications: 1. A trotting record of 2:35 or a pacing record of 2:30, or better. 2. Is the sire of two other animals with trotting records of 2:35, or pacing records of 2:30, or one trotter with a record of 2:35, and one pacer with a record of 2:30, or better. 3 Has a sire or dam that is already a standard animal.

"Fifth. Any mare that has produced a trotter with a record of 2:30, or pacer with a record of 2:25, or better.

"Sixth. The progeny of a standard horse when out of a standard mare.

"Seventh. The female progeny of a standard horse when out of a mare by a standard horse.

"Eighth. The female progeny of a standard horse when out of a mare whose dam is a standard mare.

"Ninth. Any mare that has a trotting record of 2:35, or a pacing record of 2:30, or better, whose sire or dam is a standard animal."

AMERICAN TROTTERS.

Pedigree chart for **NANCY HANKS**, showing ancestry through **HAPPY MEDIUM** and **NANCY LEE**.

HAPPY MEDIUM
- Rysdyk's Hambletonian
  - Abdallah
    - Mambrino
      - Imp. Messenger
      - Amazonia (Said to be by a son of Imp. Messenger.)
    - Chas. Kent Mare
      - Imp. Bellfounder
        - Imp. Sour Crout
        - Daughter of
      - One Eye
        - Bishop's Hambletonian Silvertail by Imp. Messenger
          - Imp. Messenger
          - Pheasant { Imp. Shark / Daughter of Imp. Medley
        - Daughter of Imp. Messenger
          - Imp. Messenger
          - Pheasant { Imp. Shark / Daughter of Imp. Medley
- Princess
  - Andrus' Hambletonian
    - Judson's Hambletonian
      - Bishop's Hambletonian
      - Not recorded in the trotting records
    - Not traced
  - Isaiah Wilcox Mare
    - Butrick's Engineer
      - Engineer
      - Not traced
    - Thoroughbred
      { Imp. Messenger / Thoroughbred }

NANCY LEE
- Dictator
  - Rysdyk's Hambletonian
    - Abdallah
      - Mambrino
        - Imp. Messenger
        - Amazonia (Said to be by a son of Imp. Messenger.)
      - Chas. Kent Mare
        - Imp. Bellfounder { Imp. Sour Crout / Daughter of }
        - One Eye
          - Bishop's Hambletonian
            - Imp. Messenger
            - Pheasant { Imp. Shark / Daughter of Imp. Medley }
          - Silvertail, by Imp. Messenger
            - Imp. Messenger
            - Pheasant { Imp. Shark / Daughter of Imp. Medley }
  - Clara
    - American Star, (Stockholm's)
      - Duroc
        - Imp. Diomed { Imp. Whirligig / Miss Slammerkin, by Imp. Wildair }
        - Amanda, by Gray Diomed
      - Untraced
    - Sally Slouch
      - Henry
        - Sir Archy { Imp. Diomed / Castianira { Rockingham / Tabitha, by Trentham } }
        - Daughter of Imp. Diomed
      - Daughter of Imp. Messenger
- Sophy
  - Edwin Forrest (Alexander's)
    - Bay Kentucky Hunter—by Old Kentucky Hunter—Highlander (Watkin's)
      - Untraced
    - Doll
      - Bertrand (Thoroughbred)
      - Daughter of Lance (Thoroughbred)
  - Sophronia
    - Brown Pilot (Parker's)
    - Daughter of

AMERICAN TROTTERS.   85

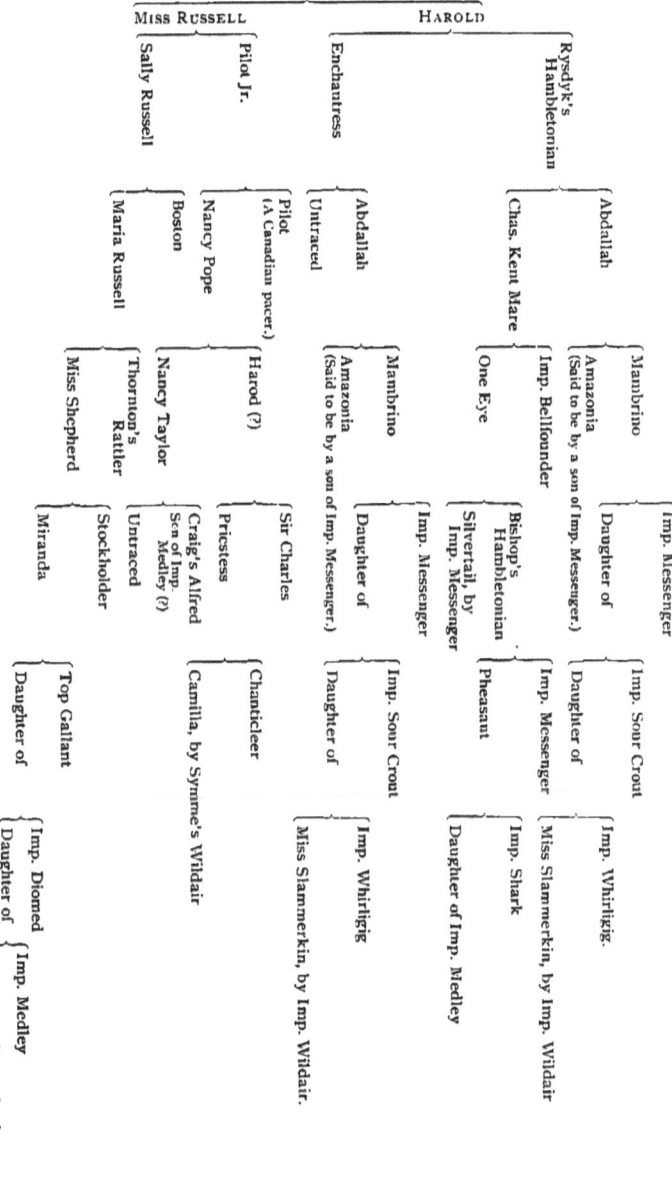

AMERICAN TROTTERS.

PHALLAS.
├─ DICTATOR
│ ├─ Rysdyk's Hambletonian
│ │ ├─ Abdallah
│ │ │ ├─ Mambrino
│ │ │ │ ├─ Imp. Messenger
│ │ │ │ │ ├─ Imp. Sour Crout
│ │ │ │ │ └─ Daughter of
│ │ │ │ └─ Amazonia
│ │ │ │   └─ (Said to be by a son of Imp. Messenger.)
│ │ │ └─ Chas. Kent Mare
│ │ │   ├─ Imp. Bellfounder
│ │ │   │ ├─ Bishop's Hambletonian
│ │ │   │ │ ├─ Imp. Messenger
│ │ │   │ │ └─ Daughter of { Imp. Messenger
│ │ │   │ └─ Silvertail, by Imp. Messenger
│ │ │   └─ One Eye
│ │ │   └─ Pheasant { Imp. Shark / Daughter of Imp. Medley
│ └─ Clara
│   ├─ Seely's American Star
│   │ ├─ American Star (Stockholm's)
│   │ │ ├─ Duroc
│   │ │ │ └─ Imp. Diomed / Amanda, by Gray Diomed
│   │ │ └─ Untraced
│   │ └─ Sally Slouch
│   │   ├─ Henry { Sir Archy / Daughter of Imp. Diomed
│   │   └─ Daughter of Imp. Messenger
│   └─ Dam of Shark
│
└─ BETSY TROTWOOD
   ├─ Clark Chief
   │ ├─ Mambrino Chief
   │ │ ├─ Mambrino Paymaster
   │ │ │ ├─ Mambrino { Imp. Messenger / Daughter of
   │ │ │ └─ Daughter of Imp. Paymaster(?)
   │ │ └─ Dam of Goliath and Downing's Bay Messenger
   │ └─ Little Nora
   │   ├─ Mambrino Paymaster
   │   │ └─ Dam of Goliath and Livingston Mare.
   │   └─ Wadkins Sir William
   │   └─ Daughter of Imp. Paymaster(?) { Sir Archy
   ├─ Ericsson
   │ ├─ Mrs. Caudle Mambrino Chief
   │ │ └─ Sir William Jr. (Prewitt's)
   │ └─ Mrs. Caudle
   │   ├─ Untraced Hannibal (Thoroughbred son of Shakespeare.)
   │   └─ Transport
   └─ Daughter of
      ├─ Daughter of
      └─ Untraced

(Right side ancestry):
- Imp. Sour Crout { Rockingham / Tabitha, by Trentham
- Daughter of
- Imp. Messenger { Imp. Whirligig / Miss Slammerkin, by Imp. Wildair
- Daughter of
- Imp. Diomed { Castianira
- Virginius { Nancy Air, by Imp. Bedford
- Imp. Whirligig { Imp. Whirligig / Miss Slammerkin, by Imp. Wildair
- Miss Slammerkin, by Imp. Wildair
- Imp. Sour Crout { Rockingham / Tabitha, by Trentham
- Daughter of

AMERICAN TROTTERS.   87

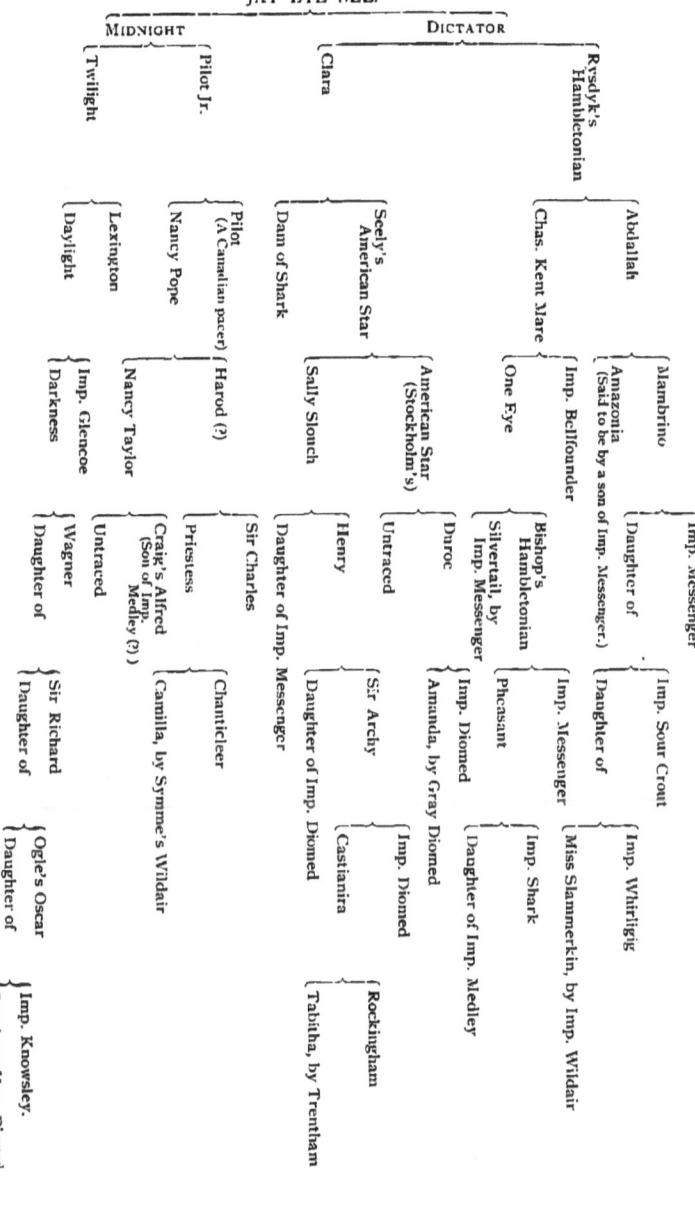

AMERICAN TROTTERS.

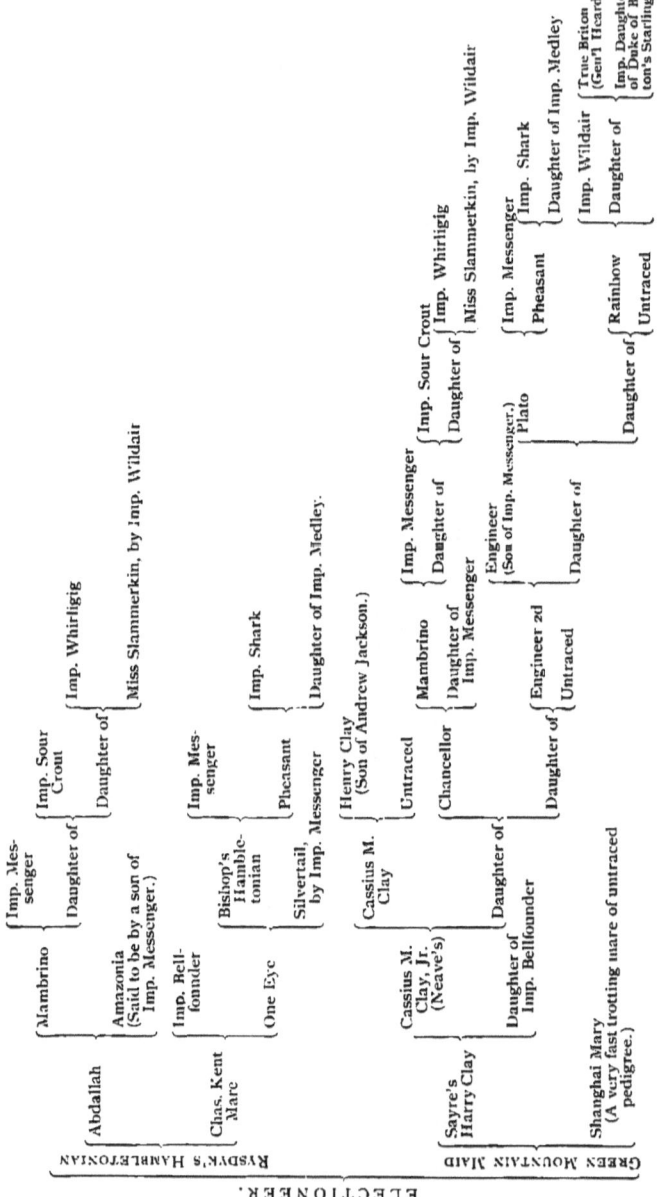

AMERICAN TROTTERS.

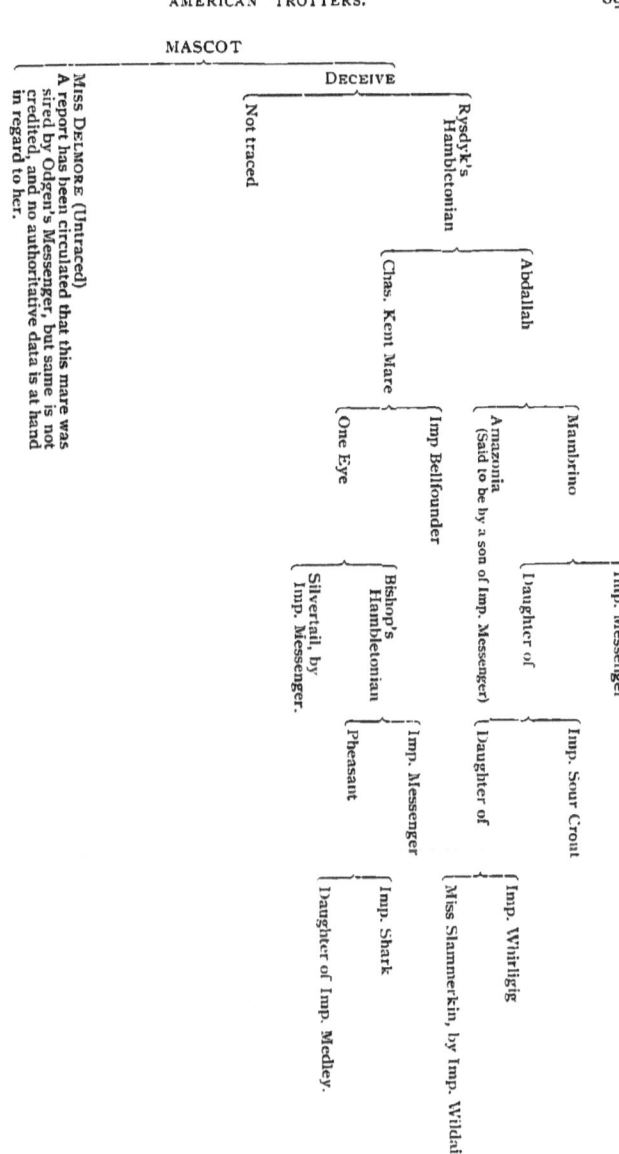

MASCOT
- DECEIVE
  - Rysdyk's Hambletonian
    - Abdallah
      - Mambrino
        - Imp. Messenger
        - Daughter of Imp. Sour Crout
      - Amazonia (Said to be by a son of Imp. Messenger)
    - Chas. Kent Mare
      - Imp. Bellfounder
        - Bishop's Hambletonian
          - Imp. Messenger
          - Daughter of Imp. Whirligig
        - Silvertail, by Imp. Messenger.
      - One Eye
        - Pheasant
          - Imp. Shark
          - Daughter of Imp. Medley.
  - Not traced
- MISS DELMORE (Untraced)
  A report has been circulated that this mare was sired by Odgen's Messenger, but same is not credited, and no authoritative data is at hand in regard to her.

(Miss Slammerkin, by Imp. Wildair)

Chapter XV.

ORLOFF TROTTERS.

The Orloff family of trotting horses derives its name from the Russian Count Alexis Orloff Tschismensky, an enthusiastic lover of horses, who is credited with producing the breed.

In 1775, he imported the gray Arabian stallion, Smetanxa—a horse of unusual size and power. This horse was used on a Danish mare, the produce being a stallion known as Polkan First, who in turn produced from a Dutch mare the horse Bars First—commonly regarded as the progenitor of the breed. Lubezney First, Lebed First and Dobroy First, three sons of Bars First, have given character to the blood of their sire, and helped to fix the trotting instinct. The count selected his stallions invariably from the foundation stock just noted, but resorted to the better class of English and Dutch mares whenever practicable.

The Orloff, like the American Trotter, is a made-up animal, but he shows neither the speed at short distance, nor the endurance on a long stretch, which characterizes so many of our American Trotters. A few have been brought to America, but they are by no means generally known.

The prevailing color is gray, but blacks are common and bays are frequently found. Possibly the Orloff may at some future time be used to relieve the inbred condition into which certain families of our American Trotters are in danger of falling; but as it stands now, the American is so far superior to the Russian Trotter that our own breeders of trotting stock have every reason to be well satisfied with the magnificent results already reached, and should feel encouraged to put forth still greater energies in the future.

Chapter XVI.

SHETLAND PONIES.

They are, as the name indicates, natives of the Shetland Islands, north of Scotland. As to their origin, one thing may be stated without fear of contradiction, and that is: No trace of racing (Thoroughbred) blood has ever found its way into their breeding.

Their resemblance to the ponies of Scandinavia, and the further fact

that the Islands were first taken possession of by Scandinavian plunderers, and for a long time (until the Fifteenth Century) remained attached to the crown of Norway, furnish good evidence that the Shetland Ponies are of Norwegian derivation. Tradition, however, has it, that some of the horses carried by the great Spanish Armada—many vessels of which were wrecked off the rugged Scotland coast—escaped to the Islands, and have since left their impress upon the native pony stock; the tradition has the color of probability, more than this cannot be definitely stated. Whatever their origin or subsequent mixture with other breeds, the Shetlands show in appearance and character the well-known influence of severe climate and scanty food. They are extremely hardy, very small—standing about 8 to 11 hands high; shaggy coated, with bushy mane and tail; always round and smooth in the barrel; with short, fine legs and round, handsome feet. All colors are found, but brown, black and spotted—black and white or brown and white, are most common.

The American Shetland Pony Club has been recently organized, and a Stud Book started. Animals are admitted to registration under the following rules, sent in by Mortimer Levering, LaFayette, Ind., the present secretary:

"Shetland Ponies 46 inches or less in height will be admitted as follows:

"1. Shetland Pony by sire and out of dam both recorded in the Shetland Pony Club Stud Book.

"2. Shetland Pony having four top crosses, in each case by imported sire, or by sire recorded in the Shetland Pony Club Stud Book.

"3. Shetland Pony examined and approved by the examining committee, as provided by rule 6 of Additional Rules Governing Entries."

The Shetlands are the safest and most popular ponies for children's use, and large numbers of them are, and have been, annually brought to the United States for this purpose. They are remarkably intelligent, and can be readily trained. Their hardiness and muscular endurance have always been marked; but they have little or no practical value outside of that already mentioned. When bred in America, the superior food and attention given causes a considerable increase in size; and—since the smallest ponies are in greatest demand—this fact has led to the practice, quite common at the present time, of importing as wanted for sale, direct from the Islands.

The illustration—engraved after a sketch from life, expressly for our use—is an accurate representation of the breed.

Chapter XVII.

WELSH PONIES.

Of late years quite a number of these beautiful little fellows have found their way to the United States; and, like the Shetlands, are in great demand for children's use. Of their origin Low says:

"The mountains of Wales in like manner give birth to a race of small horses adapted to an elevated country of scanty herbage, * * * which must be supposed to be pure with respect to their descent from the pristine race."

The typical Welsh Pony stands about 13 hands high, has a small head, high withers, smooth, rounded, close coupled body, with neat, flat legs and sound feet. Color varies; bays and browns, especially the lighter shades, are common, and blacks and other colors are frequently found.

Chapter XVIII.

EXMOOR PONIES.

This breed—a few of which have been imported to the United States—has its origin in the Exmoor Forest region, lying partly in Devonshire and partly in Somersetshire, England. They are doubtless descended from the same original stock as the Welsh breed, but differ considerably from the latter at the present time.

They are shaggy, long haired, stand about 12 or 13 hands high, and, although not so smooth and attractive in appearance as the Welsh, are said to be remarkably hardy. Bays, browns and blacks are the most common colors.

Chapter XIX.

MEXICAN PONIES.
(*Mustangs.*)

Since the conquest of Mexico by the Spaniards (1519-22) a race of so-called Mexican horses has been established, differing from their Spanish ancestry only in those things naturally affected by the semi-wild state in which they have existed, and the consequent lack of artificial care and attention. From Mexico they scattered gradually northward until the entire Southwest, including Texas, New Mexico and Arizona, was supplied with a native or wild horse stock, from the same original source. Doubtless, also, the Mexican breed has contributed largely to form the pony breeds of the more northern Indian tribes. Discussion of this point will come more properly, however, under the next heading, which see.

In Texas the Mexican Ponies have been commonly called "Mustangs," and it is by this name that they have become notorious as the most ill-tempered, unmanageable, but, withal, most wiry, tough and enduring specimens of the equine race to be found.

In height they stand about 12 to 13 or 14 hands, weighing from 600 to 800 pounds; all colors are found, but the colors which might perhaps be called characteristic of the breed are yellow clay, smoky dun and mouse, with usually a darker stripe along the middle of the back. The various shades of roan are quite common; white or pink roans nearly always showing a skin of the same color at the nose and on inside of thighs; and spotted ponies—"paints"—are frequently found.

The prominent characteristic of the Mexican Mustang lies in his wonderful powers of endurance. He will carry a heavy man on his back, and make a distance each day, for a month or six weeks' journey, that would tax the powers of the best Kentucky Thoroughbred. As to their viciousness or ill-temper, about which so much has been written, we think it entirely overdrawn. Mustang colts, taken up when two years old, and handled in the same manner that eastern horsemen handle colts of higher market value, will show a disposition entirely different from the wild, vicious temper commonly imputed to them. Indeed, the reverse is also true, since it is a well-known fact that among "American" horses—as the larger improved horses brought from the east are called—or their descendants on the range are found the worst speci-

MEXICAN PONIES (MUSTANGS.)

mens of the "bucking" or "pitching" type. While the tendency of running wild is always toward wildness, if not viciousness, yet we believe the notorious Mustang disposition is largely a product of very poor methods of breaking and handling.

Before leaving this subject, it may be of interest to note a remarkable case of prolonged gestation, reported by Mr. Z. T. Moore, of Traer, Ia., in the *Breeder's Gazette* of Chicago. The mare is said to be a Mustang; in 1887 she carried her foal 377 days, and in 1888 her foal was retained 389 days—foals in both instances doing well. The average period of gestation for mares under domestication rarely exceeds 350 to 360 days; but it is commonly observed that mares of any breed, as a rule, carry their foals longer when allowed to breed and range in pasture without care or restraint, than when kept up and favored with extra care and attention. We have no doubt that, if statistics could be as carefully kept of the service and birth dates among semi-wild horses as is done among careful breeders of improved stock, we should find a marked difference in the average length of gestation.

The illustration was engraved expressly for our use, from a photograph taken at Laredo, Texas, and is a fair representation of the modern Mexican Pony. Mr. E. H. Sauvignet, of Laredo, has our thanks for assistance in securing the photograph.

Chapter XX.

INDIAN PONIES.

As noted in the preceding chapter, Indian Ponies doubtless trace in direct line to a more or less remote Mexican ancestry. Indeed, the horse stock of the tribes of Western Texas, New Mexico and Arizona is nothing if not Mexican; but of the more northern tribes, it is probable that another factor has been potent in forming the breed. That the other factor must be sought in northern latitudes is beyond question, and we are convinced—after careful, continued observation of the ponies belonging to the various "Reservation" tribes—that the Canadian Pony, a descendant of the small horse stock of France, imported to Canada at an early date, is the animal that must bear the responsibility. We adopt this conclusion for several reasons, chief among them being the fact that Mustang colors are rarely found among Indian Ponies proper—the latter showing a great predominance of dark bay, brown and spotted (bay and white or brown and white), and the further fact that their conformation is decidedly different. The spotted marking is

INDIAN PONIES.

quite common, and it is difficult to trace its source, unless we accept the common belief that it is derived from horses inhabiting the mountainous parts of Persia and adjoining countries, through the Spanish and French ancestry.

Indian Ponies are, as a rule, kind and gentle, enduring as much in the colder regions of the Northwest as do their Mustang relations in the Southwest. There is very little ill-temper observed among northern Indian Ponies: a simple fact—whether due to different treatment or to modification by Canadian crosses, we do not pretend to say.

DESCRIPTION AND CHARACTERISTICS.

Color, dark bay, brown and spotted (bay and white and brown and white), with almost always darker points. Some of these ponies are a most beautiful blood-bay, with black points, and, when they can be obtained, make excellent saddle ponies. (As a rule the better class of Indians are loth to part with their ponies, and even when a sale has been completed, it is no uncommon thing for the Indian to become sick of his bargain before the pony is out of sight, and insist on buying it back again.)

In height they stand about 12 to 13 or 14 hands, weighing from 650 to 850 pounds; they are rather more blockily built than Mustangs, the cannons are wider, and the pasterns more on the upright order.

The illustration was engraved from a photograph taken in the Chickasaw Nation, Indian Territory, and we take this occasion to return thanks to Mr. E. J. Smith, of Woodford, I. T. (now of Denison, Texas), for his kind assistance in securing it. The ponies represented weigh about 700 pounds each, and are said by the Indians to be purely Indian bred as far back as their ancestry is known. The boy holding them is a 17-year-old full-blooded Chickasaw, by name John Turnbull.

Chapter XXI.

HINTS ON SELECTION, CARE AND MANAGEMENT OF HORSES.

In selecting a horse, more actual knowledge is needed than can be secured from books alone. The accurate judge of horse-flesh is one who has made the subject a practical, continued study for years, and who has at command not only the close knowledge gained by experience, but a good understanding, as well, of the principles which underlie Force and Action, applied in the movements of the horse. For an exhaustive discussion of this subject, the reader is referred to any one of the special works on the horse—especially such books as Sanders' Horse Breeding, and Helm's American Roadsters and Trotting Horses, with which he is doubtless already familiar. We can only undertake to give a few of the more prominent points, which may possibly aid somewhat in forming an intelligent judgment.

First. For draft, a horse must have weight; he may have fine action also, but the weight he must have, if capable of long pulls before heavy loads. The shoulders should be upright and heavy below, in order that strain on the traces may be met by collar resistance at such an angle as will utilize all of the force exerted. The draft horse should stand fairly high in front (rather prominent withers), and must have a chest of ample width to permit free expansion of lungs when under any temporary strain. The legs are best short, and should never exhibit that smooth, puffy appearance which always indicates a tendency to form fat at the expense of muscle; the cannons should be flat, and the joints, especially, hard and firmly bound together. As we have stated, fine action is not absolutely necessary, but for farm use a good, sprightly walk is certainly desirable. Right here we may say, that a horse of 1,200 to 1,400 pounds weight is about the heaviest that will be found profitable on the ordinary farm; the heavier animals will always be in demand for a different purpose, and an intelligent judgment will select in reference to the purpose for which desired. To be too "fiery" or "high strung" is an objection; the draft horse should be preeminently an animal of quiet—yet not sluggish—temperament. A strong, even puller will resist fatigue better, and do more service.

Second. For speed, the shoulders should be slanting, the withers medium to low, the loin and rump high, and the hind quarters long and furnished with powerful muscles. In the race horse, the propelling power comes from the rear, and a greater mistake could not be made than to select for running, a horse at all deficient in these parts, no matter how fully he might fill the judgment in other respects. The legs must have some length, and here may be added double caution as to their quality; not a particle of surplus flesh or fat should be apparent, and joints in particular must be closely knit together. The English government has a set of rules for the use of those who select horses for cavalry service, and we insert them here: they are called "Points for Rejection," but will answer equally well as points for selection :

"Reject a horse whose fore-legs are not straight; they will not stand wear. Stand behind the horse as it walks away from you, and you will be able to notice these defects, if they exist.

"Reject a horse that is light below the knee, especially if immediately below the knee; the conformation is essentially weak.

"Or a horse with long, or short or upright pasterns; long pasterns are subject to sprains; short or upright pasterns make a horse unpleasant to ride, and on account of extra concussions, are apt to cause ossific deposits.

"Or a horse with toes turned in or out. The twist generally occurs at the fetlock. Toes turned out are more objectionable than toes turned in. When toes turn out the fetlocks are generally turned in, and animals so formed are very apt to cut or brush. Both, however, are weak formations.

"Reject a horse whose hind legs are too far behind; good propelling power will be wanting, and disease as a result may be expected in the hocks. And a horse which goes either very wide or very close behind, and one with very straight or very bent hocks; the former cause undue concussion; the latter are apt to give way.

"Reject a horse that is 'split-up'—that is, shows much daylight between the thighs; propelling power comes from behind, and must be deficient in horses without due muscular development between the thighs.

"Reject a horse with flat or over large feet, or with very small feet; medium sized are best.

"Also, a horse with one foot smaller than another."

Concerning mental aptitude and physical conformation as related to selection of the horse for speed at certain gaits, we insert herewith the major portion of an article on "The Development of the American Trotter—A Study in Animal Physics", prepared by the author, read June 14, 1892, before the Texas Academy of Science, and printed in the "Transactions" of the Academy:

"* * * In the development of our own peculiar breeds, the American Trotter, the pacer and the American saddle horse, we have proved two things: First, that artificial gaiting may be made permanent and become transmissible, or subject to the laws of heredity; and second, that by solution of the gaiting problem the new world has succeeded where the old world always failed, save in the single instance of the Russian Orloff—a breed in no way equaling that finished product of the breeder's art, the American Trotter. Besides a feeling of pride in the fact that our breeders have succeeded beyond their most sanguine hopes, a close study of the methods pursued by leading trainers, and the physical and mental characters of the winning horses at either gait, brings up matters of interest to all, and of especial moment to the student of animal physics.

"Since the early years of the present century (1806), when a horse of unknown breeding trotted a full mile under saddle in the almost incredible time of 2:59 (but one second better than three minutes), the records show a series of descending steps—each step a tablet to the memory of some once famous horse.

"Flora Temple, the first to beat 2:20 in 1859, Dexter, Goldsmith Maid, Rarus, St. Julien, Jay Eye See, Maud S. and Sunol, the present queen of the trotting turf by virtue of her 2:08¼,* have each in turn lowered the world's mile record at the trot; while among pacers the record drops from that of Roanoke—first to beat 2:20 in 1852—past Pocahontas, Billy Boyce, Sleepy Tom, Little Brown Jug and Johnston, to the 2:06 of Direct, the black California wonder, that has earned and now holds the world's mile record at the pace †. * * * Brain capacity in the horse is of vital moment to the trainer, as is brain capacity in the student to the teachers under whom he seeks instruction. The sluggish, stupid brain of dullard, horse or human, will never show that firm yet plastic nature fitted best to carry knowledge. The brain one-sided in its make-up may receive instruction fairly well, but when forced to execute beyond a certain limit, fails by reason of its lack of balance, and fails to hold the mastery at the very moment when the muscles, strained beyond the power to respond in reflex action, most have need of mind control. A first essential for the horse that carries highest speed at artificial gait is a brain with ample room for strain in mental exercise—a perfect poise, that neither loses interest by lack of work in competition, nor overthrows its balance by undue excitement. The horse that "keeps his head" can be urged to greater effort and will break but rarely, catching quickly at the gait desired in obedience to the driver's will; while the horse with mental poise at best uncertain, carries his gait at moments to terrific speed, but just as surely follows up by breaking, losing time, and possibly a race, before he can be righted and held down to steady work.

"I have no patience with that narrow view which credits brain in so-called lower animals only as an 'instinct.' The horse that bears the highest training goes beyond an instinct, and shows a true brain action at once receptive and controlling in its functions. It cannot equal human mind, 'tis true, but to call it 'instinct' merely, is an insult to the horse creation.

---
* Since dethroned by Nancy Hanks, 2:04, and beaten also as to record by the stallions Kremlin, 2:07¼, and Stamboul, 2:07½.

† Direct still holds the world's mile pacing mark for stallions, having once again lowered it to 2:05½, but the world's mile pacing record is now held by the gelding Mascot, 2:04.

"Admitting, as a first essential, brain in horse as well as human, we may ask, is there a second necessary—a sort of corollary to the first—wherein the tape-line and the practiced eye may be relied on to select a future winner at the trot or pace? Can we find, in other words, some standard shape or measurement of certain parts, without which highest speed will be impossible? Perhaps no other subject in the breeder's realm brings forward such opposing forces as the proposition just advanced—nor can we say that either side is wholly in the wrong. Laws of motion, gravity and projectile speed, and strength by leverage of inert matter, have been investigated, and are fairly known; but when applied to life and vital action something else must be considered, and the strongest rule, as based on theory of motion, may be proved only by the plain exceptions found. To say that quality and speed in trotters can be determined by the tape-line to a certainty would be absurd at best; but we may be able often to reject the horse that lacks capacity to trot at speed, and thus save time and spare ourselves the disappointment certain to result from training trotters that can never trot. Bear in mind that best of form must not be taken as a guaranty of speed at either trot or pace; but this much may be said with certainty, if he lack the form demanded, he may be fast and game, may even trot well down among the lower 'teens' in seconds; but the records of the world will never be in danger, and the mark he does attain will be due to skill in training or to mental impulse, and cannot be credited to shape or trotting leverage.

"Severe exertion of the muscles, long continued, is only possible when the lungs are free in ample chest room. This we find best illustrated in the Thoroughbred or running horse; and here comes in an argument for the use of running blood in breeding trotters, which so many hold in favor. The highbred horse—the Thoroughbred—excels in this respect beyond all question, and the trotter that can stand the strain of long heat races must show the lung development of a Thoroughbred, with the dilating nostrils and the clean-fleshed throat that indicate the perfect freedom of the breath.

"The muscles of the leg, aside from leverage, which depends on length of bone, must be developed to the point of balanced tension, and especially be trained to work at all times absolutely under brain control.

"The leverage of motion in the horse rests almost solely in the quarters, front and rear. Front leverage (see illustration) is perhaps of lesser moment, from the fact that the main propelling power comes from rear development; but the trotting leverage in front is still of great importance, since by it alone we may determine reach and stroke, or smoothness of the stride. From a mechanical point of view the leverage in front presents an interesting double or compound lever, lifting of the knee being due to a lever of the third class, where the power acts between the fulcrum and resistance; while the bending of the knee, or flexure of the cannon on the fore-arm, shows a lever of the same class, combined with pulley action of the tendons at the knee. If the fore-arm bone—the Radius—be long, the lifting power of the muscles acting on the elbow as a fulcrum meets a greater weight resistance at the knee, the motion must be slower, and the knee will not be lifted high, as when the bone is shorter. If, too, the cannon bone be short in proportion to

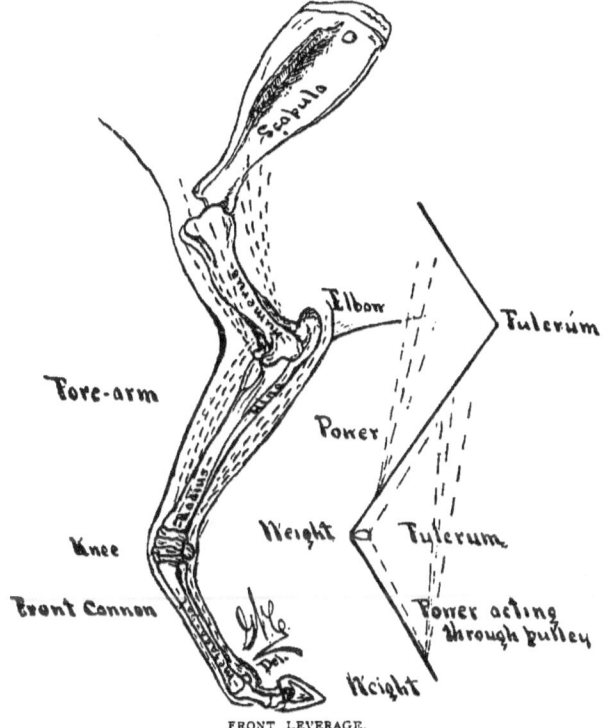

FRONT LEVERAGE.

the fore-arm the necessity for high knee action is entirely overcome, and the horse will have an easy reaching stride that covers distance without seeming to exert, and saves the feet by striking lightly even at the highest speed.

"The reverse proportion—short fore-arm and relatively longer cannon bone—insures a high and pounding action of the knees that always tends to greater wear and waste of muscle energy, as well as damage to feet and legs by heavy pounding when the horse is forced to travel fast.

"Almost all the line descendants of old Hambletonian have this easy reaching action, and the measurements of leading members of the family show a uniformly long fore-arm and short front cannon, which, together, guarantee the smooth, far-reaching action just explained. The Electioneers—descended from Electioneer, the greatest son of Hambletonian—show the feature strongest, and among them rest the records of the world at nearly every age from yearlings up. Hambletonian himself, the founder of the Hambletonian family, and the horse that should be credited as the actual founder of the trotting breed, had a cannon measurement of 11½, fore-arm of 20½ inches—a ratio of 1:1.783, and this ratio is exactly reproduced in his grandson Ansel, owned by Mr. Bonner and selected by him as the then best son of Electioneer. Sunol, the best daughter of Electioneer, measures 10¾ and 19½ inches respectively for cannon bone and fore-arm—a ratio of 1:1.823. Nancy Hanks, by Happy Medium, another son of Hambletonian, measures 10 and 19 inches—a ratio of 1:1.9. Her knee action is perfection, and her mile in 2:09 * on a regulation track is almost fairly equal to the 2:08¼ of Sunol on the Stockton kite.

"The extreme of high knee action was illustrated in the gait of Smuggler—a converted pacer of undoubted courage and recorded trotting speed, but whose every motion carried a suggestion of a cyclone. He measured 12 and 20 inches—a ratio of 1:1.666. Helm credits Smuggler with raising the knee above the horizontal to an angle of 45 degrees, and states that he 'strikes the ground with a force that is simply terrific.' It should be borne in mind, however, that the heavy muscled shoulders, high withers and well set neck which made him pace by nature made him also strike with added weight when speeding at the trot.

"While the principle of speed with least exertion is a good one always to be kept in view, we should not forget that safety lies in middle ground of conformation. The extremely short front cannon, acting with the long fore-arm, amounts to drag or dwelling motion and may even spring the knees behind the vertical, resulting in a "calf-kneed" horse—which no one can admire and few will care to use. The horse with extra short fore-arm and long front cannon will finally be knee-sprung almost to a certainty—"buck-kneed" and stumbling as he walks, a perfect picture of decrepitude. (See illustration.) For the stylish coach or carriage horse, the proud high stepper, with the short fore-arm and relatively longer cannon, will be greatly in demand; but for speed and stamina in long heat races, tie your fortunes to the horse that reaches out in front and moves the body forward on an even line at no great distance from the ground.

"Rear leverage in the horse means something more than muscle force which gives propelling power. No horse can carry speed at any

* Since reduced to 2:04.

gait with insufficient muscle, but the natural impulse of the horse to strike a gallop when he wants to travel faster may be so constrained by certain leverage in rear development as to make the artificial gait a second nature, breaking only when the brain is worried or the speed is carried past the limit which the horse can reach.

"The motion of the hind legs, from the fetlocks up, is modified by four distinct true levers, each one more or less complex in action—one especially remarkable: the muscles from the haunch or hip bone and the Illiac fossa extend in two directions—downward to the stifle, and down and backward to the leg bone (Tibia) and the hock. The upper thigh bone (Femur) works at upper end against the lower portion of the Illium in connection with the other pelvic bones, and the muscles running downward from the hip, together with the bones of upper thigh

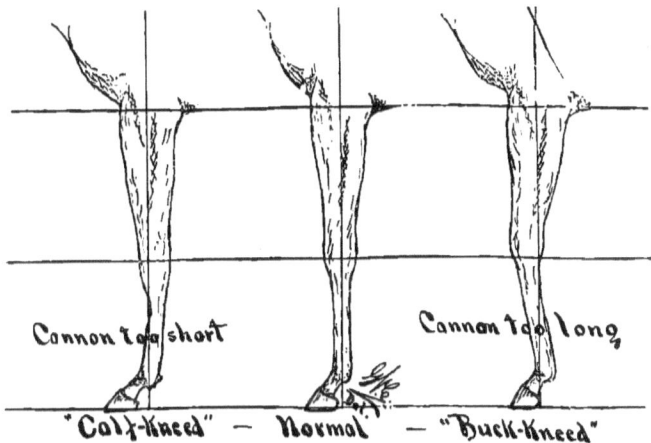

and leg, form a double compound lever—really two in purpose—moving separately or jointly in obedience to the brain's direct or reflex action. The muscles of the lower thigh which flex the cannon on the leg, present a simple lever of the third class (power between weight and fulcrum) combined with pulley action of the tendons at the hock—exactly corresponding to the leverage in front which bends the cannon on the fore-arm. (See illustration—Rear Leverage.)

"If the distance from hip to hock be fairly long in reference to the lower thigh, the horse will stand with straiter leg at rest, and the hock will swing in trotting almost underneath the stifle, somewhat with the motion of a pendulum. Such are called 'line trotters,' and our best examples bear the blood of Hambletonian through his son Electioneer. Nearly all Electioneers reach out in front and trot directly on a line behind, the hind foot passing underneath the front, and placing squarely with the body.

"The Knoxes of New England illustrate extremely narrow trotting, passing hocks in motion very close, and barely missing interference. The thigh is very short, the length from hip to hock is relatively long. They are descended from a horse called General Knox—standing 15 hands 2 inches, and with a thigh but 20½ inches.

"The reverse of this proportion, longer thigh and relatively shorter length from hip to hock, compels the horse to travel wide behind—swinging out the hocks in motion to avoid necessity for greater elevation of the stifle. The extreme in wide hock action showed in Duroc, with a thigh 24½ as compared with length from hip to hock of only 39—a ratio of 1:1.592. All of his descendants, to the present day, show Duroc blood in length of thigh, and travel with that open, straddling gait which such a conformation makes imperative.

"Hambletonian showed the middle ground in ratio, both lines being long, but lengthened so that each might correlate the other's action and insure 'line trotting' to perfection. His measurements were 24 and 41 respectively for thigh and hip to hock—a ration of 1:1.708, and his best descendants show a similar proportion. Nancy Hanks, already mentioned as the daughter of a son of Hambletonian (Happy Medium), measures 21¾ and 38—a ratio of 1:1.747. Ansel, by another son (Electioneer), measures 23½ and 40½—a ratio of 1:1.723. Maud S., by Harold (one of Hambletonian's sons) measures 23¾ and 40—a ratio of 1:1.684—and is said to have an almost perfect action. Sunol, by Electioneer, has a longer thigh and therefore has a longer stride, and carries speed at somewhat wider gait than most of the Electioneers. Her measurements are 24½ and 40—a ratio of 1:1.632. Nearly all the offspring of the so-called 'Star cross' in the Hambletonian family show the blood of Duroc through his son American Star. A horse 'Star gaited' trots with well spread hocks and carries speed without a chance of interference, front or rear.

"But by far the most important trotting leverage remains to be considered: length of Metatarsal bone (the cannon of the hind leg), as compared with length from hip to hock. As a rule the horse with hock placed low—that is, with short hind cannon—carries speed to some extent by nature at the trot; while the horse with hock placed high—that is, with long hind cannon—is a galloper from impulse. Do not understand by this that a horse with fairly long hind cannon cannot carry trotting speed—far from it; many a horse that lacks the best essentials for perfection at the trotting gait, by long and careful training, proper balancing by shoes and toe weights, and restraint by straps and hobbles, may be trained to trot at speed; but the time is past when trotting interests can be sustained by training and manipulation only. The impulse to trot—the 'instinct,' if you will—must be controlled in great degree by conformation of the parts concerned, combined with mental aptitude. Both these essentials for the future trotter may be fixed by well known laws of breeding, and become established features of the future trotting breed.

"That an animal with long hind cannon will be a galloper by nature, and with short, a trotter, is shown most clearly by a study of

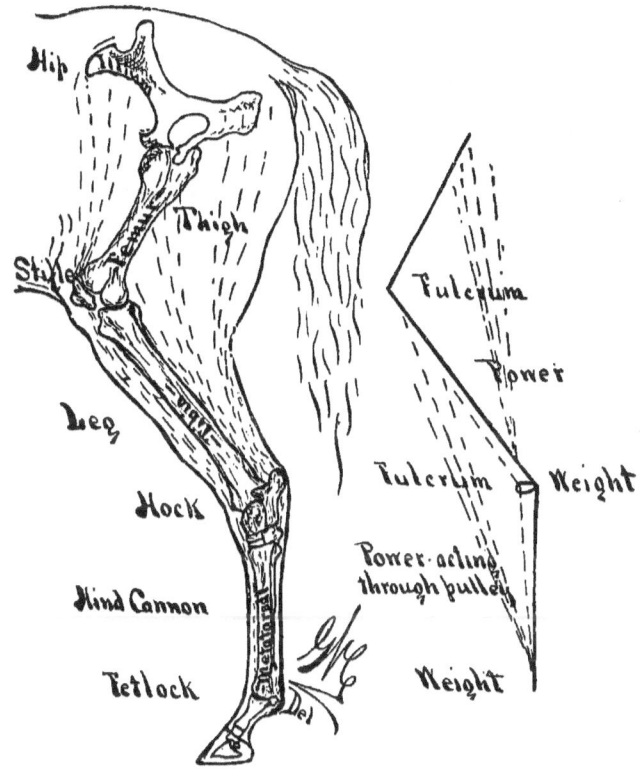

REAR LEVERAGE.

the measurements and gaits of those wild animals with which we are familiar. The elephant, whose gait is nothing but a trot, albeit verging toward a singlefoot, in spite of his enormous size and length of leg has hock placed almost on the ground—a cannon bone no longer than its breadth, and never to exceed five inches. A little study of the parts concerned will satisfy the most incredulous that the gait which he assumes by nature is a matter not of choice but of necessity—he could not gallop if he would. His leverage has been wisely placed to carry the weight of his ungainly body, and his speed becomes a matter wholly secondary. The long, strong muscles reaching from his hip to hock run almost parallel to the bones of upper thigh and leg, and could hardly be expected to exert sufficient force for lifting such enormous quarters briskly as in galloping; the motion must be swinging—not propelling—a condition which the trot fulfills exactly.

"The other extreme—the long hind cannon and the corresponding pushing or propelling gait, the gallop—may be found in all those animals of well-known speed, as deer and antelope, jack rabbits, and the like. Their natural gait, at anything beyond a walk in speed, is known to be a gallop, and the conformation correlates the gait. The pronghorned antelope (*Antilocapra Americana*) of Northwest Texas, rarely ever known to trot, although but 31½ inches high, displays a cannon measurement of 12½ inches as compared with length from hip to hock of 16¼, a ratio of but 1:1.3.

"Just what ratio in this lower lever will be most conducive to the trotting gait can be determined only by a study of the measurements of well known trotting horses now before the public, noting the peculiar points of interest in their ways of going, and especially their tendencies to break when urged to highest speed. Sunol measures 17½ and 40 respectively for hind cannon and length from hip to hock, a ratio of 1:2.285. Her hock is very low, the cannon extra short, and her mile in 2:08¼ bears witness to her speed capacity. Ansel, also by Electioneer, shows nearly equal measurement, a ratio of 1:2.222. Delmarch, by Hambrino, measures 17¼ and 38½, a ratio of 1:2.232. Jack, the steady, gray campaigner owned by Mr. Forbes, measures 17½ and 37, a ratio of 1:2.114. Mary Marshal measures 18 and 39, a ratio of 1:2.167; and Allerton, the king of racing stallions,* measures 17 and 39, a ratio of 1:2.294.

"Nearly all the great celebrities at present on the track show cannon not quite half as long as length from hip to hock; a few exceptions only prove the rule. The horses named are all pure gaited trotters, bearing voice and whip if needed in a race without a skip, and straining every muscle in a keen desire to win. The record each has made is plainest evidence that trotting blood and brain and leverage combined will carry highest speed. Mary Marshall, 2:12¼; Jack, 2:12; Delmarch, 2:11½; Allerton, 2:09¼; Maud S., 2:08¾, and Sunol, 2:08¼, are proof potential of the progress made in breeding trotters since the days of Flora Temple."

Soundness (by which is meant freedom from disease or any abnormal feature) is of prime importance, especially in selecting for stud use;

---

*Since dethroned successively by Palo Alto, 2:08¾; Kremlin, 2:07¾, and Stamboul, 2:07½.

and while we cannot undertake a description of the numerous blemishes and diseases to which the horse is subject, we may call brief attention to the nature and relative consequence of some of the more common troubles :

"Founder" (Laminitis in its various forms) is caused by overheating, over-feeding, or drinking to excess. Although a systemic disturbance, it is usually manifested in the feet, and a horse once foundered is very likely afterward to have frequent trouble in these parts. "Sweeny" (Atrophy or Shrinking of the shoulder muscles) is another manifestation of injury, which can be "cured," but is always liable to reappear on slight provocation. A sweenied horse, no matter how thoroughly he may have been "cured," it is always safe to reject.

Corns may be easily detected by tapping sharply with any blunt-pointed instrument on the sole of the foot, in the angle formed by the wall at the quarter and the inflected portion bounding either side of the frog; they never appear in any other place. Bad corns are very hard to cure, and a horse thus afflicted had best be thrown out; but mild corns —caused usually by poor shoeing—can be easily and permanently cured, and need not weigh heavily against the purchase of an otherwise desirable horse. Contracted feet, also caused by improper shoeing, may be placed in the same class as corns. Both these troubles, if mild, may be cured, as a rule, by removing shoes, paring down the foot at the quarters, and letting the animal run at grass, barefooted, for a month or six weeks.

Spavin in all its forms is a trouble we have always been afraid of ; some writer has called it "the sum of all villainy in horse-flesh"—and so it is. It affects the hind leg at the hock joint. sometimes as a watery swelling in front called "Bog Spavin," or in the rear on either side of the hamstring, when it is called "Thoroughpin," but in any case, it is liable to affect the small bones of this region, cause abnormal bone deposit, and become the justly dreaded "Bone Spavin," by which so many originally valuable animals are ruined annually. By all means reject a horse showing any indication of Spavin or of "treatment" for Spavin.

Curb, affecting the back or point of the hock, is of less moment ; it is generally caused by kicking against something hard, or habitually stepping over something just high enough to strike the heel in passing. If the injury is recent, frequent and vigorous rubbing will effect a cure ; if bone deposit has formed, it will always leave a blemish, but the horse may be—and usually is—serviceably sound. Splint—usually appearing as a hard bunch on the inner side of a front cannon, but sometimes on either side of any cannon, front or rear—is another trouble about like curb ; it leaves a blemish, and of course prevents great speed, but for ordinary use the animal is as good as ever.

Ringbone affects the bones of the pastern—making a bony bunch of considerable size—and causing, usually, serious lameness. It is considered incurable. Horses with short, upright pasterns are much more subject to this trouble and to the next than are those with pasterns of an opposite character.

Coffin joint lameness (Navicular disease) is one of those troubles about which little is really known, but much written. The Coffin or Navicular joint is just within the hoof, and hence practically inaccessible for treatment. As noted under Ringbone, horses with vertical pasterns are more subject to these troubles, and should be rejected, especially when selecting for light wagon or carriage use.

Concerning care and management, it has been our aim to secure statements from successful breeders of the actual methods employed by them in feeding, handling and breeding stock. In these statements are represented breeders of various classes of stock, and in different climates; and we present the following letters, in the firm belief that the information thus given is well worth a careful study:

French Draft, Percherons and Trotters.

"HOUSTON, TEX., July 17, 1888.

* * * *

"In the growing of horses, my object has been to produce the best horse at the least expense, and to accomplish this I have spared no pains in first securing the best of sires, and then providing clean, wholesome stables, well ventilated, with pure water and wholesome food; usually feeding oats twice a day and wheat bran once, but an occasional gradual change from oats to corn I have found advisable in maintaining the appetite. I give every sire at least five miles exercise per day. I regard this exercise as of special importance in the season for actual service. He is then always healthful and vigorous. This applies to either pure-bred or standard-bred sires that are kept up, and served to halter to choice mares, when registration of their progeny is required. Less valuable sires, when their progeny are supposed to sell only on their individual merits, I have found it more economical and raised a larger percentage of colts, to turn them out in pastures with a limited number of mares, not to exceed 25, not failing to give them a feed of oats each day to keep them strong and vigorous; and, in fact, 'turned loose' is the most natural way, and in all classes of breeding, it has been my experience that to assist nature is the best that we can do.

"In providing food for mares, we have found it most satisfactory and economical to cut and stack hay in pastures, the stacks serving as food and shelter, and with much less expense and waste than any other way. Colts, when of sufficient age to take from their mothers, we catch, halter and hitch in stable, until they learn to eat, and lose all fear of being handled, and when again caught, if not until maturity, they will not forget their early handling at the halter. We then turn them in pasture by themselves, where they have all the hay, oats and bran they will eat the first winter. They have then arrived at the age of one year, in a thrifty, growing condition, and will take care of themselves in pasture until matured to the age of three or four years, suitable to break to saddle and harness. At this time avoid 'breaking' their temper and constitution, but on the contrary, through a process of kindness, teach them to lose all fear, and when this is accomplished, the natural instincts control, and they will then intelligently respond to all reasonable calls. A little feed in winter, where circumstances and numbers will admit. would be a judicious expense. Yours very truly,

"H. B. SANBORN."

Mr. Sanborn's methods give a clear idea of handling for profit in the Southwest. The practice of breaking colts at an early age cannot be too strongly urged; once trained, the spirit of obedience to a master's will is never lost. The natural way of breeding—"turned loose"—is the practice adopted by all breeders of pony mares to common stallions, and is satisfactory so far as percentage of foals to service is concerned; but it must be remembered that to secure higher results—as Mr. Sanborn states—nature needs a large amount of assistance—indeed, a very high type of skilled "Art" is required to develop and bring to the surface the actual but latent merit of an individual or breed.

Cleveland Bays, English Shires and Clydesdales.

"SPRINGFIELD, ILL., August 10, 1888.

* * * *

"My way of handling a stallion is as follows: During the winter, whilst I give him a fair allowance of grain, mixed with bran, and cut hay or oat sheaves, I do not let him get too fleshy, giving him good exercise daily, and a few weeks prior to commencing the season, increase his allowance of grain (chiefly oats) so that on going on the stand, the horse is improving (*i. e.*, fleshing up). Whilst making a season, I give a horse all he will eat (without crowding him), and in addition to the grain feed, give where possible some green feed once or twice per day. If not available, then the best hay morning and night. I usually feed one meal per day damped with water.

"With regard to breeding or brood mares, would say: If there is sufficient nutritious grass available, they should not require anything else, but a mare to be bred should also be improving in flesh, and will be much more liable to get in foal under such conditions; a little extra feed at this time is not thrown away.

"In addition to their mother's milk, colts should have access to feed of crushed oats and bran, at least twice daily, and although many think this unnecessary, I think the growth and the superiority of colts reared under these conditions will, after being once tried, convince the most skeptical of the benefits to be derived from a generous feed in addition to that provided by nature; besides, a colt is so much more easily weaned when taught to eat and look out for himself when young. All colts should be handled, haltered and broke when three years old. * * * *

"Yours truly, R. P. STERICKER."

Mr. Stericker believes in feeding his colts, and we think the point is well taken. At no other time in the period of horse existence will a little feed give such large returns as during the first and second years, and the so-called economy of short rations at this time is really the very opposite of economy in fact.

Cleveland Bays and English Shires.

'CEDAR FALLS STOCK FARM, CEDAR FALLS, IOWA, Aug. 15, 1888.

* * * *

"Having so many stallions, it is impracticable to give them harness or saddle exercise as required. We have, however, large well-fenced exercising grounds, into which they are turned singly, daily. The exercise and rolling contact with mother earth, voluntarily taken in the sunlight, aids to keep them healthy. They have box stalls well lighted and ventilated, with earth floors and perfect cleanliness. Their food in the off reason should be clean, bright hay, oats mixed with bran or shorts, and once or twice a week some vegetables. It is also desirable to cut and save in cellar for winter, sods of grass, to give them occasionally, which are eaten with avidity and benefit. In very cold weather a little corn would aid in maintaining animal heat, but we use it very sparingly. In case of hard fæces, indicating costiveness, steep half pint of flaxseed, and feed with oats. We aim to keep them in good heart through the winter, but not fleshy. In the breeding season the ration is more liberal, and is supplemented by half pint to a pint of hempseed (which is not a drug, and is harmless) say three times a week, and raw eggs about as often, mixed with the feed. Fresh grass is always craved, and is beneficial. For mares, free run in pasture on grass—the natural food—is best, with, when necessary, some oats and bran. Toward time for stinting to the horse, half pint of hempseed is desirable three times a week, and for a short time after service. It is undoubtedly good for both stallions and mares to have reasonable, careful work at proper times, to develop stamina and muscle and give constitution to offspring. Colts should run freely in pasture and have, when on dry food, a few oats, bran and vegetables; kept growing thriftily, but not pampered; should be handled often, firmly but kindly. This should also be the rule in handling stallions.

"Very respectfully, W. M. FIELDS & BRO."

The Cedar Falls Stock Farm is well known as carrying an excellent stock of horses. Mr. Fields admits that it is impossible, on account of the number on hand, to give each stallion the exercise which should be given, but thinks they have adopted the next best plan—daily yard runs in the open air. In lieu of the green sods cut and kept for winter use, as suggested, we have understood that ensilage in small quantities has been used to advantage, and we should think the practice would involve much less trouble and expense.

American Trotters.

"WILLOW LAWN FARM, WAVERLY, IOWA, July 26, 1888.

* * * *

"As I have been away from home since July 1, have had no time to prepare statement of care of mares and colts, as requested; but our practice is to keep as close to nature as possible, giving mares entire freedom, and feeding only such grain as is necessary to keep them in fine condition at all times. Our colts are constantly handled by quiet, careful men, so that when ready to put in harness, we have seldom any trouble with them. We have about 50 high-bred mares, and we try to give each mare and colt such care as their individual condition requires.

"Very truly yours, J. H. BOWMAN"

Knowing the high character of "Willow Lawn" stud, we can only express regret that Mr. Bowman had not time to give us a more extended outline of his practice.

Draft and Trotting Horses.

"FISKVILLE, TRAVIS COUNTY, TEXAS, Aug. 27, 1888.

* * *

"In keeping stallions for public service I have handled each year, for the past fifteen years, from 50 to 150 mares; one stallion that I stood six consecutive seasons, averaged, according to accurate written records, 83 per cent. of foals to mares served, and all animals handled by me have averaged about 75 per cent., whilst I do not think the general average will exceed 50 per cent. of foals to mares served.

"My practice is to have the stallion in strong, vigorous condition, and to keep him so throughout the breeding season—say from March 1 to July 1—by constant and abundant exercise; and no plan will give this needed exercise in so desirable and economical shape as to make a business horse of him—under the saddle and in harness, one or both. The constant use, association and control by his master renders him obedient, manageable and safe; whilst it also keeps all the vital organs in full and vigorous play—which gives a larger per cent. of foals from his service, and with more constitution and vitality. I wish to emphasize this point, for it is opposite to the prevailing custom.

"Next, be sure your mare is in season (heat); * * it requires experience to determine this accurately—mares vary greatly in temperament, or nervous organization, and consequently conduct themselves differently. * * Such mares as have dropped foals will, almost invariably, be in heat in from seven to ten days after foaling. * * * I always have the colt accompany its mother, else she is fretting for it, and it is more difficult to ascertain her true condition. After the first service, * * if the mare's condition is normal, until she is safe in foal heat will recur at intervals of 21 days, varying a little with the individual; thus you will see why a reasonable degree of success attends those who practice returning mares on the seventh or ninth day after service. My observation has been that mares carry a heat on the average, five days.

"When foaling time is at hand see that the mare is exposed to no extra risks, then let her alone. When the mother's milk fails to keep the foal fat, feed her grain to enrich it, and that the colt may learn to eat and digest the grain perfectly before weaning time, which should be done at from six to eight months of age, at which time it should be abundantly and regularly supplied with nutritious food. Oats and bran are my choice, with corn added as cold weather comes on; the desideratum being to keep up thrift and growth from birth to maturity. If this is interrupted at any stage, one loses not only in size, but in style or symmetry. Where growing colts are thus constantly associated with man, the breaking-in to service is a simple thing; the transition is so easy and natural that they hardly know it, and where light and occasional work is performed by them between the second and third years, by the time maturity is reached the animals are thoroughly developed, trained and safe, and will command the very highest market price for their respective kinds. In fact, from discriminating buyers, a horse known to be thus raised and trained will command an extra price.

"Very truly yours, C. A. GRAVES."

Mr. Graves is careful to emphasize the necessity for actual use, either under the saddle or in harness, of service stallions, and brings out clearly the points in breeding on which beginners are apt to stumble. His letter contains some valuable information well worth remembering.

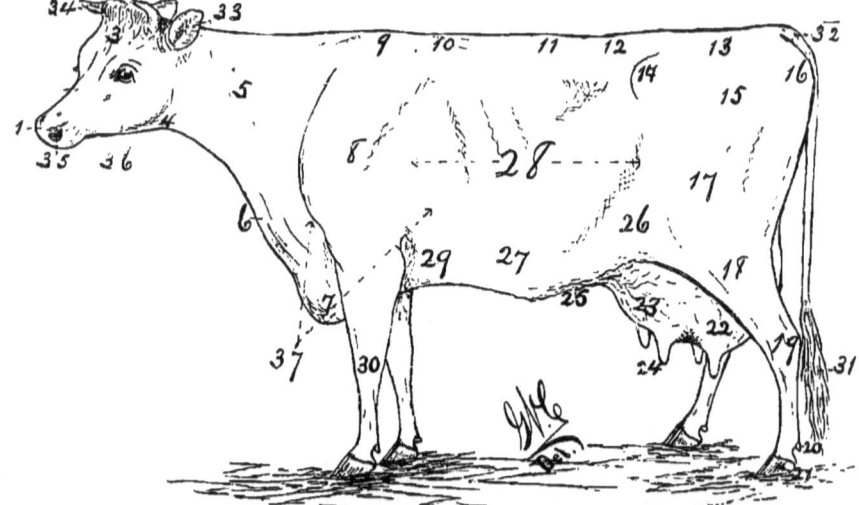

1, Muzzle; 2, Face; 3, Forehead; 4, Throat; 5, Neck; 6, Dewlap; 7, Brisket; 8, Shoulder; 9, Shoulder-tips; 10, Crops; 11, Chine, or Back; 12, Loins; 13, Rump; 14, Hip, or Hook-bone; 15, Thurl; 16, Buttock; 17, Upper-thigh, or Quarter; 18, Lower-thigh. Leg. or Gaskin; 19, Hock; 20, Onglons, or False hoofs; 21, Hoof, or Foot; 22, Hind-udder; 23, Fore-udder; 24, Teats; 25, Milk-vein; 26, Flank; 27, Belly; 28, Side; 29, Girth Arm-pit, or Fore-flank; 30, Knee; 31, Switch, or Brush of the Tail; 32, Setting-on, or Drop of the Tail; 33, Ears; 34, Horns; 35, Nostril; 36, Cheek, or Lower jaw; 37, Chest.

PART SECOND.

CATTLE.

DAIRY BREEDS.

			PAGE
HOLSTEIN-FRIESIANS	Chapter	XXII.	116
JERSEYS	"	XXIII.	125
GUERNSEYS	"	XXIV.	131
AYRSHIRES	"	XXV.	135
DUTCH BELTED		XXVI.	140
AMERICAN HOLDERNESS		XXVII.	144
BROWN SWISS		XXVIII.	148
BRITTANIES		XXIX.	152
KERRIES		XXX.	154

GENERAL PURPOSE BREEDS.

SHORTHORNS	Chapter	XXXI.	157
RED-POLLED	"	XXXII.	163
DEVONS		XXXIII.	167
LONGHORNS		XXXIV.	173
NORMANDIES		XXXV.	176
NORTH WALES BLACK		XXXVI.	180
PEMBROKES		XXXVII.	184

BEEF BREEDS.

HEREFORDS	Chapter	XXXVIII.	185
GALLOWAYS	"	XXXIX.	191
ABERDEEN-ANGUS		XL.	196
POLLED DURHAMS		XLI.	201
SUSSEX		XLII.	204
SIMMENTHAL		XLIII.	207
BRAHMINS (ZEBU)		XLIV.	210
WEST HIGHLANDS		XLV.	213
TEXANS		XLVI.	220

HINTS ON SELECTION, CARE AND MANAGEMENT.

CHAPTER XLVII., ... 223

Chapter XXII.

HOLSTEIN-FRIESIANS.

To trace the early history and establish the origin of this now firmly settled and improved breed, it is necessary to go back over the much disputed ground, until recently bitterly contested by the Holstein and the Dutch-Friesian Associations. The Friesians, or North Hollanders, from the earliest history have dwelt along the shores of the North Sea, and have possessed abundance of cattle; their history dates as far back as 300 B. C., and their cattle at that time are supposed to have been pure white. Tradition intimates that the progenitors of the breed came from India, but we have no authentic records to that effect. Two hundred years later the Batavians appear in history. They settled near the Friesians, and it is supposed that the cattle which they brought with them were black. From the crossing of these two breeds, then, might easily have arisen the black and white color of the present breed. However vague this theory of their origin may be, it is certain that these two tribes or provincial nations were afterwards known in common, and together celebrated for the excellence and great number of their cattle —so much so, indeed, that when present Holland came under Roman authority, the Friesians were required to pay an annual tax in hides, horns and cattle; the Batavians chose rather to furnish soldiers, and from this time on they seem to have relegated to the Friesians all the responsibility, labor and emolument arising from the cattle industry.

As to whether the cattle of Friesland or North Holland were originally obtained from the province of Holstein—lying in the northern part of Germany, along the border—or the exact reverse; or, indeed, as to the truth of either assertion, it is not now necessary to consider; time has only made certain what all candid breeders of either Holsteins or Dutch-Friesians never denied—that the cattle of Holstein and those of Friesland or North Holland are, and for many years have been, practically identical. The Holstein Breeders' Association was organized and the name adopted in good faith. What more suitable name for a breed than that of the country in which it has reached perfection? But gradually the cattle of Holstein were culled of the best specimens, and importers began to secure choice animals from North Holland, calling them and having them recorded as Holsteins. Possibly this fact may have hastened the organization of the Dutch-Friesian Association. Be

HOLSTEIN-FRIESIANS.

HOLSTEIN-FRIESIAN BULL, NETHERLAND PRINCE, 716 (Adv. Reg. 8).
Weight, 2,000 lbs.; imported (1880) and now owned by SMITHS, POWELL & LAMB, Syracuse, N. Y.

that as it may, the latter named society was organized in 1877, and the first volume of the Dutch-Friesian Herd Book of America appeared in 1880. To a careful observer, the name appeared to be about the only real difference between these two recognized breeds, and attempts were early made by the more conservative breeders on both sides to join forces and admit their identity, by importing and breeding under one name instead of two. The name Holstein had an undoubted priority in America, and the black and white cattle of Friesland were persistently libeled as "Holsteins" by those who were either ignorant of the Friesian name, or too partisan in their views to regard it with fairness.

The Dutch-Friesian breeders scored a strong point in their favor when they adopted for their Herd Book the Main or Advanced Register —of which we will speak later— in addition to the usual pedigree register of other breeds. Selfish interests undoubtedly operated to prevent a union of the two associations, but gradually the pressure of public opinion, combined with the good sense of a majority of breeders, effected a union. A joint committee having been appointed for the purpose of drafting a plan for consolidation, the two associations met in joint session May 26th, 1885, and formally adopted the plans prepared by the committee. The Holstein-Friesian Association (Thos. B. Wales, Boston, Mass., secretary) retained the Advanced Registry feature, and we have thought best to insert here the rules and requirements for admission to this higher record as recently modified by the association, and furnished for our use by S. Hoxie, Superintendent, Yorkville, New York.

First. An animal must be eligible to record in the Pedigree Register.

Second. If a bull, he must have shown his superior qualities by his progeny, and must scale at least 80 points of the scale adopted ; if a cow, she must have borne a calf, and made one of the following records :

"If calving on the day she is two years of age a record of not less than nine lbs. of butter in seven consecutive days, or not less than 6,500 lbs. of milk in 10 consecutive months, or not less than 354 lbs. of milk in 10 consecutive days, previous to eight months from and after date of calving, in which last case she shall have made another record of 118 lbs. in 10 consecutive days after such period of eight months. And for every day a cow exceeds two years of age at date of calving in the 'two year form' the requirement of the 10 months record shall be increased $3\frac{43}{100}$ lbs. ; the requirement of the earlier 10 days record $\frac{24}{100}$ of a lb. ; the requirement of the latter 10 days record $\frac{7}{100}$ of a lb. ; and the requirement of the butter record $\frac{9}{100}$ of an oz.

"If calving on the day she is three years of age a record of not less than 11 lbs. of butter in seven consecutive days, or not less than 7,900 lbs. of milk in 10 consecutive months, or not less than 432 lbs. of milk in 10 consecutive days, previous to eight months from and after calving, in which last case she shall have made another record of 144 lbs. in 10 consecutive days after such period of eight months. And for every day she exceeds three years of age at date of calving in the 'three-year form' the same increase per day as in the two-year form.

"If calving on the day she is four years of age a record of not less than 13 lbs. of butter in seven consecutive days, or not less than 9,300 lbs. of milk in 10 consec-

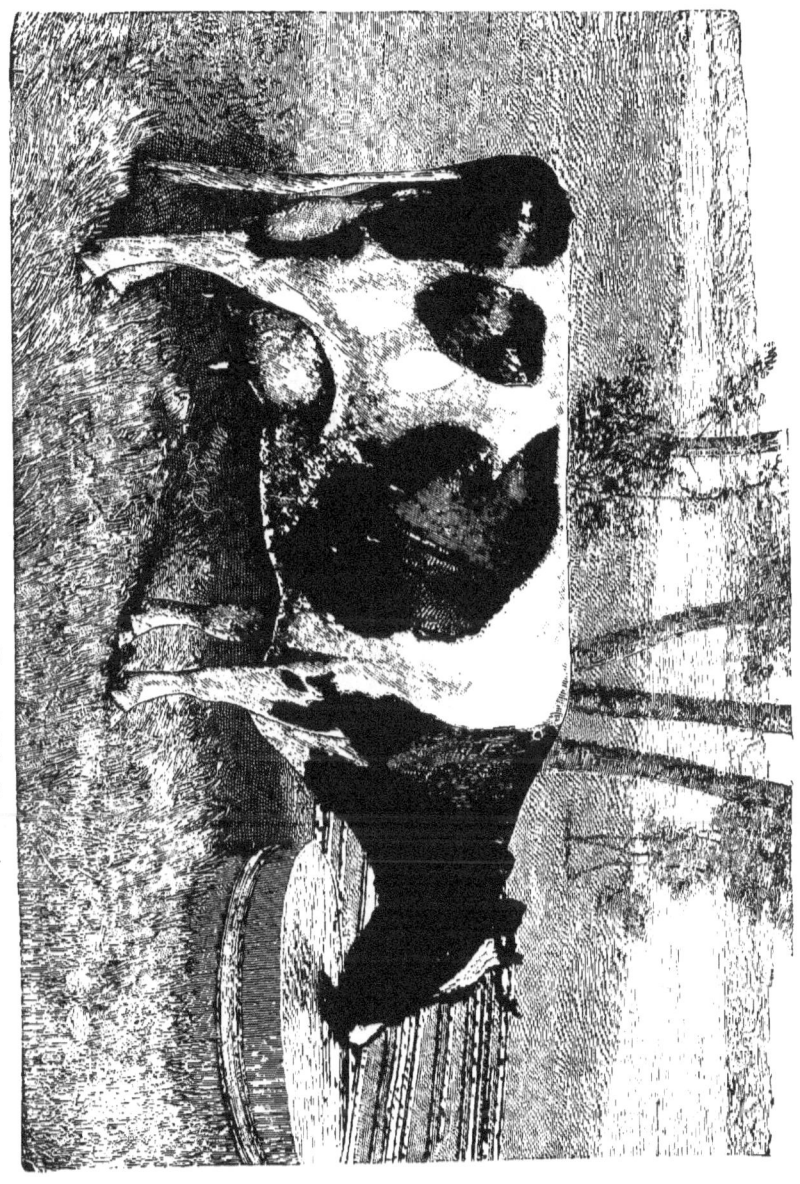

HOLSTEIN-FRIESIAN COW, CLOTHILDE, 1308 (Adv. Reg. 155).
Imported (1880) and now owned by Smiths, Powell & Lane, Syracuse, N. Y.

utive months, or not less than 511 lbs. of milk in 10 consecutive days, previous to eight months from and after date of calving, in which last case she shall have made another record of not less than 170 lbs. in 10 consecutive days after such period of eight months. And for every day she exceeds four years of age at date of calving in the 'four-year form,' the same increase per day as in the three-year form.

"If calving on the day she is five years of age a record of not less than 15 lbs. of butter in seven consecutive days, or not less than 10,700 lbs. of milk in 10 consecutive months, or not less than 589 lbs. of milk in 10 consecutive days, previous to eight months from and after date of calving, in which last case she shall have made another record of not less than 197 lbs. in 10 consecutive days after such period of eight months. No increase of production shall be required from increased age at date of calving in 'full-age form.'

"All records shall be made within a period of one year from date of calving (excepting in case of a full year's record necessarily extending a year from its date of commencement), and in no case include milk or butter produced from a second calving.

"In making each and every such record the cow shall be milked dry at its commencement, and the close shall not extend beyond the number of days reported, reckoned at 24 hours each In each and every butter record reported the butter shall be of good marketable quality, salted at not higher than one ounce of salt to a pound of butter, and worked free from any excess of water or buttermilk.

"In reporting each and every record, the date of calving shall be given, age of cow at such date, the date of commencement of record, the date of close of record, and the number of pounds of milk or butter produced; and in records of butter production, the average number pounds of milk required to produce one pound of butter during the whole period covered by the record. At the option of the owner the number of milkings per day during any part of the time covered by the record or records may be given, or other matters of interest, to occupy in the Register not to exceed two lines as published.

"Every such record shall be sworn to by each and every person assisting in making it, including in every case the owner of the animal. Such affidavits shall set forth that the record or records were made in accordance with these rules, and that they are true in each and every particular to the best knowledge and belief of the subscriber thereto. The inspector shall also certify that in his judgment the animal is capable of making such record or records.

"A cow, to be eligible to this registry, shall also be found by the inspector to conform to the structural requirements provided in connection with the Scale of Points.

"A cow shall also be eligible to this registry on a record of pure butter fat, determined by composite test of samples of her milk, taken from each and every milking for a period of seven consecutive days. The samples to be taken, in every instance, from the whole milking immediately after it has been thoroughly stirred and mixed. This composite test shall be determined by the Babcock or other equally accurate apparatus or method approved by the Association of Official Agricultural Chemists. The total amount of milk given during this period of seven consecutive days shall be multiplied by the per cent. of pure butter fat thus found in the milk, and the product obtained shall be the record. The requirement for entry on such a record of pure butter fat shall be $83\frac{1}{3}$ per cent. of the requirement for entry on a record of marketable butter of a cow of the same age. Full particulars shall be reported and affidavits made as in cases of milk and marketable butter records."

The recent quarrel in the Holstein-Friesian camp between Eastern and Western breeders, and the attempted starting of a second Herd Book, will have a depressing effect on the really best interests of the Holstein-Friesian breed, and may result in even greater disaster. We have no "side" to take in this controversy, but in the interests of the whole breeding fraternity would say: One registry is ample; one association all that is necessary. If honest differences of opinion exist, let them be settled by other means, and keep the good name of the Holstein-Friesian breed from any further damage which the warring breeders may unintentionally inflict.

DESCRIPTION.

In outline they present the typical milk wedge, with narrow shoulder points and wide, strong hips; color jet black and pure white, more or less evenly variegated over the entire body; the brush of the tail must always be white, no matter how strongly black may predominate elsewhere; the tastes of breeders differ as to markings, some preferring an excess of white, or at least evenly variegated, while others prefer to breed for a predominance of black, confining the white to the belly line, brush and star in forehead. In size they are fully equal to the Shorthorn or Hereford—bulls weighing from 1,900 to 2,300 lbs., and cows from 1,200 to 1,600 lbs.—lacking the square, heavy appearance of these breeds, but suggesting magnificent constitutions by their powerful frames. The head is long, with very little flesh, and prominent muzzle-veins; the mouth large and coarse; nostrils large and flexible; eyes not especially prominent, but large, bright and wide apart; face beautifully dished; horns small, clear at base, with black tips, usually pointing forward; ears large, thin, quick in movement and of yellowish, oily texture within; neck long, slender and finely tapered in the cow, with small dewlap suspended from lower one-third—in the bull the neck should still be fine at the head, but heavy, muscular and well set on at the shoulders. The shoulders are thin above, but long and very deep, giving a much greater shoulder-beef capacity than would appear at first thought. The rib arches gradually increase toward the loin region, giving ample room in the abdominal cavity, and by no means crowding the chest. The barrel gradually deepens to the region of the flank, which is low and well-muscled. The loin is full; hips wide apart, and on a level with the back; back straight throughout—although in some of the best milkers, there is more or less drop from the sacral regions; buttocks large, and the angle between them in the cow wide, giving ample room for passage of fœtus at parturition; tail long, slender and delicately tapering to the brush; hind quarters very heavy; legs rather longer than in the Shorthorn or Hereford, but straight and finely formed—crooked legs, as a necessary accompaniment to milking qualities, no longer exist. The udder should be broad, square, close up to the body and spreading well forward on to the abdomen—long, low-hanging, meaty udders, that are nearly as large after milking as when distended with milk, are very objectionable; teats are nearly always even, good shape—not conical—and the reservoirs supplying them of about equal dimensions in the four divisions of the udder; escutcheon varies, and to select well requires an accurate knowledge of these peculiar "mirrors," which we cannot give in a work of this kind. (For a very exhaustive exposition of the indications of escutcheons, we most heartily recommend the American translation of Guenon's Milch Cows.) The milk veins are remarkably developed in the best specimens, and the brisket, while not so low as in some other breeds, is broad and full. The skin is of medium thickness, soft and mellow to the touch, and the hair short, fine and close lying. The following Scale of Points was adopted August 12th, 1885, and is now in general use:

COWS.		BULLS.
2	Head	2
2	Forehead	2
2	Face	2
1	Ears	1
2	Eyes	2
2	Horns	2
4	Neck	5
3	Shoulders	4
6	Chest	8
2	Crops	4
3	Back	3
5	Barrel	6
5	Loins and Hips	5
4	Rump	5
4	Thurl	4
4	Quarters	5
2	Flanks	2
5	Legs	6
2	Tail	2
10	Hair and Handling	10
10	Mammary Veins	10
12	Udder	
8	Escutcheon	8
	Rudimentary Teats	2
100	Perfection	100

CHARACTERISTICS, USES AND ADAPTABILITY.

The prominent characteristic of the Holstein-Friesian cow lies in her wonderful milk production; and of the bull, in his power to transmit superior milking qualities to his offspring. They are admittedly a superior milk breed, giving a large quantity of milk, especially rich in casein, and fairly good in butter content. Clothilde produced 26,021 lbs. 2 ozs. of milk in one year—the second largest record ever made by a cow of any breed; she has also a record of 28 lbs. 2¼ ozs. of butter in seven days. Recently some astonishing results have been obtained in the butter line; a Mercedes heifer, property of Thomas B. Wales, Jr., of Iowa City, Iowa, dropped her first calf February 13, 1887, and when she was two years and twelve days old, commenced a seven days' test. (See rules of admission to Advanced Register.) She produced 21 lbs. 8 ozs. of unsalted butter in seven days, from a yield of 312 lbs. 6 ozs. of milk—said to be the largest certified record, with one exception, ever made by a heifer.

Still more remarkable is the record of Pauline Paul, 852 A. R., 2199 H. H. B., owned by J. B. Dutcher & Son, Pawling, N. Y. Dropping her calf January 19, 1890, when eight years of age, she produced in 365 successive days, beginning February 8, 1890, and ending February 7, 1891, 18,669 lbs. 9 ozs. milk, from which was made 1,153 lbs. 15¾ ozs. well worked, marketable butter. This record is truly remarkable, and has, of course, had to pass through the same gauntlet of doubting remarks and publications which are always launched when any world's records are broken. It is attested, however, under oath by the owners, and by H. D. Warner, Geo. Vail and W. H. Johnson, and we have no reason to doubt the truthfulness of what these gentlemen affirm. It will be seen that on an average it required a little over 16 lbs. of milk throughout the year to make one pound of marketable butter. Not only the owners but the whole Holstein-Friesian breeding fraternity are to be congratulated on the record of this wonderful cow. It is not only the largest butter record among Holstein-Friesians, but the largest butter record for an entire year ever made by a cow of any breed. She has also a record of 128 lbs. 13½ ozs. of butter in 30 days.

Pieterje, 2d, property of Mr. Dallas B. Whipple, of Cuba, N. Y., has lately completed the greatest milk record, not only to date, but that is likely to be made for some time to come; she is truly a wonderful animal, having to her credit 112 lbs. 7 ozs. of milk in one day; 3,289 lbs. 10 ozs. in 31 consecutive days, and the enormous amount of 30,318 lbs. 8 ozs. in one year of 365 days—surpassing the great yield of Clothilde by 4,297 lbs., and proving herself the largest milker in the world. She was bred by T. K. Cuperus, of Boxum, Friesland, Holland; calved April 25, 1877, and imported November 1, 1882, by Mr. A. Bradley, of Lee, Mass.

Touching their beef qualities we have yet much to learn; their exponents claim for them finely marbled, rich, juicy flesh, while the opposite faction assert that they are good for nothing but milk; probably a mean between these two views will be found more nearly correct. That the grades produced by using Holstein-Friesian bulls on native stock rank well in size and thrift with the grades of either Shorthorn, Hereford or Galloway lineage, cannot be denied; but to claim as fine beef qualities for a typical milk breed as may be found in cattle bred especially for the butcher's block, is too much like the theory of the individual who claims the earth. They have size and vigor, two things of prime value in grading up a herd of native stock, and are especially valuable for the great Southwest for the reasons: First, that they rapidly improve the milking value of native stock by grading; and second, that so far as we have been able to collect statistics, they acclimate in the fever belt with greater ease than any other known breed of improved cattle. They are ravenous eaters, bear forced feeding well, and give good return for extra care.

Our illustrations are from the famous Lakeside Herd at Syracuse, N. Y. Clothilde we have already mentioned; Netherland Prince has proved his great value, not only to his owners, but to the entire Holstein-Friesian fraternity. An animal of fine parts in himself, of untarnished ancestry, and showing by his superior get a wonderful power of transmission.

Chapter XXIII.

JERSEYS.

This breed—the best known and most widely distributed of the Channel Island groups—has long held a high place in public favor. Although there is no doubt that the Jerseys were originally from Normandy, in France, they were long ago transplanted, and became the peculiar breed of the Channel Islands. There are four of these Islands: Jersey, Guernsey, Alderney and Serk—named in order of their size—the last one, Serk, being so small as to have received scarcely any notice in the records of the Island Breeds. The people of the islands are essentially Norman in habits, appearance and dialect; but ever since Normandy was severed from English sway, these islands have remained, as their inhabitants evidently desired, a dependency of Great Britain, subject to her rule, and, what is more to the point, her protection. The cattle of the islands, although at first considered as one breed, have within the last 50 years gradually drifted apart, until now there are recognized two distinct breeds, corresponding in name respectively to each of the two largest islands. Prof. Low (1842) seems to have recognized only one breed, describing that one under the name "Alderney," and merely mentioning the Jersey and Guernsey breeds in an incidental way. In America this condition of things has been continually reversed—Jerseys receiving most marked attention and entirely absorbing the Alderney name; while the Guernseys, until late years few in numbers, have been frequently compelled to struggle even for recognition as a distinct breed.

Improvement of both groups was effected by the kindly care and attention lavished upon them. In no portion of the world, probably, is there more attention given to the comforts of the cow; she is the mainstay and source of revenue to her owner, and holds a place in his affections justified by her financial importance. Under these conditions, supplemented by judicious selection in breeding, they have risen to their present merited position. In the United States, superior inducements have caused extra effort toward improvement and the establishment of so-called fancy strains, until it may be safely asserted that there are as good Jerseys bred in America as can be found among those bred in their native islands. Their importation to America dates from as early as 1830, and from 1850 to the present time has been rapid and systematic.

DESCRIPTION OF THE MODERN JERSEY.

There are four different markings or styles of color to be found among registered Jerseys; and, as tastes differ, each style is in sufficient demand to justify the continued supply. (1) Fawn and white, evenly variegated; (2) solid fawn; (3) brown and white; and (4) solid brown. Solid color means all one color—that is, without admixture of white. The solid browns, however, gradually deepen to almost pure black at the head and lower joints of the legs, forming what are termed "black points." With the solid fawns there are also darker points, so that the term "solid color" may now be understood to include several widely different shades of the same color.

In all of these styles of color there is invariably a peculiar light, mealy-colored ring of hair just at the edge of and encircling the nostrils—generally considered the distinctive mark by which even low-grade Jerseys may be recognized; this same mark, however, in slightly different shade, is frequently met with among the unimproved Texas cattle—a fact which may serve to trace some possible relation between them, through the old Spanish cattle from which the Texas stock originally sprang.

The head is small, close fleshed, broad at the forehead and narrow between horns, with strongly dished face; large, expressive eyes, set wide apart; thin, delicate ears, and small, crumpled, amber colored horns. The neck is thin, long, fine at the head, and set into the shoulders, "ewe-necked;" shoulders thin and light; forward ribs flat, "fish-backed," but increasing in curvature to the loin; hips fairly wide, but rump narrow, and buttocks lean; body deepest at the flank, presenting the V-shaped outline of all milk breeds; front legs short, fine boned, straight and small—hind legs somewhat coarser, and, in the less improved animals, rather crooked. The best improved specimens have been bred away from the crooked hocks of their ancestors, and can present as straight and clean a pair of heels as one would wish to see. The Jersey udder as a rule is not large, but its capacity is good, and the escutcheon, in all its forms, is built upon a rich orange yellow skin, which clearly marks the dominant characteristic of the animal—butter. The general appearance of the Jersey is that of all highly sensitive, nervous temperaments; and, taken in connection with its peculiar color, furnishes a striking resemblance to the well-known Southern deer.

The following Scale of Points was adopted May 6th, 1885, by the American Jersey Cattle Club (J. J. Hemingway, of New York city, secretary), and is now in general use:

JERSEY BULL.
Bred by J. H. Hart, Nova Scotia.

COWS.		BULLS.
2	Head	2
1	Eyes	1
8	Neck	8
1	Back	1
6	Loin	6
10	Barrel	10
10	Hips and Rump	10
2	Legs	2
1	Tail	1
5	Skin	5
13	Fore Udder	
11	Hind Udder	
10	Teats	10
5	Milk Veins	
5	Disposition	5
10	General Appearance and Constitution	10
	Progeny (for Bulls when exhibited in a separate class with their progeny)	29
100	Perfection	100

In judging heifers, use same scale as for cows, omitting numbers 11, 12 and 14.

CHARACTERISTICS.

As indicated above, the all-absorbing trait of the Jersey cow is the uniform richness of her milk in butter content; the globules are large, causing the cream to separate easily and quickly from the body of the milk; and the butter produced from it is usually more highly colored, under the same conditions as to food and care, than that of any other breed except, perhaps, Guernseys. In size the Jersey ranks with the small breeds, mature bulls weighing from 1,000 to 1,300 lbs., cows from 650 to 950 lbs.

As a family cow to supply cream or butter, or both, for the home table, the Jersey has no superior. For the butter dairy, as a special-purpose cow, she is also excellent, if not queen.

Landseer's Fancy made 936 lbs. 14¾ ozs. in one year; Massena made 902 lbs. 3 ozs.; Matilda, 4th, made 927 lbs. 8½ ozs.; more recently Bisson's Belle, 31144—owned by Maury Jersey Farm, Columbia, Tenn. —made 1,028 lbs. 15 ⅝ ozs. butter in one year, from a yield of 8,412 lbs. 7 ozs. of milk; and still more recently, and heading the Jersey list for butter yield in 365 successive days, comes Signal's Lily Flagg, 31035 —owned by Matthews and Moore, Huntsville, Alabama—with a year's record of 1,047 lbs. 0¾ oz. butter from a yield of 11,339 lbs. milk.

These records are phenomenal, of course, and represent high feeding and still higher care, but none the less are they important as showing the recognized butter value of the Jersey breed. The yield of Bisson's Belle is really most remarkable on account of the small yield of milk reported as producing such an enormous yield of butter. A simple operation in long division shows that it took, in round numbers, a trifle less than 8¼ lbs. (about a gallon) of her milk on an average throughout

JERSEY CATTLE.

the entire year to produce a pound of "well-worked, marketable butter, salted not heavier than one ounce to the pound." The ratio of butter to milk is so remarkable, indeed, that many doubt the record reported, and declare it a physical impossibility. Signal's Lily Flagg, the present Jersey Queen, averaged throughout the year one pound of butter to a trifle less than $10\frac{3}{4}$ lbs. milk. She is certainly a wonderful cow. Her record and that of Bisson's Belle were reported in good faith by honorable gentlemen, whose personal integrity cannot be questioned, and we see no reason to doubt their published and certified statements.

It is unfortunate that the breeders of all classes of dairy stock have not been able to agree upon at least co-ordinate chemical tests for actual butter fat at stated intervals throughout the churn test period. Every maker of good butter knows that the churn is but a tool in the hands of the churner, and that very many conditions surround to influence the churn result. The chemical test can do no harm, and may do untold good in checking up the churner, not the churn. In our opinion those who fight against the well-known accuracy of tests for butter fat—on one excuse or other—are standing in their own most-needed light and holding back the wheels of dairy progress.

The beef capacity of the Jersey breed is small. If sex in offspring could be controlled, it might be profitable to breed Jerseys on a large scale for their butter feature alone, but since the number of steer calves is usually equal to the number of heifers, and since there is always a greater or less number of heifers deficient in milking quality, which must be fed for the butcher, it is evident that breeding Jerseys for home use—not for sale as breeding stock—might prove a losing business.

The farmer who keeps a few cows, and depends on the annual sale of a few fat steers to meet his expenses, demands a breed of larger frame and greater aptitude for beef; but in their legitimate sphere, Jerseys must always rank deservedly high.

It is very commonly stated that the bulls of this breed are vicious and ill-tempered. We think this opinion is based upon nothing more than the fact of their extremely nervous temperament, already referred to. They undoubtedly require skillful handling; but when so managed, are not more inclined to viciousness than the bulls of other breeds. Because there are at present so many Jerseys in the Southern states, there has arisen a very popular but erroneous notion that they acclimate with greater safety than cattle of other breeds; the real facts in the case are, that at least three of the improved breeds rank ahead of them in this respect—their greater number in the South being due to their earlier importation, and hence longer period for the breeding of acclimated stock.

A study of the illustrations, engraved after sketches from life by a well-known artist, will give a good idea of this valuable breed.

Chapter XXIV.

GUERNSEYS.

This breed, having an origin probably identical with that of the Jersey, has rapidly but surely increased, both in popularity and inherent worth. Near the large cities of the United States, Guernseys are now found in considerable numbers, and there is a growing sentiment in their favor throughout the entire country. They were introduced into America about the time of the first Jersey importations, but have not become so widely distributed or so generally known.

IMPORTED GUERNSEY COW, SELECT, 2205.
Property of J. W. Fuller, Catasauqua, Pa.

DESCRIPTION AND CHARACTERISTICS.

These points may be best studied by comparing them briefly with the full description of the Jersey already given. They are larger and coarser, being rather inclined to appear bony. Color varies; yellow, yellowish or reddish fawn, and brown, of solid colors, frequently with considerable spotting of white, and showing the same mealy-colored ring—although less marked—about the nostrils. Bones are larger, head longer, and general appearance indicative more of utility than beauty. She is, like her Jersey sister, a milk and butter cow, and in her place ranks as good as the best. The butter made from Guernsey cows is claimed to be even more highly colored than that from the Jersey.

At the New Jersey Agricultural Experiment Station the recently conducted breed tests show very strongly in favor of the Guernsey as a profitable dairy cow, placing her ahead of the Jersey on a basis of net profit, as shown by the following summary:

Total milk in 300 days.	Total butter fat in 300 days.	Total value butter fat @ 25 cts. per lb.	Total cost food in 300 days.	Total profit per cow.
Guernsey, 5,730 lbs.	291 lbs	$72.75	$44.70	$28.05
Jersey, 5,535 lbs.	270 lbs.	$67.50	$48.30	$19.20

Of course "one swallow does not make a summer," but the single test made as above stated shows that the Guernseys selected for the test were superior animals—certainly superior to the Jerseys with which they were there compared.

The following Scale of Points has been adopted by the American Guernsey Cattle Club (Edward Norton, of Farmington, Conn., secretary):

Quality of milk, 30	Skin deep yellow, in ear, on end of bone of tail, at base of horn, on udder, teats and body generally	20
	Skin loose, mellow, with fine, soft hair	10
Quantity and duration of flow, 40	Escutcheon wide on thighs, high and broad, with thigh ovals.	8
	Milk veins long and prominent	6
	Udder full in front	6
	Udder full and well up behind . } 18*	8
	Udder large but not fleshy . .	4
	Udder Teats squarely placed	4
	Udder teats of good size	4
Size and substance 16	Size for the breed	5
	Not too light bone	1
	Barrel round and deep at flank	4
	Hips and joints wide	2
	Rump long and broad	2
	Thighs and withers thin	2
Symmetry . . 14	Back level to setting-on of tail	3
	Throat clean, with small dewlap	1
	Legs not too long, with hocks well apart in walking	2
	Tail long and thin	1
	Horns curved and not coarse	2
	Head rather long and fine, with quiet and gentle expression.	3
	General appearance	2
100	Perfection	100

* For bulls deduct the 18 points for Udder from above.

Of our illustrations we may say, in brief: Imported Select brought with her from the island a record of 22 lbs. 8 ozs. of well-worked and salted butter in seven days, and of milk showing 18.05 per cent. total solids, of which 8.09 per cent. was fat, with a yield of about 22½ quarts a day, on a ration of three quarts of crushed oats and three of wheat

GUERNSEY BULL, MIDAS, 2003—CHIEF OF THE "ELLERSLIE" HERD.
Owned by Levi P. Morton, Rhinecliff, Duchess Co., N. Y. (Engraved by *Rural New-Yorker*, N. Y.)

GUERNSEYS.

IMPORTED GUERNSEY COW, JOLIE 2d, 2206.
Property of J. W. Fuller, Catasauqua, Pa.

bran a day, and grass. (Select is now dead.) Jolie, 2d, is perhaps the best cow in Mr. Fuller's herd, and gives when in full milk 33 quarts per day. In 1884 this cow won the first Island prize over her famous half-sister, Flukes. Windfall is also a wonderful milker, and although well advanced in years, may still be ranked as one of the prime Guernseys in America.

Midas, the pride of Vice President Morton's Ellerslie herd, is a magnificent bull, both in blood and individuality, and is justly recognized as one of the best Guernsey bulls in the world.

IMPORTED GUERNSEY COW, WINDFALL, 2216.
Property of J. W. Fuller, Catasauqua, Pa.

Chapter XXV.

AYRSHIRES.

The Ayrshire breed—which takes its name from the county or shire of Ayr, Scotland—is of comparatively recent origin; in Cully's work on Live Stock (1790) it is not even mentioned. Aiton in 1825 mentioned it, but described an entirely different animal from the present improved Ayshire. Even as late as 1842 Prof. Low closes his history of their origin as follows:

"We may assume, then, from all the evidence which, in the absence of authentic documents, the case admits of, that the dairy breed of Ayrshire owes the characters which distinguish it from the older race to a mixture with the blood of races of the continent, and of the dairy breed of Alderney."

AYRSHIRE BULL, SIR HUGH, 2582.
Property of H. R. C. WATSON, West Farms, N. Y.

Afterwards, in the same chapter, he gives us a pretty definite idea as to how the later improvement was effected in the statement that "some breeders in Ayrshire have begun to cross the breed with the Shorthorns." Allen (American Cattle) makes a shrewd "guess" as to how the improvement was brought about. He says:

"It could be from no other than the direct cross of small, compact Shorthorn bulls, descended from the best milking cows in the northeastern counties of England, on the cows descended from the Holderness bulls of Lord Marchmont, and their crosses from the 'conjectured' Dutch bulls brought in by Mr. Dunlop. From no other race of cattle, either Scotch, English or Irish, could the improved Ayshires get their shape, color and milking qualities combined."

They are undoubtedly based on the hardy West Highland or Kyloe stock; that the Alderney or Jersey breed was used in the crosses, would appear from the early descriptions given; and that the "guess" made by Allen may at least approximate the truth, is evidenced by the present appearance of the breed and the gradual change it has made within the past 40 or 50 years.

DESCRIPTION OF MODERN AYRSHIRE.

Color varies almost as much as in Shorthorns, and is, indeed, very much the same—red and white predominating; but in many individuals black hairs scattered through the red give a blue and white color which we have never seen among pure Shorthorns. Roans are quite common, and roan and white, or patched roans, were formerly very abundant. Later breeders, however, require colors, of whatever shade, to be distinct.

The general outline of the body is similar to that of all milk breeds —being light and narrow in front and gradually deepening toward the hind quarters. The head is narrow and close fleshed—in the bull wider, but still showing the more delicate contour peculiar to bulls of milking strains—with bright medium sized eyes, and small horns, showing a tendency, among cattle of our acquaintance, to assume more or less irregular positions; ears thin and well coated; neck fine, without dewlap —in the bull naturally arched; body deepening toward the flank; ribs, at first flat, arching toward the loin; loin, hips and rump full and even with the back; tail dropping squarely; legs straight with rather thin twist, and brisket close and firm fleshed. The udder of the Ayshire cow is her special peculiarity; it is large but so broad and vertically flattened as to appear small; it spreads out well both in front and to rear—divisions strongly marked, with small cylindrical teats, wide apart and evenly placed. Her escutcheons are usually of a high order— especially the front ovals being well developed, and the milk veins show with considerable prominence.

In general appearance, the Ayrshire of the present day has lost much of the lean, ungainly outline once supposed to be necessarily co-existent with dairy excellence, and assumed a neat, trim, well rounded, though not beefy, form, which cannot fail to increase its popularity.

CHARACTERISTICS.

We regard it as a waste of argument to try to convince the public— as many have attempted—that the Ayrshires are general-purpose animals; they are, and have been, a distinctive class of milk stock, differing from all known breeds in the high per cent. of casein or cheesy mat-

AYRSHIRE CATTLE.
Property of COLDREN & LEE, Iowa City, Iowa.

ter of the milk. For butter, the Ayrshire has not been classed among the best, for the reason that the globules are not equal in size, causing the cream to rise unevenly, and injuring the grain of the butter by reason of protracted churning ; the use of the centrifugal in cream separation practically does away with the first objection, but the second has yet to be overcome before they can take high rank as butter producers. In quantity of milk they excel the Jersey, but fall short of the Holstein-Friesian ; the percentage of fat in the milk is good, and, taken in connection with the large amount of casein, renders the milk from an Ayrshire dairy pre-eminent for cheese.

AYRSHIRE COW.
Property of H. R. C. Watson, West Farms, N. Y.

Their beef claims must be accepted with some latitude. Unquestionably they produce excellent beef under favorable conditions, but there is too great a tendency toward milk to admit of any very marked aptitude for fattening. In size they rank with the small breeds—mature bulls weighing from 1,200 to 1,500 lbs., and cows from 900 to 1,100 lbs.

As showing the average yield under ordinary conditions, and with very light feed, we give the public record of the herd owned by C. M. Winslow, Brandon, Vt.:

Average of	10	cows for	year	1880,	each	6,035	lbs. milk
"	11	"	"	1881,	"	6,176	"
"	9	"	"	1882,	"	6,672	"
"	15	"	"	1883,	"	6,168	"
"	16	"	"	1884,	"	6,814	"
"	15	"	"	1885,	"	7,025	"

The following Scale of Points to be used in connection with description given was adopted by the Ayrshire Breeders' Association, C. M. Winslow, secretary, Feb. 4th, 1885:

COWS.		BULLS.
10	Head	10
5	Neck	10
5	Fore quarters	7
10	Back	10
8	Hind quarters	10
33	Udder	
	Scrotum and Rudimentary teats	10
3	Legs	5
5	Skin and Hair	10
3	Color	3
8	Live Weight	10
10	General appearance	15
100	Perfection	100

Referring to our illustrations: Dutchess of Smithfield, 4256, has a record of 10,748 lbs. of milk in one year, and 19 lbs. 6 ozs. butter in seven days; she won first prizes at Rhode Island State Fairs of 1879 to 1881; at Woonsocket, 1879; and second prize at New York State Fair in 1882. Sir Hugh, 2582, won first prize at New York State Fair in 1882, and second for bull and four of his get, at New York Dairy and Cattle Show, 1887. The large engraving—group from the herd of Coldren & Lee—shows the variety in color markings common to the breed by a predominance of white, and represents a fair sample of the excellent herd from which it is taken.

Chapter XXVI.

DUTCH-BELTED CATTLE.

Natives of Holland, and of a pure black and white color, they have been frequently described as peculiarly marked Holstein-Friesians. It must be remembered, however, that no matter how closely these two Dutch races of cattle may have been related at first, they are now justly recognized as pure and distinct breeds.

The original name of the Dutch-Belted cattle, and the one still used in Holland is "Lakenfield" cattle—the name having reference to the peculiar white belt or sheet passing completely around the body. From the first volume of the Dutch-Belted Cattle Herd Book, we quote:

"Their breeding dates back to beyond the seventeenth century;"

And again :

"These cattle were solely controlled by the nobility of Holland, and they are to the present time keeping them pure, but are not inclined to part with them"—

A fact which may account for the comparatively small number found at present in America.

The peculiar color markings of these cattle show an attainment in the science of breeding really wonderful. Prof. Low attributes the first appearance of the belted marking to a cross between two fixed original breeds of opposite color, and this theory is doubtless correct; but to found a breed which will transmit such peculiar points with certainty—as do the Dutch-Belted cattle—was a task, the magnitude of which is only excelled by the result attained.

Among the first importers to America were D. H. Haight, of Goshen, N. Y.—who made the first importation to the United States in 1838 ; W. R. Coleman, and P. T. Barnum—the nation's showman. Mr. Barnum says :

"They struck my fancy in Holland. I imported them, and found their unique and singular appearance not their best recommendation, for they are excellent milkers."

DESCRIPTION AND CHARACTERISTICS.

Color, as already mentioned, jet black with a broad band or "belt" of purest white passing completely around the body. The milk outline is beautifully shown in long head, fine, rather thin neck—well arched in bull, but still fine at head, small horns, wide chest, straight back, broad, level hips, deep quarters, and square, well-placed udder. In size they are somewhat above medium—mature cows weighing from 900

DUTCH-BELTED BULL, EDWARD THE GREAT.

to 1,200 lbs.; and bulls from 1,600 to 2,000 lbs. They are strong and vigorous; usually kind and docile in disposition, and transmit, with great certainty, all their original qualities.

In addition to the above we give the following standard description, combined with Scale of Points, which has been formally adopted by the Dutch-Belted Cattle Association of America:

COWS.		BULLS.
8	Color	13
	(Body color black, with a clearly defined continuous white belt. The belt to be of medium width, beginning behind the shoulder and extending nearly to the hips.)	
6	Head	6
	(Comparatively long and somewhat dishing—broad between the eyes; poll prominent; muzzle fine; dark tongue.)	
4	Eyes and Horns	4
	(Eyes black, full and mild; horns long, compared with their diameter.)	
6	Neck	6
	(Fine and moderately thin, and should harmonize in symmetry with the neck and shoulders.)	
4	Shoulders	9
	(Fine at the top, becoming deep and broad as they extend backward and downward, with a low chest.)	
10	Barrel	10
	(Large and deep, with well developed abdomen; ribs well rounded and free from fat.)	
10	Hips	10
	(Broad, with level chine and full loin.)	
6	Rump	6
	(High, long and broad.)	
8	Hindquarters	8
	(Long and deep, rear line incurving; tail long, thin, tapering to a full switch.)	
3	Legs	3
	(Short, clean, standing well apart.)	
20	Udder	
	(Large, well developed front and rear; teats of convenient size and wide apart; mammary veins large, long and crooked, entering large orifices.)	
	Rudimentary teats	10
	(Size and wide-spread placing.)	
2	Escutcheon	2
3	Hair and Skin	3
	(Fine and soft; skin of moderate thickness, of a rich dark or yellow color.)	
4	Disposition	4
	(Quiet; animal free from excessive fat.)	
6	General condition and constitution	6
100	Perfection	100

They are a dairy breed, the cows producing a large quantity of milk, which is above the average in butter content. For beef they are fair, standing fully equal to other dairy breeds in this respect. Our illustrations are from the herd of Mr. H. B. Richards —the genial secretary of the society and editor of the "Dutch-Belted Cattle Herd Book"—and are excellent portraits of his celebrated cow, Lady Aldine, and the bull, Edward the Great, now owned, we believe, in Illinois.

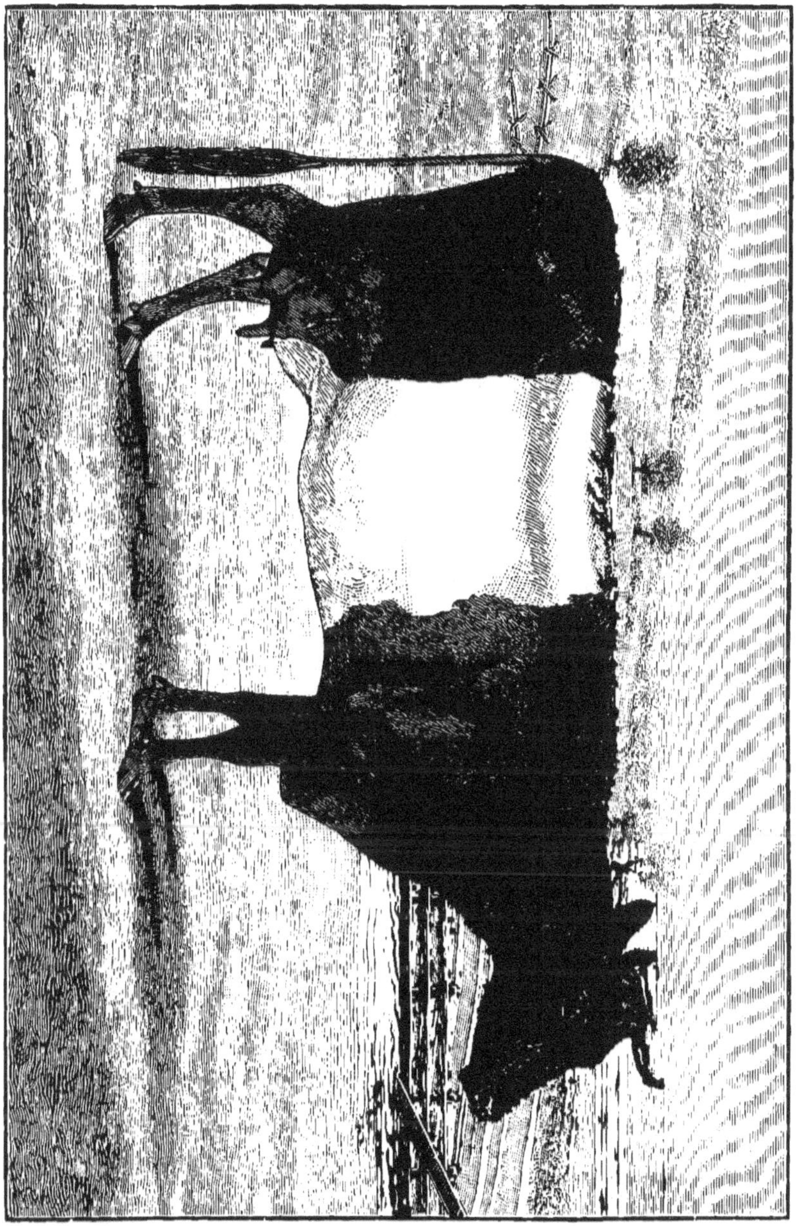

DUTCH-BELTED CATTLE. 143

DUTCH-BELTED COW, LADY ALDINE, 124.
Property of H. B. Richards, Easton, Pa.

Chapter XXVII.

AMERICAN HOLDERNESS.

The origin and history of this breed are fraught with singular interest as illustrating the peculiar methods used by breeders in fixing type.

Some fifty or sixty years ago, Mr. Truman A. Cole, of Solsville, N. Y., purchased a cow of imported stock called "Holderness"—originally from the West Riding of Yorkshire, England; she was red and white in color, of large size, an excellent milker, and was at the time in calf by a bull of the same breed. Her offspring proved to be a male; when this calf was a yearling, he was bred to his own mother, the result being a heifer calf, which was afterwards bred to the same bull. To put the history of their improvement in a nutshell: Mr. Cole has continually and closely in-bred, never admitting a single drop of outside blood until he has produced a breed thoroughly fixed in type, and accurately transmitting even the least of its distinguishing qualities. A remarkable change has taken place in their color markings as seen from the following

DESCRIPTION OF AMERICAN HOLDERNESS.

When first dropped, the sides, neck and head are reddish brown; as they increase in age this color changes to a dark brown or jet black, while the white lines on the back and belly remain unchanged from birth. The legs correspond in color with the sides, except at the belly line, where a white band is thrown across, presenting a novel and attractive design. (This change from the former Shorthorn colors of the Yorkshire cattle can only be accounted for by assuming that the close incestuous breeding practiced by Mr. Cole has caused them to revert to the colors of their original Dutch ancestry.)

In size they are nearly equal to the Holstein-Friesians; and in outline also very similar. The head is neat, close-fleshed, long in the cow and shorter in the bull; horns short and curving forward; neck fine at head—in the bull arching—and well set on at shoulders; back keeping up an even, straight line from the shoulders to the drop of the tail; flanks deep; udder large, broad, well forward, with good-sized teats, placed evenly and wide apart.

They are emphatically a dairy breed, as illustrated by the fact that nineteen cows of Mr. Cole's herd—two years old and upwards—actually made 5,860 lbs. of butter during the season of 1879—an average of a

HOLDERNESS BULL ACME.
AT 20 MONTHS.
BRED AND OWNED BY T. A. COLE, SOLSVILLE, N.Y.

little over 308 pounds of butter to each cow. Mr. Cole states that he could easily have brought up the average to 350 pounds, if he had not raised the calves. While not equaling the Holstein-Friesians in quantity of milk, they are said to excel them in richness of product for butter. Their beef qualities are also good, and taken all in all, we predict for them a popular reception in strict keeping with their merits. They are by no means generally known ; yet they have found a foothold in nearly all of the Northern states, and wherever found are rapidly growing in favor.

Our illustrations, better than any description, will give an excellent idea of their appearance. Mr. Cole's herd has become justly celebrated ; and by his skill and carefulness, he has won for himself a most enviable reputation as a patient and painstaking breeder, and as the originator of the American Holderness breed.

HOLDERNESS COW, ADELAIDE 17.
BRED AND OWNED BY T. A. COLE, SOLSVILLE, N.Y.

Chapter XXVIII.

BROWN SWISS.

The history of this breed may be given briefly by stating that it has been built up step by step from the common bovine ancestry of Switzerland and neighboring countries. Improvement has been effected almost solely by selection and light in-breeding, and is most noticeable in those districts or "cantons" of Switzerland, like Schwytz, which are peopled by progressive, well-to-do farmers—men who have always taken great pride in their cattle, and, prompted no doubt by local jealousies, have striven, each, to make his herd the best and purest of the race.

IMPORTATION TO AMERICA.

In the United States the Brown Swiss have been slow to find purchasers until within the last few years. The first importation was made by H. M. Clarke, of Belmont, Mass., about 1870, since which time several importations have been made, and the demand in the United States is now quite active. The Brown Swiss Breeders' Association has been organized, and Volume I. of their record appeared in 1881. N. S. Fish, Groton, Conn., is secretary of the association. In the Eastern states this breed has already attained considerable prominence, while in the West and South it is little known.

DESCRIPTION AND CHARACTERISTICS.

Color solid chestnut bronze, somewhat lighter at the back and belly line, and showing the same mealy ring at the muzzle, so well known as characteristic of the Jerseys. The hoofs, tongue, nose and switch of the tail are always black, while the light belly line extends more or less over the escutcheon and inner surface of the legs. In size they are above medium, mature bulls weighing from 1,700 to 2,100 lbs., and cows from 1,100 to 1,300 lbs. The head is large ; horns short and waxy, with black tips ; ears well covered inside with long. light-colored hair ; neck short, with rather heavy dewlap ; legs short and straight, with wide thighs and deep quarters, and general outline showing the milk breed. The cows have excellent escutcheons, well formed udders, and give a good quantity of rich milk.

The remarkable record of the Brown Swiss cow. Brienz, 168, made during the Fat Stock Show, Chicago, Ill., Nov. 1891, has brought prom-

BROWN SWISS BULL, ELMO, 306.
Owned by N. S. Fish, Groton, Conn.

BROWN SWISS COW, MUATTA, 155.
Owned by N. S. Fish, Groton, Conn.

inently forward the claim of the breed to a position in the front rank for butter. Brienz gave in three days 245 lbs. milk, which by the Babcock test contained 9.32 lbs. of fat. The first day her yield was 81.05 lbs. of milk, containing 3.25 lbs. of fat; and her average was 81.5 lbs. milk, containing 3.1 lbs. fat per day, the largest official yield of pure butter fat ever made by a cow of any breed, when under show excitement away from home.

As to the ease with which they acclimate in the fever belt, we have as yet no information. The cattle are thrifty, mature early and promise to find abundant favor in the Western states for the dairy.

The following Scale of Points has been adopted by the Brown Swiss Breeders' Association:

Head 2	Forward 39
Face. 2	Thighs 4
Ears 1	Legs 4
Nose 2	Tail. 4
Eyes 1	Hide 3
Horns 5	Color 6
Neck 4	Fore-udder 10
Chest. 4	Hind-udder 10
Back 6	Teats 5
Barrel 8	Milk-veins. 4
Hips 4	Escutcheon 7
	Disposition 4
Forward 39	
	Perfection 100

In judging bulls and heifers, omit the points for Fore-udder, Hind-udder and Teats, as above given; and in color they should be dark brown.

Our illustrations—all originally from photographs—may be accepted as accurate representations of the breed.

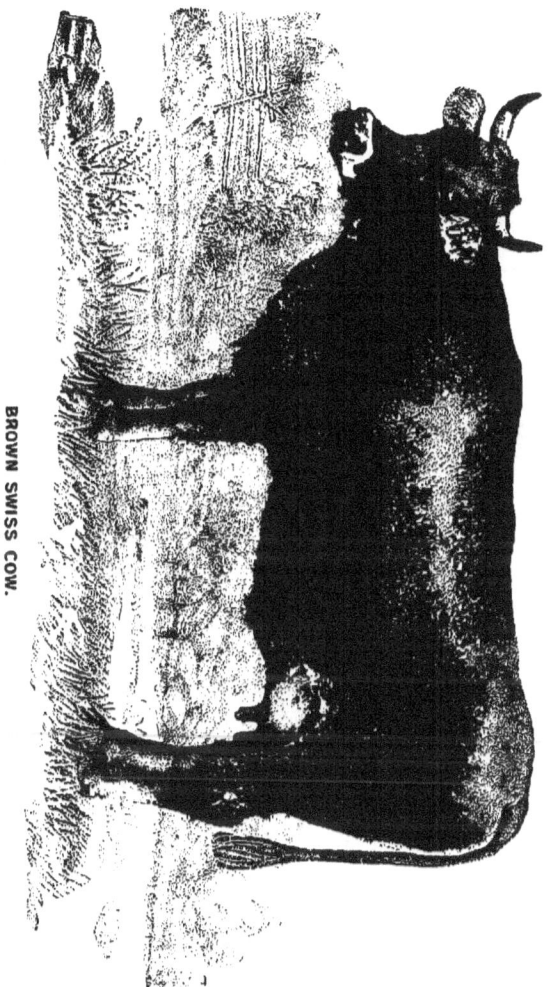

BROWN SWISS COW.
(Re-engraved, by permission, from lithograph made for the Department of State.)

Chapter XXIX.

BRITTANY CATTLE.

From best authority obtainable, this breed of cattle has an origin much in common with that of the Holstein-Friesian; difference in climate, soil and vegetation having, through years of time, made the difference in size and in other respects as now observed. The breed is now said to be "native" to the five departments of France which for-

BRITTANY BULL.

merly made up the province of Bretagne, and in support of the statement as to origin, it may be noted, that considerable variation among the cattle, as to size and milking capacity, is found in the various localities of their native province.

A few have been imported to the United States at various times within the last decade, but they are by no means generally known. Mr. W. B. Montgomery, of Starkville, Miss. (better known as a breeder of Jerseys) has a herd of 12 or 15 cows and two bulls. Writing to the author under date August 6, 1888, this gentleman says:

"They are the hardiest of all the breeds of which I have any knowledge, and on scant pasturage and poor soil will give better results in the butter dairy than any breed with which I am acquainted. On moderately fertile land, and with proper care and attention, Jersey cattle are greatly to be preferred, but the Brittanies, on scant feed and rough mountain lands, will prove superior to the Jerseys."

DESCRIPTION AND CHARACTERISTICS.

Color clear black and white—almost exactly similar to that of the Holstein-Friesian—the white showing a tendency to appear over shoulders and hips, and along the belly line; the membrane surrounding the tongue is always white—a mark which may be called a distinguishing characteristic of the breed.

In size they are classed as small—about equal to the Jersey—mature bulls weighing from 1,000 to 1,300 lbs., cows from 650 to 950 lbs. The head and neck are fine, even delicate, with little or no dewlap. The horns small, always black at the tips, and sometimes black throughout, rather longer than Jersey horns, and approaching more nearly those of the Devon in curvature; the back is even, chest large, and haunch and buttock bones wide apart. The legs are well proportioned to size of body, hair fine and short, and skin mellow and of medium thickness.

The Brittany cows are strictly dairy animals, giving a good quantity of rich milk, and are claimed to give a greater yield on scant grazing than cows of any other breed. Much allowance must be made for extravagant claims of partisan breeders, yet we believe the Britanny breed will find, in our districts of less fertility, ample favor with those best qualified to judge.

Our illustrations were re-engraved, by permission, from lithographs used by the Department of State in the recently issued volume of Consular Reports on Cattle and Dairy Farming—and were originally from photographs taken in France.

BRITTANY COW.

Chapter XXX.

KERRY CATTLE.

This breed—the only one of any prominence native to Ireland—has of late years found its way to America, and is attracting considerable attention. In the volume of Consular Reports on Cattle and Dairy Farming, previously mentioned, Mr. Gumbleton refers to the "Kerry Cattle, which are very pretty (small in size and black) and very good milkers." Mr. Richard Good says the Kerries "are attracting more attention than they did formerly, owing to the ease with which they are managed;" and that "they are particularly suited to mountain districts, which would not properly feed Shorthorns." It may be here stated that the County of Kerry, whence they derive the name, is the most mountainous, as it is the most western, portion of the island. The Kerries form as nearly an aboriginal breed as possible, tracing back to the wild "Forest" stock, and showing the stages of improvement all through their history.

Within the last three years, several small importations have been made to the United States. The largest of which we have any knowledge, numbering eleven head, was made by Mr. Edward Kemp, of the well-known firm of Lanham & Kemp, of New York city, in 1886.

Mr. Kemp is proprietor of the "Locust Farm," Rumson Neck, New Jersey, where his Kerries, Holstein-Friesians and Hambletonians are now kept.

DESCRIPTION AND CHARACTERISTICS.

Color black, but this is only a fashionable point of the last 10 or 15 years, so that black and white—"line backs"—and even reds are still found. Low, in 1842, described them as "generally black, with a white ridge along the spine;" he further says that a white streak along the belly was common, and other colors, such as brown, red and spotted were met with. Breeders are now strictly adhering to the black coats, and will in time eliminate all other colors.

In size, the Kerry cattle are small, mature bulls weighing 800 to 1,100 lbs., and cows from 600 to 800 lbs. The head is small, with long clean muzzle and thin lips; eye expressive; horns fine, short and white —"middle horns"—usually turning upward; neck fine at head and well set on to deep but narrow shoulders; body gradually deepens to the flank, but the rump is narrow and the thighs light. The dewlap is rather scant, and the brisket small and close fleshed; legs are neat and

KERRY COWS.
(English Engraving.)

fine, but rather long, and the tail slender and dropping squarely. The hair is rather long and thick, but the skin is mellow, with good handling properties. In general appearance the Kerries are neat, small-sized dairy animals, showing the typical milk wedge, and possessing the quiet disposition so essential to dairy excellence.

They are bred exclusively for milk, and their partisans claim for them an unrivalled production on scanty hill or mountain ranges. To explain their dairy worth in more definite manner, we appropriate from the weekly edition of the *National Live Stock Journal*, of Chicago —issue of July 24, 1888—the following clipping, referring to four Kerry cows, which were recently entered at The Royal Counties Show:

"One of the four was reserve number, and very highly commended, and another commended; moreover, it will be seen by the following figures that the 'reserve' Kerry gave more butter in proportion to quantity of milk than even the first or second prize cows, though one of them was a Jersey. The first prize cow, a Shorthorn, gave 2 galls. 2 pints of milk, yielding 1 lb. 3½ ozs. butter; the second prize, a Jersey, gave 3 galls. 3½ pints of milk, yielding 1 lb. 4 ozs. butter; the Kerry, very highly commended and reserve, gave 2 gallons of milk, yielding 1 lb. 1½ ozs. butter."

Nothing is said as to conditions or food for the three cows mentioned, but we may reasonably infer that these points were made as nearly equal as possible.

The Kerries are certainly hardy for more northern latitudes, but we can say nothing as to their acclimation in the South. The "Dexter" strain of Kerry cattle has been quite extensively fostered, and we mention briefly the points of difference; it gets the name from that of its founder, who is supposed to have changed the type by selection. The head is coarser; horns thicker and more nearly straight; the body round and blocky, and the legs short and thick.

Chapter XXXI.

SHORTHORNS OR DURHAMS.

The origin of this valuable breed has always been a subject of more or less dispute—ardent admirers of the Shorthorn claiming an almost unbroken line of pure descent, and improvement solely by careful selection, feeding and management; others, perhaps partisans of other breeds, claiming that whatever improvement has been made, and in fact, whatever excellence the breed might possess, has been brought about by judicious but stealthy crosses with superior individuals of other breeds. That there was a time when the Shorthorn ancestry were only native cattle, even the most earnest advocates of their purity must admit; but it is also true, that, if there have been any radical out-crosses since the breed became definitely known as such, they have been exceedingly stealthy ones.

EARLY HISTORY.

Their probable history begins with the cattle of the mainland of Europe, in the provinces bordering on the Baltic and North Seas. These cattle possessed many of the qualities now claimed by Shorthorns, including color and size; but there was a general disposition toward excellence in milking qualities rather than the full, rounded, symmetrical, beef outline of a majority of modern Shorthorns as bred for range improvement in the Western states.

Prior to the conquest of England by William of Normandy, the northern and eastern portion was occupied by Danes and other warlike races from the mainland. These people did not confine their operations to war and pillage alone, but, while holding the eastern coastline of the island, established a considerable trade in merchandise and agricultural products to and from the mainland. In this way, it is claimed, were the Shorthorn progenitors introduced into England; and what renders the claim more probable, is the fact that the first Shorthorns were found in and confined to those counties or shires lying along the northern and eastern boundaries.

IMPROVEMENT.

As early as 1740, permanent records were kept by the more careful breeders; and, according to Mr. Bates, there were fine Shorthorns upon the estate of the Earl of Northumberland as early as the year 1600. Mr. Millbank, of Barningham, and Sir William St. Quintin, of Scampston, were among the early noted breeders previous to 1750, but it was not until the Colling Bros. began raising them for profit that the Shorthorns obtained anything like general notice or favor. They established themselves about 1780—Chas. Colling at Ketton and his brother Robert at Barmpton, both places near Darlington, on the river Tees. While keeping their herds distinct, they worked more or less together, freely interchanging the use of their bulls. The method pursued by them was to select the best animals, male and female, that could be found among neighboring and even quite distant breeders, breed them together, keeping up the best conditions as to food and management, and carefully in-breeding to fix the type. (By the term in-breeding, which we have frequently used, is meant the breeding together of animals more or less closely related; the object being to perpetuate certain characteristics, common to both parents, in the offspring. While very valuable if carefully used, the principle of in-breeding is dangerous if carried to extremes, and should be used lightly unless by the most skillful breeders.) Early in their history (1786) Chas. Colling purchased, for $42, the bull Hubback; he proved a most excellent stock-getter, and now ranks as one of the most celebrated bulls in Shorthorn history. In 1810, Comet—the direct offspring of Bolinbroke and Phœnix, and a lineal descendant of Hubback—was sold for $5,000, showing to what extent these cattle had advanced both in merit and popular favor. After Colling Bros., in point of time, came Thos. and Richard Booth and Thomas Bates. These men secured their stock from Colling, but while Booth Bros. persisted in breeding for beef, and the full, rounded points so much admired for the butcher's block, Bates was carefully selecting and breeding with main reference to milking qualities. Thus it happened that Shorthorn improvement was started in two parallel but distinctly different lines. From these two main lines of improvement, the tastes of different individuals have given rise to numberless "strains" or "families" all having the same general characteristics, but differing in color, beef and milk qualities, or other particulars.

EARLY IMPORTATION INTO THE UNITED STATES.

It is probable that importations were made very soon after the close of the Revolutionary War with England, as cattle answering the description of Shorthorns were found in Virginia as early as 1790, and in 1797 some of these cattle were taken across the line to Kentucky by a Mr. Patton, soon becoming quite well-known as the "Patton Stock." Authentic importations were made direct from England by Mr. Cox in 1816; by Col. Lewis Sanders and Brutus J. Clay, both of Kentucky, in 1817; and from this time on importations on a small scale were quite frequent. In 1834-5-6, Shorthorns were brought over in considerable numbers by a company made up for this purpose among breeders in the Scioto Val-

SHORTHORN BULL, MARIUS, 70744.
(Young Mary family.) Property of Wilcox & Leggitt, Benson, Minn.

ley in Ohio, and acting through an agent who was supplied with almost unlimited funds. The first introduction of the celebrated Duchess strain was made about 1840, by a Mr. Vail of Troy, N. Y., who secured a bull and a heifer direct from the herd of Thomas Bates. Among the earlier noted breeders in America, we may mention Samuel Thorne, of Thornedale, N. Y., and R. J. Alexander, of Kentucky—the latter a Scotch nobleman, who purchased the Woodburn estate of 3,000 acres, and used his annual income of $80,000 to establish and maintain a model American herd of Shorthorns.

DESCRIPTION AND CHARACTERISTICS.

Widely varying in color, we find almost all markings except black, brown and brindled; in some families pure, deep cherry red, in others snowy white, and between these two extremes are red and white in all grades as to size and arrangement of spots—red roan, white roan, roan and white, and speckled or "turkey" roan. In size the Shorthorn ranks among the largest of known breeds, bulls of mature age ranging from 1,900 to 2,300 lbs., and cows from 1,200 to 1,600 lbs., with occasional individuals considerably exceeding these figures. The general form is square with well-filled points, straight back, keeping the line even and well up at the rump; quarters deep and full, but not bulging; ribs well sprung, giving a wide back and rounded barrel; muzzle clear orange yellow (in some families, light drab); wide open nostrils, and rather thin-fleshed lips; eyes clear, bright and surrounded by rings of orange colored flesh; horns clear or cream-flecked, short and usually curving inward; ears thin and delicate, showing clear orange wax; neck short and fine in the cow—in the bull heavy, and rising with age; back level; loin full; buttocks wide apart; tail small just above the brush; brisket wide and full; and legs close, fine boned and well-proportioned to size of body.

The Shorthorns are emphatically general purpose animals, although perhaps, the majority of breeders persist in classing them with the purely beef breeds. When selected and bred for milk, they are exceedingly valuable as dairy stock, but it must be admitted that the general tendency to breed and feed for show has greatly increased their beef capacity at the expense of milking qualities. In some of the strains or families —as notably the Princess and Duchess strains—the dairy features have been carefully preserved, and even among the most pronounced beef families, an occasional excellent dairy cow will be found.

The American Shorthorn Breeders' Association (J. H. Pickrell, of Chicago, secretary) has never adopted any standard Scale of Points for the animal. Their adaptability seems not so great as that of some other breeds; they find their most congenial home and give best returns for investment in latitudes of the more central and northern United States.

IMPORTED PRINCE CHARLIE AND FOUR OF HIS GET.
Owned by C. W. Norton, Wilton Junction, Iowa.

In the Southern states—comprising what is known as the "fever belt"—they have not proved easy to acclimate, averaging a high percentage of mortality when brought into this region. Good animals, old enough for service, and recorded in the American Herd Book, can be obtained at from $100 to $200 of any responsible breeder.

The individuals so well represented by our illustrations need no introduction to any one familiar with Shorthorns. They are representative animals of the strains to which they belong, and their breeders are men of unquestioned integrity.

Chapter XXXII.

RED-POLLED CATTLE.

The Red-Polls, while tracing their history well back into the last century, have only recently attracted any considerable attention. Their origin is somewhat clouded in obscurity. Suffolk county, England, had from very early times a breed of polled cattle, and it is more than probable that this Suffolk breed had much to do with moulding the type of, and dehorning the Norfolk breed, which was the first to attract attention from outside parties. From their general resemblance to the Devons (excepting horns) we would look for a common ancestry somewhere in the early history of the breeds. Marshall, in his Rural Economy of Norfolk, states that the breed of Norfolk, about 1780, was a "Herefordshire breed in miniature," and that the color was "blood-red, with a white or mottled face." He further traces the changes of the breed, by crosses with Suffolk bulls, stating in substance that size was increased and form improved. To trace the origin further, it would be necessary to go back of the old polled Suffolk breed, and bring up the question as to how the various breeds of hornless cattle were established in their peculiar feature. We need only say in this connection that polled animals were found in most portions of the British Islands from time immemorial. According to Youatt, there seem to have been two distinct breeds of aboriginal cattle occupying the central and northern portions of the British Island; one of these had medium horns, while the other had none; from the first were probably produced the Devon, Hereford, Sussex and West Highland cattle, while as a continuation of the second, we have now the Galloways, Angus and Suffolk and Norfolk Reds—the latter now collectively called Red-Polls.

Improvement of the breed has been steadily carried forward—the Suffolks dehorning, while the Norfolks were firmly fixing the blood-red color mentioned by Marshall—and both breeds came gradually nearer a common standard, until, about the middle of the present century, breeders from both counties began to meet in honest competition, and select their breeding animals with reference to perpetuating the red color and the hornless trait. In 1874, Mr. H. F. Euren, of Norwich, succeeded in establishing the English Red-Polled Herd Book, and through the stimulus thus applied, these cattle have since been making rapid strides toward perfection. In 1883, the American Red-Polled Cattle Society

164   RED-POLLED CATTLE.

ROYAL HERD OF RED-POLLED CATTLE.
Owned by J. C. Murray, Maquoketa, Iowa.

RED-POLLED COW, PAULINA, 315.
Property of Wm. Steele, Merton, Wis.

(J. C. Murray, of Maquoketa, Iowa, secretary) was organized, and two volumes of the Herd Book have already appeared. The first importation was made in 1873 by G. F. Taber, Patterson, N. Y., since which time many have been brought in, and more bred, until we have in the United States at present writing some 1,800 or 1,900 head.

DESCRIPTION AND CHARACTERISTICS.

Color a deep rich red, with only the brush of the tail white, occasionally white on the udder in cows, but this, while not regarded as an absolute disqualification, is not favored. Size above medium, mature bulls weighing from 1,700 to 2,100 lbs., and cows from 1,100 to 1,400 lbs. The head is neat, with a tuft of hair curling over the narrow frontal points, and a light-colored, clear-cut muzzle. The neck is clean and fine, with little dewlap; ribs springing—not broadly arched, but filling the demand for rounded outline of barrel; legs clean, fine and short. In the cow the udder should be large, but not meaty; when empty it should hang in creases or folds; milk veins should be prominent, and knotted or puffed.

It must be confessed that most of the modern breeders of Red-Polls have been too intent on securing size and beauty of contour to preserve, as carefully as they should, the really valuable dairy qualities of the breed. If a change be not made in this direction, we shall soon be compelled to say of them, as we might now say of the Shorthorns, that they were originally excellent dairy stock, but have been greatly injured by the pernicious custom of feeding high for the show ring.

Red-Polls are, in general appearance, hornless Devons (see also illustrations), and they are bred and advertised as general purpose cattle. They are claimed, and we think fairly, to be the rivals of the Shorthorns for general use in the western United States. As to their adaptability in the fever belt of the South, we cannot speak to a certainty, from the fact of there having been so few importations to this region. They are quiet, good feeders, easy to handle and ship, and—as all must admit—attractive in color and form. If the Red-Polls are carefully bred, we may expect to see them grow rapidly in public favor, and secure on their merits high rank as a combined milk and beef breed.

In view of the present increase of the practice of dehorning, we may be pardoned for saying, that among the bulls of the established polled breeds now in America the advocates of surgical dehorning will certainly find more formidable rivals than have hitherto appeared in print.

Chapter XXXIII.

DEVONS.

Lying south of the Bristol Channel, on the map of England, may be found the county or shire of Devon. Much of its physical geography, as also that of the county adjoining it on the west, Cornwall, presents characteristics strikingly similar to that of Wales—indeed, the people of these lower western counties were as safe from Roman incursions behind the vast forests which covered the alluvial deposits of lower England, as were the people of Wales in their rugged mountain fastnesses. As a result of this immunity from invasion, the wild or "White Forest" breed of cattle described by Low increased greatly in numbers, and, in the counties named, became more or less subject to partial domestication.

In Wales, we have at present the North Wales and Pembroke breeds as undoubted descendants of these wild cattle; and in the shire of Devon, occupying more especially its northern slope, has existed for generations the ancestry of the Devon breed—familiarly known in England as the "North Devons" to distinguish them from the cattle occupying the low lands of Devon and the counties to the east. That the breed is of remarkably pure descent is attested by the wonderful impressiveness in marking offspring. Surely no breed of modern improved cattle has a better claim to be called aboriginal than this. As their merits became known, they were gradually distributed to other and more northern counties, and the demand thus found to exist induced a more systematic effort toward improvement. Within the present century their size has been increased, beef capacity improved, and milking qualities especially advanced. The Earl of Leicester was among the most noted of early English breeders, followed by Lord Somerville and Lord Western, who were not only breeders but did much, also, to improve the quality of the animals bred.

Their introduction to America dates from a very early period, a few head of what were undoubtedly Devons being brought over in the ship Charity (1623) for a Mr. Winslow, of Massachusetts. In 1817, however, probably the first authentic importation of pure bred improved Devons was made by a Mr. Patterson, of Baltimore, direct from the herd of the Earl of Leicester (at that time Mr. Coke, of Holkham). The next year (1818) a few were imported to Long Island from Mr. Coke's herd.

Other importations were made from time to time, notably in 1836, by Mr. Vernon, of New York state, and in 1853 by L. G. Morris, also of New York. Since that time, the Devons have been widely distributed throughout the United States, and have taken a settled place among the popular breeds of the country.

DESCRIPTION OF MODERN IMPROVED DEVON.

Color a rich, deep red throughout, excepting a central tuft of long white hair in the brush of the tail, and a white spot on the udder in cows, and about the purse in bulls. Upper line almost perfectly straight from the head to the tail; in the bull, the neck is of course somewhat arched above this level. The head is neat and trim, rather long in the cow but short and masculine in the bull, and well pointed to a bright flesh-colored muzzle; eyes prominent, bright, wide apart, and encircled by rings of flesh-colored skin; horns rather long, slender, curving outward, forward and upward, waxy clear at base, and tapering to almost needle-like points of darker shade. The ear is sprightly; neck small at head, without dewlap, and full and broad at the shoulders; forequarters wide apart, showing good lung power, and slanting well back, a feature in strict keeping with their well-known activity. The barrel is round and close-muscled; loins even; hips square; rump smooth; tail long, slender, and invariably tipped with white; flank low cut; brisket deep, and legs short, straight and clean fleshed. We believe the above to be a just and fair description of the breed as now known in the United States, and to show the improvement which has taken place, we quote the following from Low's Domestic Animals of Great Britain (previously quoted), published 1842:

"Although the Devon ox presents a symmetry of parts which pleases the eye, yet his form is not precisely what the breeder seeks for in an animal destined to fatten quickly and arrive at great weight. His neck is too long, his chest too narrow, his sides are too flat, his limbs are too long in proportion to his body; or, in other words, his body is too small in proportion to his height. The Devon ox is a kindly enough feeder, but he requires good pasture, and a somewhat favorable climate, and could barely subsist on food which would suffice to fatten some of the hardier mountain breeds of nearly his own size."

The following Scale of Points adopted by the American Devon Cattle Club (L. P. Sisson, Wheeling, W. Va., secretary) is now in general use:

COWS.		BULLS.
8	Head	10
	Cheek	2
4	Neck	4
4	Shoulders	6
8	Chest	10
8	Ribs	10
16	Back	20
48	Forward	62

DEVON BULL.

COWS.		BULLS.
48	Forward	62
8	Hind quarters	12
20	Udder	
2	Tail	2
4	Legs	4
8	Skin	8
2	Size	4
8	General appearance	8
100	Perfection	100

CHARACTERISTICS

Probably the most prominent trait of the Devon is his sprightly energy. In the early days of the present century, when the fertile prairies of the Great West held their virgin soil unbroken, the farmers of New England found abundant exercise in removing the stones, stumps and saw logs with which their land was covered. For this purpose oxen were employed almost exclusively, and the grades from those early imported Devons were eagerly sought. The writer has in mind an amusing incident related by his father concerning a yoke of grade Devon steers, which, for two good miles, in response to the fun-loving spirit of their youthful driver, succeeded in keeping behind them a span of fine carriage horses belonging to a neighbor, and 'driven by the neighbor's son.

As work oxen, the Devons have no superior in the world; they lack, perhaps, the weight necessary to move enormous loads, but their remarkable quickness, combined with an intelligent observance of the driver's will, make them invaluable for work of certain kinds. For beef, little recommendation is needed; the improvement of the breed has, with many breeders, been almost entirely in this direction. Allen, in his valuable treatise on American Cattle (previously quoted), after speaking of the excellent milk qualities of the cows in a herd of Devons owned by him, says:

"It is but fair to say, however, that after we commenced crossing our cows with bulls of later importation, some 15 years after the commencement of the herd, the large milkers were not so numerous, although the cattle from these crosses were somewhat finer. The bulls we used were apparently bred from stocks highly improved with an effort more to develop their feeding properties than for the dairy."

We are glad to note that not all of our Devon breeders have followed these points so closely as to lose sight of the capabilities of the breed for dairy purposes, and, in this connection, quote the following from the report of Wm. Brown, Professor of Agriculture in the Ontario (Canada) Agricultural College, for 1886:

"Of this distinctly intermediate class of cattle (Devons), milk and beef combination, we have to repeat the observation that none can make better calves, few so content and hardy, and but one richer in dairy product. The Devon has not held the world's patron-

DEVONS.

DEVON COW EDITH.
Owned by Jos. Hilton & Sons, New Scotland, N. Y.

age because of under size, and possibly also, of moderation in maturing and milk quantity, but it is difficult to conceive of a more desirable cow on upland rangy pastures for the butter factory."

A most excellent step was taken by the Devon breeders when the so-called "Red-Letter" Registry was adopted. The plan follows that of the Holstein-Friesian Association's "Advanced Registry," and is designed to stimulate actual performance of Devon cows in the dairy as well as higher scaling by the score card, certifying beef or feeding form improvement. The following synopsis of requirements for Red-Letter registration will best indicate the purpose and explain the objects of the club in adopting this feature:

"1. All animals must be recorded in American Devon Record.
"2. No bull is eligible unless first dam is in Red-Letter Register.
"3. No bull under two years old is eligible.
"4. A bull, to be eligible, must score at least 80 points in the Devon Scale.
"5. A cow to be eligible must score at least 80 points in the Devon Scale.
"6. A cow under three years old must have made not less than seven pounds of well-worked butter in seven days, and show a yield of at least one pound butter fat in one day, as determined by chemical test.
"7. A cow over three and under four years old must yield 8¾ lbs. butter in seven days and 1¼ lbs. butter fat in one day.
"8. A cow four years old and over must yield 10¾ lbs. butter in seven days and 1½ lbs. butter fat in one day.
"9. Bulls and cows may be scored at any time after two years old.
"10. Scorers must be officially appointed by the club."

The Devons are probably as nearly general purpose animals as may be found among the present known breeds, In size they are medium, bulls when matured weighing from 1,200 to 1,600 lbs., and cows from 900 to 1,100 lbs. One thing more we must notice—their introduction into the Southern states. In Mr. Allen's work, the author intimates that the Devon acclimates unusually well in the South. We cannot agree with him; information from various portions of the South has shown a high proportion of mortality among Devons brought from the North, only one breed—Shorthorns—showing a greater average per cent. of loss. To counterbalance this, however, it is a well-known fact that the Devons when acclimated will thrive and keep in good condition on scant pasture where many other improved breeds would starve to death. This high per cent. of mortality in acclimating Devons may be due to the unnatural forcing which the breed has undergone of late years in the hands of unskillful breeders, as it is well known among successful importers of Northern cattle that the introduction of over-fed or pampered stock from the North is apt to result fatally to both profits and cattle.

There are now a goodly number of fine herds of Devons in the South, and their certain increase, both in numbers and favor, is fast becoming an accomplished fact.

Chapter XXXIV.

LONGHORNS.

These cattle, so little known at present in the United States, have their origin in the district of Craven, England. Probably the Irish Longhorns, mentioned by Youatt, were identical with the English breed, and for many years were bred in parallel lines.

When Bakewell (see also Leicester sheep) took hold of the breed, he found it already somewhat improved, but there can be no doubt that a large proportion of whatever merit or popularity the English Longhorns once possessed was due to his wonderful skill as a breeder. His methods were kept secret, and his ability considered extraordinary; but, to state the case plainly, we have no doubt that many of our modern improvers and breeders possess just as much ability, and are producing just as great results.

Concerning their importation to America, we can say little. A few head were imported into Kentucky as early as 1817, but they were crossed with the Shorthorns and soon lost sight of. We know of but one other importation, although several are said to have been made at different times. In 1872 or 1873, the writer attended the Iowa State Fair, then held at Cedar Rapids, in Linn county; there was exhibited a herd of some four or five cows and a bull of the genuine English Longhorns; they were marked somewhat similar to the modern Hereford, with white faces and lined backs and bellies; their sides, however, were of a dun or light red, almost a yellow, and on one or two individuals patches of brindle and roan were visible. We do not remember the name of the exhibitor, nor have we since been able to locate the herd.

DESCRIPTION AND CHARACTERISTICS.

We describe as we remember them, and find that our observations agree with the description given by Allen (American Cattle). Size equal to Shorthorn or Hereford; color dun or yellowish fawn, sometimes red, brindled or roan, with frequently white faces and white lines on back and belly. Their distinguishing feature lies in the peculiar horns, which are long, ungraceful, curving forward and downward, sometimes crossing under the jaws, and frequently requiring amputation to prevent a threatened puncture of the muzzle.

They were claimed to be general purpose animals, but with especial

LONGHORN STEERS.
Winners first prize at Birmingham, England, 1860.

tendency to milk, and were exhibited as would-be rivals of the Shorthorns—at that time in the height of popular favor. Their general appearance was very like the description given of the earlier unimproved Herefords, and this, with the similarity in their markings, would lead us to suppose, that they may have originally sprung from the same channel.

Our illustration was re-engraved by permission, expressly for this purpose, from a lithograph made for the Department of State, and was originally from a photograph.

Chapter XXXV.

NORMANDIE CATTLE.

From the report of United States Consul Williams, of Rouen, we clip the following :

"The origin of the Norman breed seems unknown ; in fact, has never been traced. It is considered that the nature of the soil has produced the breed. It seems to have changed very little in the last century and is very remarkable. The center of production of this fine breed is comprised in the departments of Eure, Manche, Calvados and Orne."

The above, while not very definite information, is the best we have been able to obtain regarding the origin of Normandie cattle. As the breed grows in favor, doubtless some one will be encouraged to more extended—and, we trust, more successful—search for their early history.

Improvement has been slow but constant, and has been brought about by care in selection and management. Attempts to improve the breed have been made by crossing with Shorthorn or Durham blood, resulting—as might be expected—in a more rounded contour, but decreasing at the same time the milking value and fixedness of type ; in fact, producing that most unreliable of all animals for breeding purposes—a cross. For beef the Normandie is undoubtedly improved by the use of bulls of any of our best beef breeds ; but when we say this, we have neither added to the claims of one, nor detracted from the merits of the other.

Importations to the United States have been few, and only during recent years. The first of which we have any knowledge was made in 1885, by Mr. J. C. Duncan, of Normal, Ill. Regarding this importation, Mr. Levi Dillon writes under date August 20, 1887 :

"* * * * He [Mr. Duncan] imported from France two years ago, one Normandie bull and one Normandie cow ; they are registered, both recorded in France. They are brindle in color, and are noted for their great milking qualities as well as for their beef qualities. They are said to be the equal of the Jerseys as milkers, and the equal of the Shorthorns as beef cattle. I am not a cattle man, but our leading cattle men here speak highly of these cattle. * * * * Combining, as they do, the good qualities of the Jersey and the Shorthorn, I believe they are the coming cattle of this country."

Another small importation was made to New York city in 1886, and one to Chicopee, Mass., in 1887. Probably others have been made of which we are not aware.

NORMANDIE BULL.
Re-engraved expressly for this work, by permission, from a lithograph made for the Department of State; originally from photograph.

178 NORMANDIE CATTLE.

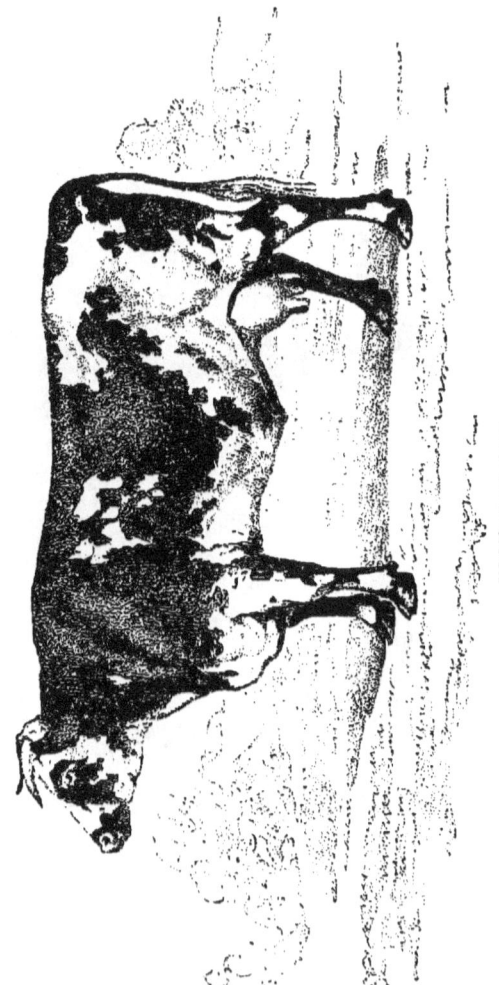

NORMANDIE COW.

Re-engraved, by permission, expressly for this work, from lithograph made for the Department of State; originally from photograph.

DESCRIPTION AND CHARACTERISTICS.

Color brown, roan and red or spotted—varying considerably as to marking, but never failing to preserve the brown stripes peculiar to the breed, which have earned for them the term "brindled." The head is long and coarse, with large mouth—fit emblem of an enormous appetite. The horn is irregular, commonly twisted and curved toward the forehead; the body long and deep at the flank, with rather narrow hind parts, showing an escutcheon well marked for milk. The legs are short and the skin rather thick and heavy.

The Normandie cow is classed as a combined milk and beef animal, with tendency more towards milking excellence, especially in the Cotentine strain of Normandies. In size they rank with the large breeds, mature bulls weighing from 1,800 to 2,200 lbs., cows from 1,100 to 1,500 lbs. The illustrations were re-engraved by permission from lithographs made for the Department of State, and were originally from photographs taken in France.

Chapter XXXVI.

NORTH WALES BLACK CATTLE.
(*Anglesea.*)

As a separate and distinct breed, this race of cattle has received attention only of late years. Descended from the same original stock (the wild Forest breed of Wales and West England) as are the Pembrokes or Castle Martins of South Wales, and partaking largely of the same general appearance, they yet show decidedly different characteristics, which, by right, stamp them as a separate breed.

Of the gentlemen in Wales who have been so actively advancing the interests of Anglesea cattle, we can make only brief mention; they well deserve more extended notice. Col. Henry Platt, of Gorddinogg, Bangor; Lord Harlech, of Glyn Hall, Talsarnau; R. B. Smith, Esq., of Tynewydd, Bangor, and the editor and honorary secretary (now deceased) of the association, Wm. A. Dew, have been among the most active workers.

Only one importation of which we are aware has been made to America. In 1885, Mr. J. B. Warren, of Larchwood, Ia., imported 13 head for the Larchwood estate. Answering our inquiries, under date Sept. 12, 1887, this gentleman says:

"We have had our herd for the last 18 months, and are prepared to say that they are a very large breed, quite as large as the Shorthorns, and much hardier. They are excellent milkers, are very docile and thrifty. Last year most of our cows ran out until the middle of January, and were at that time in much better condition than the natives."

DESCRIPTION AND CHARACTERISTICS.

Color black, with occasionally white about the udder in cows and scrotum in bulls; all other spots of white, while not necessarily a mark of impurity, are discouraged, and will soon no doubt be known only as an occasional reversion. The hair is long, fine and wavy; head rather large; neck medium; quarters full, and general outline approaching very nearly that of the Devons. In size they are classed with the larger breeds, mature bulls weighing from 1,800 to 2,200 lbs., and cows from 1,100 to 1,500 lbs. The Earl of Cawdor, whose answer is published in a report to the Department of State, goes still higher, and places the "live weight of the bulls 24 cwt.; oxen, 22 cwt.; cows, 18 cwt." The horns

NORTH WALES BLACK BULL, AP GWILYM, 70.

Property of Col. Henry Platt, Gorddinogg Estate, Stanfairfechan, North Wales. Reengraved by permission, from a lithograph copyrighted in Great Britain.

NORTH WALES BLACK COW, VICTORIA (Vol. 1, 62).
Property of Mr. G. W. Duff Assheton Smith, Vaynol, Bangor. Re-engraved by permission, from a lithograph copyrighted in Great Britain.

of the North Wales cattle are middle sized, long and yellowish, with darker tips; the legs are short, and waste portions of the body generally are reduced to a low percentage. Their dairy qualities on an average are counted good—an ordinary herd yielding annually from 125 to 150 pounds of butter to the cow, and occasional herds are found which considerably exceed these figures.

The partisans of the breed claim for them a rank equal to the highest as a combined milk and beef breed; we are willing to file the claim, and shall give them ample time to prove it. The establishment of the North Wales Black Cattle Herd Book—the first volume of which appeared in 1883, and the second volume in 1886—will doubtless do much toward improving and keeping pure this really valuable breed of stock.

Chapter XXXVII.

PEMBROKE CATTLE.

("*Castle Martins*," *or Black Cattle of South Wales.*)

Although we know of no Pembrokes in the United States, we insert the chapter on account of the close relationship between this breed and the Black Cattle of North Wales. Until within a score of years, the Pembroke breed has included all of the black mountain cattle of Wales. From the report of the Hon. Stephen B. Packard, United States Consul at Liverpool, we quote :

" There are two breeds of cattle in Wales. The North Wales breed [see North Wales Black Cattle] is found in greatest perfection in Anglesea and Caernarvonshire. The South Wales breed was called "Castle Martin," and the animals are very big, large boned and coarse, but they are not in favor in the north of the Principality. * * * * Both breeds are black, producing occasionally specimens dun colored and red. Characteristic points require that bulls should have white testicles and the cows white udders."

They are supposed to be directly descended from the *Bos primogenius,* and are hence allied to the wild "Forest" breed—still preserved in Chillingham Park, the Devons, and still more closely to their new rivals, the Black Cattle of North Wales.

DESCRIPTION AND CHARACTERISTICS.

Color black, with the white marks already mentioned. As compared with the North Wales breed, they have shorter hair, lighter hind parts, narrower shoulders, and coarser bones. The best specimens of each breed would bear close inspection to decide between them on merit alone ; but it is now admitted that a much larger number of the North Wales cattle answer the requirements of an improved modern breed.

The particular characteristics claimed for the Pembrokes are hardiness, dairy qualities and aptitude to range well. They cannot be said to bear forced feeding, but for rough grazing they would doubtless find much favor upon our western ranges. As to their dairy qualities, we confess to some degree of skepticism; it does not seem reasonable that a breed reared under the rough "no care" conditions—which their breeders are careful to claim—can have any very great tendency to large yields of milk. Their flesh is said to be as good as any, and the oxen are docile, easily trained, and make strong, active teams.

The first volume of the Herd Book appeared in 1874, and since that time improvement of the breed has taken a more decided and systematic turn.

Chapter XXXVIII.

HEREFORDS.

There is much to be said of the Hereford cattle, as they existed in Herefordshire, and adjoining counties, England; and also of the cattle of Wales. Previous to the time of Tomkins, the cattle of these districts had a reputation for the best of quality, and were of uniform character—varying in size according to elevation and fertility of the range. It was from cattle of this uniform character that the Hereford breed had its origin.

The more reliable records place Mr. Benj. Tomkins as the improver, if not the founder, of the breed. Mr. Tomkins was born in 1745, at the Court House, Canon Pyon, and began farming at Black Hall, King's Pyon. 1766—then in his 21st year. He afterward lived at Wellington, and then at Brookhaven, King's Pyon, where he died in 1815. His herd was sold in 1819, and brought (for breeding stock) as follows:

15 cows	$11,245 00	—an average of	. . . . .	$750 00
2 two-year-old heifers . .	1,415 00	"	. . . . .	460 00
2 one-year-old " . .	780 00	"	. . . . .	390 00
4 bulls	5,355 00	"	. . . . .	1,335 00
2 bull calves	1,810 00	"	. . . . .	905 00
Total, 26 animals	$20,605 00	"	. . . . .	$792 00

Mr. Tomkins came from a line of ancestors who were prominent men of the county of Hereford as cattle breeders, and many of them were prominent men of the nation. He pursued a steadily systematic course in his breeding, and stands, undoubtedly, as regards the history of the improvement of Hereford cattle in the west of England, as do the Colling Bros. in improvement of Shorthorn or Durham cattle in the east. Other noted breeders may be mentioned, among them such men as Yarmouth, Walker, Hoskyns, Penn, Jellicoe, Smith, Lord Talbot, Price, Sherif and others; but the blood of Tomkins' cattle was always found strongly diffused throughout their herds—as may be seen by consulting the Herd Book records.

To show the recognized value of the Hereford breed for beef at that early day, we give the following prices of cattle sold by Mr. Westcar, and obtained from his books by Mr. Smythies, of Marlow. The figures represent 20 Hereford oxen, selected from the entire record as each

bringing a figure upwards of £100. Sales of 20 oxen from 1799 to 1811 —the average price of which was £106, 6s., or $530 each:

1779, Dec. 16	2 oxen	£200
1800, Dec. 4	1 "	147
1800, Dec. 13	1 "	100
1801, Nov. 26	6 "	630
1802, Nov. 26	1 "	100
1802, Nov. 30	1 "	126
1802, Dec. 4	2 "	200
1803, Dec. 4	1 "	100
1803, Dec. 19	1 "	105
1803, Dec. 29	1 "	105
1804, Dec. 5	1 "	105
1805, Dec. 4	1 "	100
1811, Nov. 28	1 "	105

The Smithfield Club at London, England, held its first cattle show in 1799. The winner of the first prize was a Hereford ox, shown by Mr. Westcar, bred by Mr. Tully, Huntingdon Court, Hereford, and for the first 20 years of this show Herefords won the first or champion prize for the best ox or steer exhibited. During the years from about 1820 to 1834, there was a very warm contest carried on between the respective breeders of Herefords and Shorthorns as to the merits of the two breeds—a condition of things which has been kept up with more or less warmth ever since. (We cannot see why there should be such violent temper displayed by the respective champions of these two popular breeds. Each has a certain definite place in our midst, and it is no secret that any successful breeder is quite likely to regard his own success as a reflection of superior merit in the breed he handles. "Live and let live" is a pretty good motto, which both breeders of Herefords and Shorthorns would do well to heed.)

Mr. Geo. T. Turner, writing to the *National Live Stock Journal* of Chicago in 1880, says:

"The Hereford bullock in London is quite a season animal, and comes only as a grass beast in the late summer and autumn, when it tops the market."

And we might add, the Hereford steer has held his own in this respect for more than 100 years.

The Hereford Herd Book was first published in 1846 by Mr. T. C. Eyton—the second volume appearing in 1853. At this time, the markings of the breed were not as uniform as now, and Mr. Eyton classed them according to color as Mottle Faced, White Faced, Gray and Light Gray. In his preface to the second volume, Mr. Eyton says that many breeders neglected to forward any account of their stock or pedigrees of their bulls, and that it is not his intention "to continue the work unless the breeders generally come forward to assist me more than they have done to the present time. I would willingly give my own time and

HEREFORDS.

HEREFORD, BULL, SIR CHARLES, 543.
Imported by T. L. Miller, Beecher, Ill.

trouble if I thought all would join in working out the truth, and afford the work sufficient patronage to cover its expenses." While some few of the breeders were willing to aid in the support of the work, the interest was not general enough to induce Mr. Eyton to continue his labors. In 1856, Mr. W. Styles Powell purchased the copyright, and published the first part of volume III., containing 236 pedigrees. July 15th, 1857, a letter to the Herefordshire Agricultural Society was read, from Mr. Underwood, solicitor to Rev. W. Powell—uncle to W. S. Powell—stating that the cost of the Herd Book to his late nephew was £30; yet he was willing to place the work as it then stood in the hands of any gentleman recommended by the society on payment of £10. Mr. Powell's offer was accepted, and Mr. Thos. Duckham was requested to carry on the publication of the Herd Book. The conditions were that he should publish it annually, and that an entrance fee of one shilling (25 cts.) should be paid for each head of stock entered. Mr. Duckham proceeded to revise and reprint the first portion of Volume III., adding a second part for bulls and a third part for cows, with their produce; and in September, 1858, the revised volume was issued. In 1859 Volume IV. appeared, with a list of 247 subscribers; and Volume V. followed in 1862, with a list of 317. Mr. Duckham continued the work on his own responsibility until Volume IX. was issued, when—March 5, 1878—the Hereford Herd Book Society was formed, and the Society purchased the copyright, becoming responsible for its publication through an editing committee, of which Mr. Duckham was an active and influential member until his resignation, which occurred about six years ago. Volume XVII. of the Herd Book was issued in 1887.

While Mr. Duckham was editor and publisher, he gave a large portion of his time to the advancement of Hereford interests, and the breeders of England and America owe much to him for the records and data that have been preserved to the breed.

In Scotland, Ireland, Australia, South America and the island of Jamaica, Hereford cattle are now well-known, and rank second to none in public favor for early and economic production of beef.

IMPORTATION TO, AND BREEDING IN, THE UNITED STATES.

The Hon. Henry Clay brought two bulls and two heifers to this country in 1817; one bull and the two heifers reached Kentucky, and contributed to the improvement of beef cattle in that state. In 1824 Admiral Coffin brought to Massachusetts the Hereford bull Sir Isaac. The bull was owned for several years by Isaac C. Bates, of Northampton, Mass., and was used on the cows in that vicinity with the uniform testimony that for all purposes combined, his produce formed the best stock ever kept in that neighborhood. In 1839-40 a large number of Hereford cattle were imported by Mr. William Sotham, of Albany, N. Y.

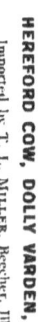

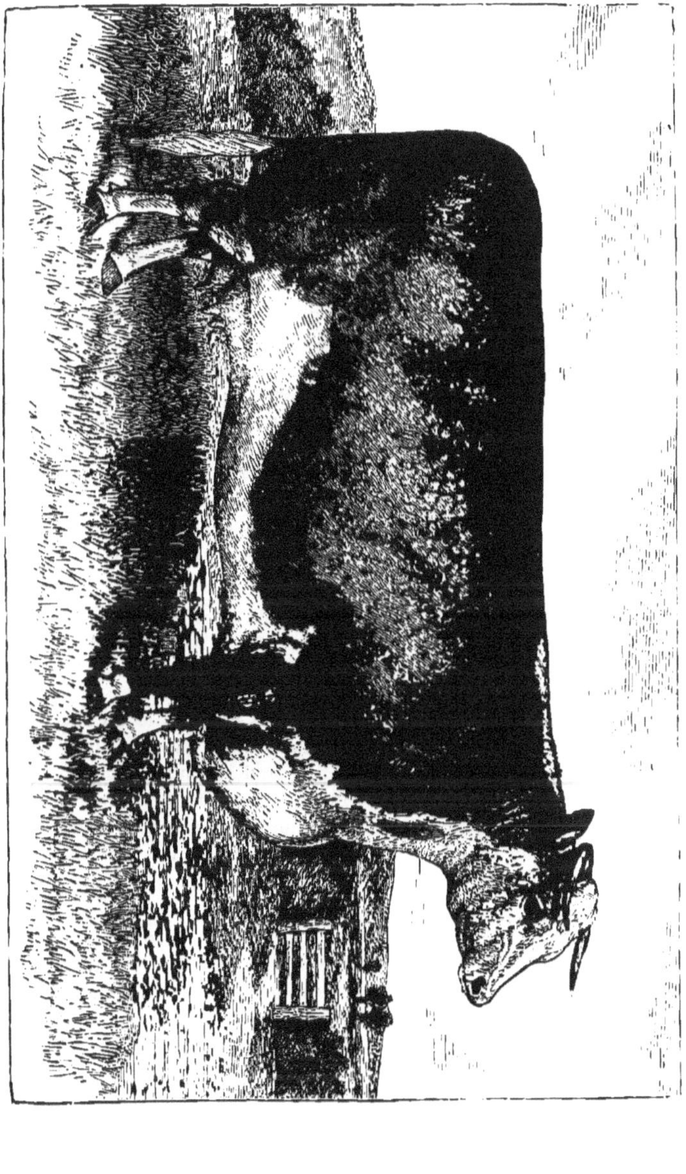

HEREFORD COW, DOLLY VARDEN, 5-
Imported by T. L. Miller, Beecher, Ill.

They met with a good deal of favor, and were soon well distributed throughout the northeast portion of the United States. In 1851 Messrs. John Humphries and Thos. Ashton brought to Ohio two bulls and two heifers; and since 1879 there have been many importations, and some very large ones. They have gone into all parts of the country, and have uniformly become very popular with all who have handled them.

C. R. Thomas, of Independence, Mo., is the present secretary of the American Hereford Breeders' Association.

DESCRIPTION AND CHARACTERISTICS.

In color the Hereford is a red of varying shade, generally dark, with clear white face, white line—extending from head to tail in some specimens, in others abreviated to merely a white mane, or what is even more fashionable at present, an oblong spot above and between the shoulders—white belly, white brush and white feet. The horns are medium to long, white, waxy and generally turning outward, forward and sometimes downward. In form they are blocky, square built, with rather short legs and all meat points full and rounded; the tail drops squarely from rumps even and high; the quarters are heavy, muscular and low down on the hocks; the ribs well sprung, but rounded neatly to a long, deep barrel; the head and neck both short and close fleshed; in fact the whole make-up of the animal indicates strongly the marked characteristic of the breed—beef.

The Hereford is emphatically a beef or range animal, and while good milkers are occasionally met with among the cows, most of them do little more than raise wonderfully vigorous calves. The "white faces" have found considerable favor on the great cattle ranges of the Panhandle of Texas. In acclimating, they are well located as standing even with the Aberdeen-Angus—about third on the list—Holstein-Friesians and Galloways ranking first and second respectively. They are hardy, prepotent to a strong degree, and are classed with the largest of modern breeds, mature bulls weighing from 1,900 to 2,300 lbs., and cows from 1,200 to 1,600 lbs., with occasional animals exceeding these weights.

Probably no other man in America has done so much to advance the interests of Hereford cattle as T. L. Miller. His latest great undertaking, to push the white faces on irrigated lands in Arizona, for shipment by train loads to the large markets of the country, is an enterprise which, if successful, will rank as almost phenomenal; and that it will be successful is almost assured by the simple fact that Mr. Miller has undertaken it.

Chapter XXXIX.

GALLOWAYS.

These cattle derive their name from the province of Galloway, lying in the southwest portion of Scotland, to which locality they trace a long line of polled ancestry. The breed is among the oldest, authentic history carrying it back to the beginning of the Sixteenth Century, and tradition asserting that there was never a time when Galloway cattle did not exist in their native province; moreover, the main distinguishing points of the breed were the same then as now, subject only to progressive change from careful selection and management.

Improvement in the Galloway breed was largely stimulated by the extensive purchases of Scotch polled cattle by the English soon after the union of England and Scotland. The Scotch breeders, knowing that the cattle sold were to travel on foot throughout the greater part of England, vied with each other in attempting to furnish the best animals. It is worthy of note that the improvement of the Galloway has been effected almost entirely by skillful selection, judicious feeding and careful management—a fact which accounts, in fixedness of breeding, for their present remarkable prepotency.

Although an old breed, the records date only from recent time—all pedigrees and papers relating to the breed having been destroyed by fire at Edinburgh in 1851. From 1851 to 1878, they were recorded with the Angus and other polled stock in the Polled Herd Book; in 1878 Galloway breeders published separately the first volume of the Galloway Herd Book of Great Britain, and in 1883 appeared the first volume of the North American Galloway Herd Book—the register now used for American-bred Galloways.

While black has always been the prevailing color, there were formerly many well bred individuals of other colors, and one of the most apparent improvements made by later breeders has been to eliminate variety in color and reduce the breed to its present standard, namely, black—in winter with a brownish tinge. It must be borne in mind, however, that this peculiarity still shows itself in an occasional reversion to dun or drab; and such animals, while inferior in selling value, are nevertheless as purely bred as the most sable of their kind. We had on the College Farm, a heifer—now dead—dropped in 1886, got by Admiral Good, 1184, Am. G. H. B., out of Admiration, 1186, Am. G. H.

B., both black—which was a pure dun in color, but a typical Galloway in all other respects.

DESCRIPTION OF THE GALLOWAY.

No horns are admissible, not even scurs; they are emphatically a polled or hornless breed. The color should be black—in winter showing a brownish tinge, from the fact that the long hairs turn brown at the extremities. The skin should be of medium thickness, but soft and pliable, and the hair long, soft and wavy, giving a silken, shaggy appearance—with a soft thick coat of wool underneath. Coarse, straight, or closely curled hair is objectionable, especially when the mossy undercoat is wanting. The head should be short and wide between eyes, with full forehead and open nostrils; eyes large and prominent; ears medium sized—rather broad in proportion to length—pointing upward, fringed with long hair, and well provided, both inside and out, with a soft woolly covering; neck short, tapering finely in the cow, and becoming wonderfully enlarged with age in the bull; quarters long, deep and fleshed well onto the leg; breast wide, brisket heavy, loin well filled and flank low. The body is round and long, back straight, tail thick, with a heavy brush, and legs short and very muscular. The Galloway, in brief, is a heavy bodied, short legged, hornless, black, beefy looking animal. No scale of points has yet been adopted for the breed.

CHARACTERISTICS.

The Galloways are mainly a beef-producing cattle—their flesh finely marbled, sweet and juicy; in proportion of live weight, they dress remarkably well, averaging nearly 60 per cent., and frequently reaching as high as 65 or 66 per cent. of live weight. As range stock they have proved exceedingly valuable, being hardy, easily handled, close shippers, and amply able to find their own food on any reasonable range.

The practice of dehorning, which we have mentioned, although advocated by breeders of horned cattle, must surely work to the advantage of all of the polled breeds, inasmuch as the average man will consider it much safer, more economical and much less cruel to remove the horns by using a naturally hornless bull. One of the prominent traits of Galloway cattle is their prepotency when crossed with other breeds—fully 80 per cent. of resulting offspring being without horns. As to maturity, there is considerable difference of opinion, due, we believe, to the fact that Galloways vary greatly in ages at which individual animals reach maturity; as a rule we cannot say that they are early maturers—although perhaps comparing favorably with most of their rivals in this

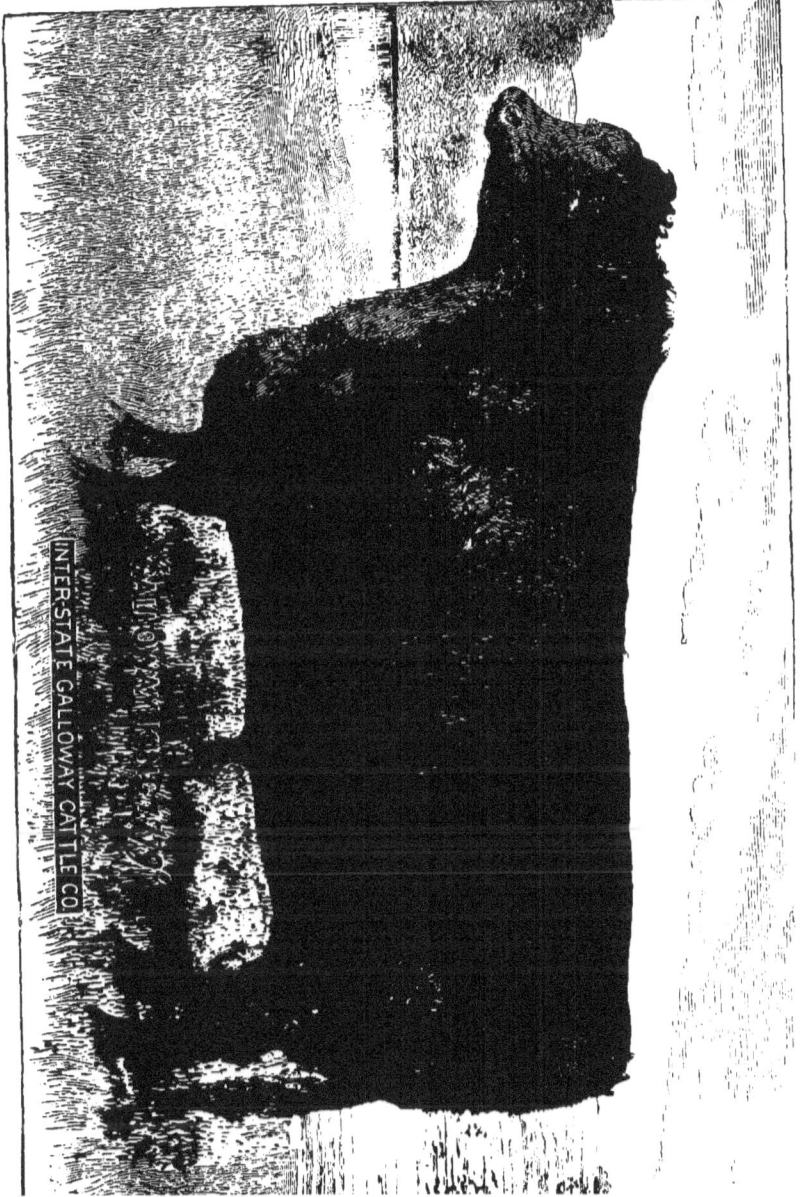

respect; neither do they as a rule attain so great weight as several of the other beef breeds—bulls weighing from 1,700 to 2,100 lbs., and cows from 1,000 to 1,400 lbs., with occasional animals exceeding these figures. We believe there is truth in the following statement: Let a Galloway steer alone, and he will do what he can with credit to himself and profit to his owner; but attempt to crowd him for extra results, and beyond a certain point the forcing process will not prove a financial success.

In the dairy little is claimed for the Galloway cows, by even their most ardent admirers. It is only fair to state, however, that among them are found some very excellent milkers. The practice of allowing the calf to run with the cow and making the herd find both food and shelter on its own account, while it may have, and doubtless has, increased the hardiness to a considerable extent, has certainly worked great injury to whatever milking superiority the breed may have originally possessed.

Another and economically important outlook for Galloway breeders is indicated in a letter to the author written under date December 3, 1892, by L. P. Muir, secretary of the association, Independence, Mo. He says:

"* * * The Galloways are proving one of the best of breeds for hardiness, thriftiness and general usefulness. Robes, coats, cloaks, gloves and various articles of use and wear are made from first-class hides. * * *"

We understand that there are already a number of breeders who are handling grade Galloways primarily for their hides, as indicated by Col. Muir. In the South, Galloways stand second on the list as to ease of acclimation; and this fact will doubtless tend to gradually increase the number of pure bred Galloway bulls annually shipped to Texas ranges for improvement of native stock.

MARION FIFTH OF CASTLEMILK, 8194.

Chapter XL.

ABERDEEN-ANGUS.
(*Polled Angus or Polled Aberdeen.*)

As to the origin of this now well-known breed, little is definite beyond the commonly accepted belief that the two polled Scotch breeds—Galloway and Aberdeen-Angus—are descended from the polled variety of the original Forest breed. Of the long controversy, between Galloway and Angus breeders regarding the merits of their respective breeds we have nothing to say; by many the two breeds are considered identical. Some of our best judges predict that at no distant day the Aberdeen-Angus and Galloway Associations will follow the example so lately set by the Holstein and the Dutch Friesian breeders, by combining forces to advance the interests of all concerned.

We cannot say that we agree with such expression. While both breeds have undoubtedly descended from the same original stock, yet selection, feeding, care and systematic breeding have changed the characteristics and appearance so greatly as to fully warrant the present recognized distinctions between them. What these differences are will be understood from a study of the description and characteristics of the two breeds—which see.

Improvement of the Aberdeen-Angus was first begun in a systematic way about the opening of the present century. Probably no man has contributed more to advance the merits of Angus cattle than Mr. Hugh Watson, of Keillor, Scotland. Mr. Watson began his herd in 1808 with 2 bulls and 14 cows—the "best and blackest" that could be found—and by continually breeding in and in, putting the "best to the best," without regard to relationship, and carefully weeding out all freaks or reversions, he established a reputation for his herd, and for himself as a breeder, which the most successful of breeders might'well envy. The early improvers brought to the work superior ability, practical experience and sound sense. Following up the demand for an animal that should range well, and at the same time prove a kindly feeder, quick maturer and an animal of large size, they kept steadily at work, until the foundation of the Angus breed was thoroughly laid, tested and received. Among the later breeders of note we may mention William McCombie, of Tillyfour. His herd was started about the year 1830—just at the time when the pure bred Aberdeen-Angus was threatened with total extinction

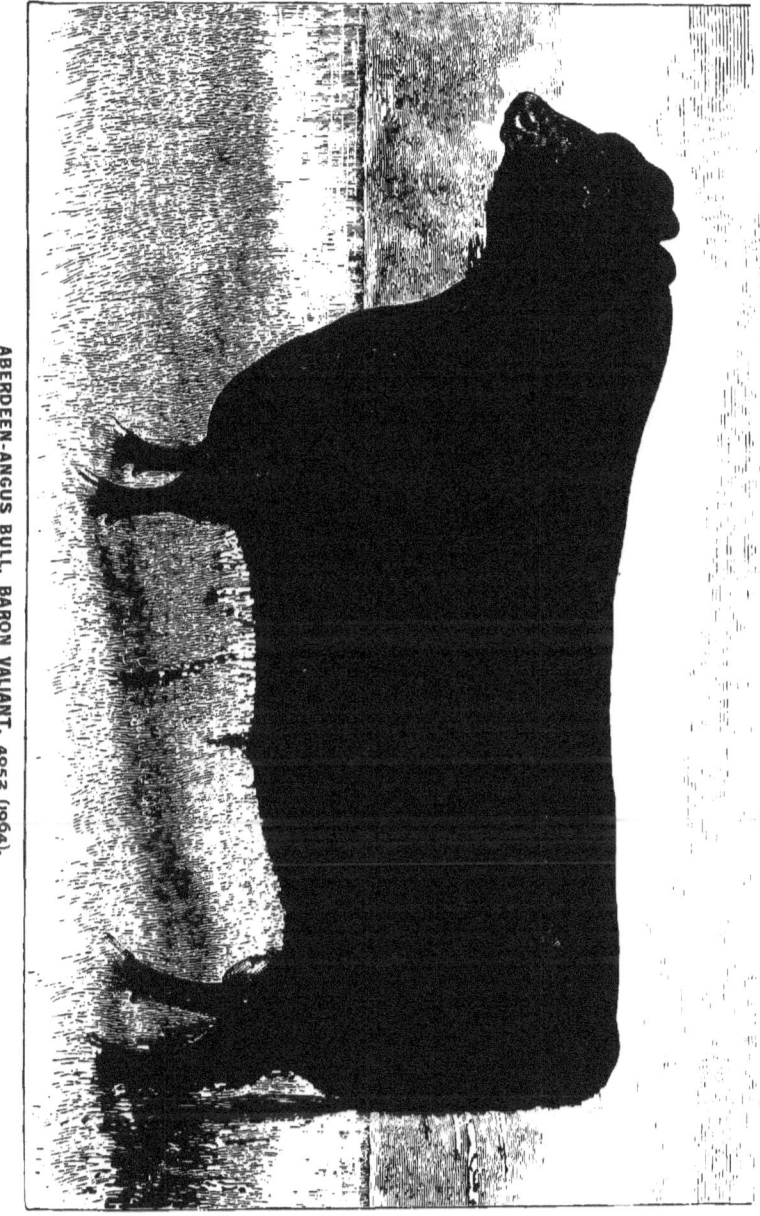

ABERDEEN-ANGUS BULL, BARON VALIANT, 4052 (1964).
Property of A. B. Matthews, Kansas City, Mo.

through the exceeding popularity of the Angus-Shorthorn crosses for feeding purposes. Mr. McCombie believed that the Angus breed was eminently worthy not only of preservation, but of improvement as well, and steadily directed his energies toward the accomplishment of this end.

IMPORTATION TO THE UNITED STATES.

The first of which we have any record was made in 1873 by Mr. Grant, of Victoria, Kan.; this was followed in 1878 by an importation of five cows and a bull for Messrs. Anderson & Findlay, of Lake Forest, Ill., and the next year a few head were brought over by Mr. F. B. Redfield, of Batavia, N. Y.; since that time importations have been numerous and breeding rapid, until there are at present writing probably not less than 4,500 to 5,000 head of pure bred Aberdeen-Angus in the United States.

DESCRIPTION AND CHARACTERISTICS.

We can best distinguish them by a comparison with the close description of the Galloway already given: There are no horns. The color is pure shining black—without the brown tinge of the Galloway—and the hair is fine, smooth, short and close-lying. In this respect, alone, the Angus cattle show a greater nicety of breeding, and, taken in connection with their size, illustrate perfectly the aim of both early and modern improvers of the breed, namely: To produce an animal which could be forced with profit, attain large size, and attract attention by his neat and meaty appearance.

In size they are considerably ahead of the Galloway, mature bulls ranging from 1,800 to 2,200 lbs., and cows from 1,100 to 1,500 lbs.; the forehead is less inclined to fullness, the back broader; flanks deeper, and general form more nearly filling the beef rectangle.

To the ordinary observer, not interested financially, in either breed, the Aberdeen-Angus would undoubtedly rank first from looks alone; to those who go further, and demand not only looks, but hardiness and other qualities combined, it is difficult to decide between them. From our own experience, and what we have gathered from others, the Aberdeen-Angus is the better animal to buy where feed is plenty and pasture luxuriant; but for the range, where the animal has to look out for himself, we would prefer the Galloway. The fact already stated—that Galloways acclimate somewhat better than Angus in the southern fever belt—the latter standing next below the former—bears considerable weight with breeders in the great Southwest. To offset this, Angus cattle mature earlier, and attain greater size. Each breed claims preeminence in beef qualities, and we candidly confess our inability to see any difference between them on this point. As a milk cow, the Aberdeen-Angus gives an ample supply for her calf—no more is needed for the range. Either Angus or Galloway bulls are excellent dehorners.

ABERDEEN-ANGUS. 199

ABERDEEN-ANGUS COW, ELAINE OF ABELOUR, 2720 (8203), AND CALF.
Property of Mossom Boyd & Co., Bobcaygeon, Ont., Canada.

The following Scale of Points was adopted by the American Aberdeen-Angus Breeders' Association, Nov. 20, 1890:

COWS		BULLS
2	Color	3
10	Head	10
3	Throat	3
3	Neck	3
6	Shoulders	6
10	Chest	10
4	Brisket	4
8	Ribs	8
10	Back	10
8	Hind Quarters	8
3	Tail	3
8	Udder	
4	Underline	4
3	Legs	4
3	Flesh	4
10	Skin	10
5	General Appearance	10
100	Perfection	100

When bulls are shown in separate class with progeny, add 25 points for progeny.

The first volume of the American Aberdeen-Angus Herd Book was published in 1886 the two main requisites for record being: (1) The animal itself or its sire and dam must be recorded in the 8th or prior volumes of the Polled Aberdeen or Angus Herd Book of Scotland. (2) The animal must be the produce by registered sire of a cow that has produce in the 8th or prior volumes of the Polled Aberdeen or Angus Herd Book of Scotland. Thos. McFarlane, Harvey, Ill., is the present efficient secretary of the association. The illustrations of both Galloways and Angus represent excellent specimens of their respective breeds, and will well repay a careful study.

Chapter XLI.

POLLED DURHAMS.

The Polled Durham breed is of recent origin; indeed it is only within the last three years that it could at all lay claim to the title. Since, however, the blood lines have become so fixed, and the features sought to be perpetuated are therefore transmitted with a great degree of certainty, their breeders have banded together and propose to place before the world the merits of their favorites on a blood parity with other breeds. In November, 1889, the American Polled Durham Breeders' Association was organized and the Herd Book started. The association now has a membership of between forty and fifty, and there are registered in the Herd Book something over 200 animals. Mr. Wm. W. Crane, Tippecanoe City, Ohio, is president, and Mr. A. E. Burleigh, Mazon, Ill., secretary.

As the name of the breed indicates, its basal blood is drawn from Shorthorn or "Durham" ancestry. The best "muley" or polled cows were selected from among the common or native herds in the central-western and Mississippi Valley portions of the United States, and these cows were bred to registered, selected Shorthorn bulls. Only the best hornless heifers were selected from the calves thus bred, and these were in time returned to registered Shorthorn bulls. This plan was persistently followed by several conscientious and thoroughly reliable breeders independently of each other, and, indeed, each without the other's knowledge, until after several generations of selective breeding, the Shorthorn outline, and especially the best beef or feeding characteristics of that old and popular breed, were firmly fixed in combination with the potent hornless feature of the "muley" cows, and the modern breed of Polled Durhams was established.

Of the breeders who, in this quiet way, have worked so faithfully to bring about what now has been so worthily attained, we can only mention those most prominent, whose names must live in Polled Durham history as do the names of Booth and Bates in that of their Shorthorn ancestry. Dr. Wm. W. Crane, Tippecanoe City, Ohio, now president of the association; Salem R. Clawson, Clawson, Ohio; Peter Shafor, also of Ohio; J. L. Burleigh, Mazon, Ill., now secretary; and T. Dunham, of Iowa.

Among the later breeders we may mention Mr. J. H. Miller,

Mexico, Ind., who in 1891 purchased entire the fine herds of Dr. Crane and Mr. Clawson, and is now vigorously and successfully pushing the Durham "doddies" into popular favor. Our illustration represents two of his best cows, and shows the symmetry and beauty of the breed. The engraving is an artist's faithful reproduction from photographs taken on the grounds of the Illinois State Fair Association at Peoria, in September, 1892.

DESCRIPTION AND CHARACTERISTICS.

Color varies—red, red and white, roan. and, indeed, as with the Shorthorns, all colors except black, brown or brindle. Size fully equal to the beef families of Shorthorns—mature bulls weighing from 1,900 to 2,300 lbs. and upwards; cows, 1,200 to 1,600 lbs. and over.

The appearance is exactly that of a typical Shorthorn of beef proclivity without the horns. Full rounded barrel; wide, straight back; heavy muscled shoulders, with neck well set on; wide, deep chest over heavy brisket; well filled quarters, especially low at the twist; short, straight legs, set wide apart and easily supporting all the weight of body a breeder could desire; short, firm-fleshed neck, with little dewlap, and short, neat head, with intelligent face and large, expressive eyes. The dominant characteristic of this new American breed is feeding quality for beef production, although, as Mr. Miller states, "they have the color, the contour and general make-up of the grand old breed from which they have been mainly builded; besides, in their production, their milking qualities have not been lost sight of, and among them are some excellent milkers."

We have thought best to class this new breed with the beef producers of the world, admitting Mr. Miller's statement that some excellent milkers are found; but shall insist, what the facts regarding different families warrant, that the grand old Shorthorn breed, from the more beefy types of which the new breed has arisen, be still classed as distinctively and usefully "general purpose," regardless of the fact that some families have been bred directly into beef production and out of dairy excellence.

POLLED DURHAMS. 203

POLLED DURHAM COWS, ABBESS AND LORENA.
Property of J. H. Miller, Mexico, Indiana.

Chapter XLII.

SUSSEX CATTLE.

This breed is closely allied to the Devon—indeed, some writers assert that it is folly to class them as separate breeds. We cannot think so. Certainly their origin is found in the same stock, but this is also true of the Galloway and Aberdeen-Angus breeds. The early writers on the breeds of cattle of Great Britain certainly looked upon the Sussex as a breed well worthy a class by itself. Youatt and Martin, while acknowledging the common origin of both Devon and Sussex cattle, yet speak of the Sussex ox as possessing not only the activity of the Devon, but the strength of the Hereford, "with the propensity to fatten, and the beautiful fine grained flesh of both."

The breed takes its name from the county or shire of Sussex, in England, adjoining Devonshire, and differing from it in contour, elevation and fertility of soil. As already mentioned, the Devons occupied the elevated slopes bordering the Severn; the Sussex cattle held the lower regions of rich, luxuriant pasture farther east; and this fact alone —when we consider the long period of time involved—would naturally lead to a very supposable difference between the two breeds.

Improvement of the Sussex has not been rapid, but rather marked by the slow, steady conservatism of their English breeders. In America they have obtained a foothold, and already claim a large share of favor from American stockmen. Mr. Overton Lea, the energetic and popular breeder, of Mont Eagle, Tenn. (now secretary of the recently organized association), has done more towards pushing the Sussex to the front in the last ten years than all their breeders in England combined —and only because he has freely advertised and fully exhibited his cattle, courting inspection at all times, and asking only an honest opinion as to their merits.

DESCRIPTION AND CHARACTERISTICS.

Color, like the Devon, a rich dark red, with white brush to the tail; in size they excel the Devon considerably, mature bulls weighing from 1,700 to 2,000 lbs., and cows 1,100 to 1,400 lbs. Comparing further with the Devon, we may say: The head is coarser, with thicker horns; neck heavier, shoulders deeper, barrel longer and general form showing more of a beef tendency; they mature as early; are fine feeders, hardy, dress well, and produce an excellent quality of flesh.

SUSSEX CATTLE.

SUSSEX CATTLE.
Property of Overton Lea, Mont Eagle, Tenn.

At the Fat Stock Show, Chicago, 1885, a yearling Sussex steer received the Class prize on the butcher's block, and was only defeated by one vote for the Sweepstakes prize open to all ages. At the Kansas City Fat Stock Show, 1886, a two-year-old Sussex heifer, shown by Fowler and Van Natta, of Indiana, won both the Class and the Sweepstakes prizes. When we consider the great number of magnificent carcasses exhibited in competition, we may readily accord to the Sussex for beef a place among those in the front rank.

As milk stock, they cannot claim much. Improvement of the breed has been rather with a view of increasing size, appearance and feeding value, than with any idea of enhancing their dairy qualities. What milk they do give, however, is quite rich in cream, and occasionally a cow is found capable of an excellent record as to quantity.

The engraving was prepared expressly for our use, and we do not hesitate to say that the animals represented are second to few if any in America in point of general merit. Mr. Lea, as a breeder of Sussex, has been remarkably successful, and his uniform courtesy and fair dealing have secured for him a host of well-wishers.

Chapter XLIII.

SIMMENTHAL (BERNESE) CATTLE.

The Simmenthal cattle came originally from Canton Berne, Switzerland, but the best specimens are found in the valleys of Bernese Overland and on the rich pastures of western Switzerland and southern Germany. In southern Germany, especially, the fertile valleys have been found very favorable to steady improvement, and to the late King William of Würtemberg, who was especially interested in their importation to Germany, the breed is largely indebted for its present improved condition.

So far as we can ascertain, only two importations of these cattle have been made to the United States. In 1886, the Rev. F. von Schluembach, of Perry, Tex., while on one of his periodical visits to Germany, became much impressed with the idea that just such cattle as the Simmenthal were needed in the United States, and if properly handled would grow rapidly in favor. He accordingly secured and brought over successfully four head—two bulls and two heifers, all yearlings—the first Simmenthal cattle ever brought to America. (The second importation of Simmenthal cattle was made in May, 1887, by John Dick, of Quincy, Ill.) Writing to the author, under date February 14th, 1888, Rev. von Schluembach says:

" * * * * The weight of the cattle in Switzerland is very great; bulls up to 3,000 lbs.; cows five years old, upwards of 1,800 lbs. Height, from 1.34 to 1.4 meters [54 to 56 inches]; length, 2.15 to 2.2 meters [85 to 87 inches], well and equally developed animals. * * * * Edelweiss [referring to one of the heifers imported in 1886], three-year-old cow, May 1st, gives about four quarts per day now, but she will come in with second calf very soon. They are not a distinctly dairy breed, but are rather for meat purposes; but, at the same time, I believe good milkers if properly attended to. Although I imported my cattle in spring, and after quarantine in New York, had to bring them to Texas in August, by steamer to New Orleans, they have done finely from the start, and are easily acclimatized. The success I had with them in this respect I attribute in no little measure to your excellent and very reliable suggestions. * * * They are easy kept in food, are fully satisfied with Texas prairie hay and loose bran, feed up well, and fatten easily. * * *"

Wishing to present an accurate description of this valuable breed, the author made a personal inspection of Rev. von Schluembach's herd in March, 1888, and from notes made at that time, gives the following

DESCRIPTION AND CHARACTERISTICS.

Color light yellowish red, spotted with white—in one strain of the breed, evenly variegated; in the other strain the white is confined mainly to the legs and belly line, with white marks about the flanks, and usually, also, about head and neck. Further than this there is no distinctive arrangement of color markings. In size they are fully equal to the largest Herefords or Holstein-Friesians—bulls weighing at maturity 1,900 to 2,300 pounds, cows from 1,200 to 1,600 lbs. The head is broad and short, rather beefy, with a neck which in the bull fills up grandly as the animal develops, and in the cow is short, not delicate, but neat and well carried. There is a characteristic mark in the peculiar pendent skin beneath the throttle in both sexes—especially so in the bull—and in the rather long and finely shaped ears well fringed with hair. The horns are white and waxy to the tips, pointing outward and upward, sometimes forward, much like those of the Hereford, but shorter and better curved. The shoulders are deep and surmounted by a mass of dense muscular tissue, filling the crops to an even line; ribs well sprung to a neatly rounded barrel; haunches smooth, not prominent—indeed, the even, rounded appearance of the haunches, as seen from rear view, may be called a prominent characteristic of the breed. The tail is placed well up, and drops squarely between full buttocks; legs medium to short, with large, strong bone closely held in firm tissue —almost the perfection of bovine symmetry and strength. The general appearance indicates beef and feeding capacity; and the long body, squarely placed on legs of moderate length, gives a framework of sufficient size to carry an enormous carcass.

As we have already indicated, the Simmenthal should be classed with the beef breeds. As to their merit for use in grading up on the range, we can only conjecture, as they have not been tried long enough to exhibit many grade offspring. We believe, however, that the Southwestern rangemen have a very valuable addition to their stock in this breed, and we shall await further trial with interest.

The engraving has been prepared expressly for our use from a photograph of Rev. von Schluembach's cattle, by Baron von Hollweg, and is remarkably accurate in all details. The bull in front is Czar; a fine model, with evenly variegated color. The one showing escutcheon (rear view) is Sultan; he represents the type in which the white markings are limited to lower line, legs and head. The view of Sultan displays fully the characteristic rounded haunches, and shows a thigh well turned and extremely muscular. The cow Edelweiss is unfortunately almost hidden by the two bulls, but is fully their equal in breed markings and characteristics.

[Rev. von Schluembach's address is now Cleveland, Ohio.]

SIMMENTHAL CATTLE.
Property of Rev. F. von Schuenbach, Perry, Texas.

Chapter XLIV.

BRAHMIN (ZEBU) CATTLE.

Referring to the name by which these cattle are known in America, it may be well to state that it has no authentic foundation other than the prevalent but mistaken idea—that but one breed of cattle is found in India, and that one connected in some mysterious way with the Brahmin religion. There are, in fact, several breeds of cattle in India, each one transmitting its peculiar qualities with as much certainty as do any of the modern breeds so well known in America. True, all of these families possess many characteristics in common, but they differ sharply in those distinctive qualities by which American breeders must judge of their value.

Mr. Albert Montgomery, of New Orleans, has kindly placed at hand a number of private letters from reliable parties in various portions of India, written in response to queries prior to his importation of Brahmins in 1885. According to the unanimous testimony of these men—well qualified to judge—the family best calculated to find favor in America is, in India, known as the "Buchour," and it is from cattle of this family that most of the shipments to America have been made. The name "Brahmin," however, is so firmly fixed among those who have bred or known them in the Southern States, that it would be impracticable, at least, to attempt a change. We have therefore adopted the nomenclature which heads this chapter, and shall refer solely to the cattle as now known in the United States.

The Brahmins—as noted above—form one of the common domestic breeds of Indian cattle, are found also in China and East Africa, and are the only breed which can endure the intense heat and insect pests of the countries named. They differ from our domestic cattle in the following particulars: The period of gestation is about 300 days, while the average period with the common cow is 283 days; they have a hump of fat over the shoulders, and 18 caudal vertebræ as against 21 in our ordinary cattle. These characteristics have led naturalists to class them as a distinct species (*Bos Indicus*), but the bulls breed as freely with all varieties of the common cow (*Bos taurus*) as with females of their own peculiar breed.

Introduction to the United States dates from the year 1849, when Dr. James Bolton Davis, of Charleston, S. C., secured from the Earl of Derby and imported the first pair of Brahmins ever brought to the

United States. Dr. Davis, who died in 1859, was a typical southern gentleman of the old school, whose thorough knowledge of medicine was combined with not only a close knowledge of, but also an enthusiastic love for, progressive agriculture. In 1846, on the recommendation of President James K. Polk, Dr. Davis was engaged at a salary of $25,000 per year by the Sultan of Turkey, Abdul Medjid, to attempt the introduction of cotton into the Turkish Empire, and to instruct certain selected pupils in the cultivation of cotton and the general principles of the then modern American agriculture. As a matter of interest it may be stated that the Doctor was successful in introducing three varieties of cotton—the White, the Nankeen and the Silk—and continued his work of instructing the Sultan's selected pupils for a period of three years. During his three years' stay in Turkey, the Doctor obtained pure-bred specimens of the Indian Buffalo (*Bos gaurus*) or "water ox," the Cashmere goat, the Thibet shawl goat, and the Scind goat. These were brought first to Turkey in Asia, thence to Turkey in Europe, and thence to America *via* Liverpool. While in England with his family on his way home, Dr. Davis became acquainted with the Earl of Derby, who had some pure Brahmin cattle—secured by him direct from India, through the agency of the East Indian Co., a short time before. The Earl had no Cashmere goats and the Doctor had no Brahmin cattle. Negotiations were therefore made which resulted in a mutually satisfactory exchange—the Doctor leaving some Cashmere goats in England, and adding to his already unique collection for shipment to America a pair of pure Indian-bred Brahmins.

For a time after reaching South Carolina the Brahmins, with the other animals imported from Asia, were kept on the rice plantations in the lower part of the state, but after a time were taken to the Doctor's old homestead, in Fairfield county. About the time of the removal Dr. Davis sold the original imported pair of Brahmins for $4,500 to a Mr. Eades of Kentucky—their increase and most of the grade offspring from common cows being afterwards sold to Col. Richard Peters, of Atlanta, Ga., who purchased also some of the pure bred Cashmere goats. From the best information obtainable the cattle sold Eades finally found their way to the McHatton farm above St. Louis; but it was too far north for them, and they were afterward sold at auction.

Brahmin cattle found their way to Mexico about 1867, when Mr. F. McManus & Sons shipped 20 head—descended from the Davis importation—to the "Brachimba Farm," near the city of Mexico. No attempt was anywhere made to keep them pure, but the grades were much sought, and were soon widely scattered through northeast Mexico and southern Texas. Col. Peters also made an importation of pure Brahmins before the war, and descendants of his stock have been scattered all over Florida and the coast regions of Georgia, Alabama, Mississippi, Louisiana and Texas. In southern Texas especially, the Brahmin blood has played an important part in improving the native stock, and its value is attested by the constant demand for Brahmin grades from practical stockmen in the region named.

For the imformation concerning Dr. Davis' importation of Brahmins we are indebted to a valued friend, Mrs. Harriet Davis White—daughter of Dr. Davis, and now the charming wife of Major H. K. White, a wealthy Brazos bottom planter, and member of the Texas House of Representatives, residing in Bryan, Texas. We sincerely hope that Mrs. White may be prevailed upon to prepare—as she has been urged to do—what could not fail to be a most interesting account of her father's life, especially that portion of it covering his three years sojourn in Turkey, and his experience in importing and handling Brahmins and other Asiatic stock.

DESCRIPTION AND CHARACTERISTICS.

They may be best described by calling attention to those peculiar points which distinguish the grades—even when as low as 1-16th of Brahmin blood is present. The ears are long and drooping; the horns, in the thoroughbred, point upward and backward; in the grades this peculiarity is retained, but greatly modified. The dewlap is voluminous, especially at the throttle; the hips are rather narrow, and the rump slopes rapidly from sacrum to the tail. The loose fold of skin at the navel is remarkably developed, swinging from old males so as to almost touch the ground : this latter may be called the distinguishing mark of a Brahmin grade. We have seen a great many of these grade steers— some of them not having more than 1-16th of Brahmin blood, but every one retained this peculiar mark. In the grade heifers or cows, it is not so strongly marked, but even a novice would have no trouble in detecting the Brahmin blood. The color of the thoroughbred Brahmin is a sort of silver gray, with darker (iron gray) fore and hind quarters, and a large percentage of the grades from native cows exhibit similar markings.

As to the economic value of this breed for the Southwestern ranges, we have already written. The great advantage they have over any other breed capable of improving the so-called "native" Texan, lies in the fact, that they acclimate with perfect safety. Their native home is subject to about the same conditions (in concentrated form) as obtain in the Gulf regions of the United States; and a change to the latter seems only to act as a sort of strong tonic, increasing the general vigor and health.

We cannot say that we admire them—in fact an American ideal of a thoroughbred bull is likely to be considerably shattered on first inspec-

BRAHMIN (ZEBU) CATTLE. 213

BRAHMIN CATTLE.
Property of Albert Montgomery, New Orleans, La.

tion of a typical Brahmin; but there can be no doubt as to their utility in the region named. The cross improves the quality of native beef, and adds quantity by increasing size. For the dairy, some of the cows are said to be superior; they give a large quantity of milk, but the quality is rather deficient; moreover, the wild nature of the animal is liable to crop out in a variable and sometimes vicious temper. The grades from good quiet cows, are of course more nearly free from this objection, and in many places dairies of Brahmin grades are giving good satisfaction.

The previously published experience of Col. Peters is interesting in this connection, and we quote:

"The animals did excellent, and I thought I had solved the problem. They made fine beef cattle—wonderful—and some of them were extraordinary milkers. I had one grade Brahmin cow that gave 36 quarts of milk per day; I exhibited her at the fairs, and took premiums everywhere; but I discovered that the milk lacked butter-making qualities. * * * * And then the Brahmins were the most malevolent animals in the world, with a distinctive aversion to women. I don't think I ever saw a Brahmin cow that a woman could milk. * * * * I never knew one animal to die of murrain. They made the best work oxen I ever raised."

The place for the Bramins is on the Southern ranges, and the grade bulls—half bloods—with which Mr. Albert Montgomery, of New Orleans, and his partner, J. M. Frost, of Houston, Texas, are supplying the market, find ready sale at good prices. Mr. Frost, writing to the Author under date of July 9th, 1888, says:

"I defy any man to name the time when he ever saw a tick on either pure or half-breeds, or a worm from the blow fly [screw worms]. Further than this, I defy any man to say that he ever saw any of them to die from a severe winter. They are the grandest cattle that exist for southern climates."

The illustration represents the imported Brahmin bull Khedive, and two of his grade offspring from native Texas cows—property of the gentlemen just mentioned—and was engraved for our use from photographs taken in Houston, Texas.

Chapter XLV.

WEST HIGHLAND CATTLE.
(*Kyloes.*)

This breed is undoubtedly native to the Highlands of West Scotland and the islands along the coast. The mountain breeds of Scotland may all be referred to the same original stock and their variations at the present time, ascribed to climatic or other natural and artificial conditions under which they have been reared. As in Wales we have the Pembroke and North Wales Cattle, so in Scotland we have the West Highlands, as direct descendants of the original Forest stock.

Improvement of the breed has been effected mainly by selection and careful in-breeding. About the middle of the last century, the Duke of Argyle commenced a systematic course of breeding, which soon called public attention to the herds of Argyleshire; in course of time the superior quality of his stock was communicated to all the cattle of the Highlands, and has since served as a basis for their continued excellence and improvement. The Hebridean farmers especially, declare that the Kyloes are as nearly perfect, for that locality, as may be, and assert positively that outcrosses, whenever tried, have only tended to render the offspring less hardy without increasing either quality or quantity of beef. Several importations have recently been made to the United States and Canada, and we may confidently look for more extensive introduction in the future.

DESCRIPTION.

Color black; until late years, this color was not so strictly adhered to—brown, brindle, dun and other colors were nearly as common as black; even now, while the fashionable Kyloe must be black, there are many animals of equal merit showing other colors; indeed we are inclined to agree with Prof. Low when he says:

"The breeders should look to the essential character of form, without limiting themselves to a black color of the hair, which is a property altogether secondary."

The face is broad, tapering to a narrow muzzle, and showing a gradual dish or curvature from the horns to the nose. The eyes are prominent, bright and restless; ears well carried, and thickly covered with hair; horns middle sized, broad and waxy at base, and curving upward to sharp points of a darker shade; neck short, with considerable

WEST HIGHLAND BULL.
(English Engraving)

dewlap; back wide and straight, with full crops and even loin; ribs well sprung, and dropping to somewhat flattened sides. A striking peculiarity of the Kyloe is found in the small space between the hips and the last floating ribs. The lumbar region is remarkably short and strong, a provision rendered necessary by the mountainous character of their native country, and admirably fitting them for mountainous or hilly ranges wherever found. The hind quarters are full, deep and fleshed well down to the hock—twist low; fore quarters wide apart, deep and heavy; brisket very full and projecting well forward; legs short, straight and strong boned. The skin is mellow, "handling" remarkably well, and the hair is long, thick and more or less wavy—curled hair is considered an objection. In general we may say: The Kyloe is a compact, blocky built, neat looking, middle horned animal of dark color and medium size. Mature bulls weigh from 1,100 to 1,600 lbs.; cows from 700 to 1,000 lbs.

CHARACTERISTICS.

The West Highland breed has two very strongly marked characteristics—(1) hardiness; and (2) excellent beef qualities. To use a western expression, the Kyloe is a good "rustler"—that is, he is entirely capable of taking excellent care of himself if given a reasonable opportunity. Trained for generations to range over pastures always hilly and sometimes scant, and sheltered only by the rocks and ravines of his native range, it is no wonder that the modern Kyloe is superlatively hardy. Why they have not been introduced more extensively in the ranges lying along the foot hills of the Rocky Mountains, is only explained by the push and energy of Hereford, Angus and Galloway breeders, and the mania—we can call it nothing else—among Americans, for breeding size without regard to vigor. Certainly it would be hard to imagine a better stock for the broken range country of the western United States than is found in this vigorous and impressive breed.

And now comes the second point in his favor—meat excellence. Facts are stubborn things, and the fact that Kyloe or West Highland beef has almost invariably commanded a higher price in the London markets than beef of other breeds, speaks volumes in its favor. We must remember, however, that the Kyloes have never yet been in such demand as to shut off the annual supply of thoroughbred beef; while with some of the more popular breeds, nothing has found its way to the shambles, except the inferior animals—too poor for breeding purposes. That the West Highland beef is really better than the marbled beef of either Galloway, Angus or Hereford, we are much inclined to doubt; but that Kyloe beef is as good as the best there can be no question. As work cattle, we have little knowledge concerning them; the people of the Highlands have always been essentially stock raisers,

WEST HIGHLAND COW AND CALF.

and there has been consequently small demand for oxen trained to the yoke. They possess the essential properties—activity and strength—and with training, would undoubtedly rank high for this purpose. Nothing is claimed for the Kyloe cow in the dairy; she gives sufficient milk to bring up her calf in excellent condition, and, for the range, nothing more is desired.

The engraving of cow and calf was prepared expressly for the *Breeder's Gazette* of Chicago, and the kindness of the *Gazette* people in parting with an electro for our use is acknowledged, with thanks.

Chapter XLVI.

TEXAS CATTLE.

On the ranges of the Southwest have existed for many years vast herds of cattle, which by their peculiar characters—effectually transmitted to their offspring—may be classed as a breed. Although known as "Texas Cattle," the same race extends throughout Mexico, and has been pretty well scattered through the more northern and western territories of the United States. According to Allen (American Cattle), "they are the descendants of the early Spanish stock introduced into Mexico in the 16th century;" and this is undoubtedly correct, as a comparison of Texas cattle with the modern cattle of Spain would show—even at this time, after centuries of changed conditions—a marked similarity.

The same original stock must also have furnished a nucleus for the now almost countless bovine population of South America. In this connection we quote Prof. Low (Domestic Animals of Great Britain):

"The origin of those amazing herds which cover the plains of Paraguay, Buenos Ayres and other noble provinces is traced by Spanish writers to the arrival, by way of Brazil, of seven cows and a bull from Andalusia, at the City of Assumption, on the Paraguay, in the year 1556."

DESCRIPTION AND CHARACTERISTICS.

Color varies; light dun and mouse color are, perhaps, most common, but red, yellow and black—and each with all styles of white markings—are found. A point already mentioned in the chapter on Jerseys is the usually lighter color of the hair bordering the muzzle—a peculiarity doubtless derived from the cattle of Spain, where it is commonly observed. In size they vary according to the quality of range, but as a rule are small—bulls weighing from 1,000 to 1,200 lbs.; cows from 600 to 900 lbs. Texas steers at four years old, grass fat, generally weigh from 900 to 1,200 lbs. The distinguishing feature lies in the extraordinary size of the horns; these assume various wide, spreading shapes, sometimes measuring upwards of four feet from tip to tip.

The cows are practically worthless for the dairy—few giving more than one or two gallons per day on good feed; but the value of the race to the whole country where it finds a natural home can hardly be overestimated. The improved breeds have found in this hardy stock a basis which receives most kindly the blood of improvement; indeed, but

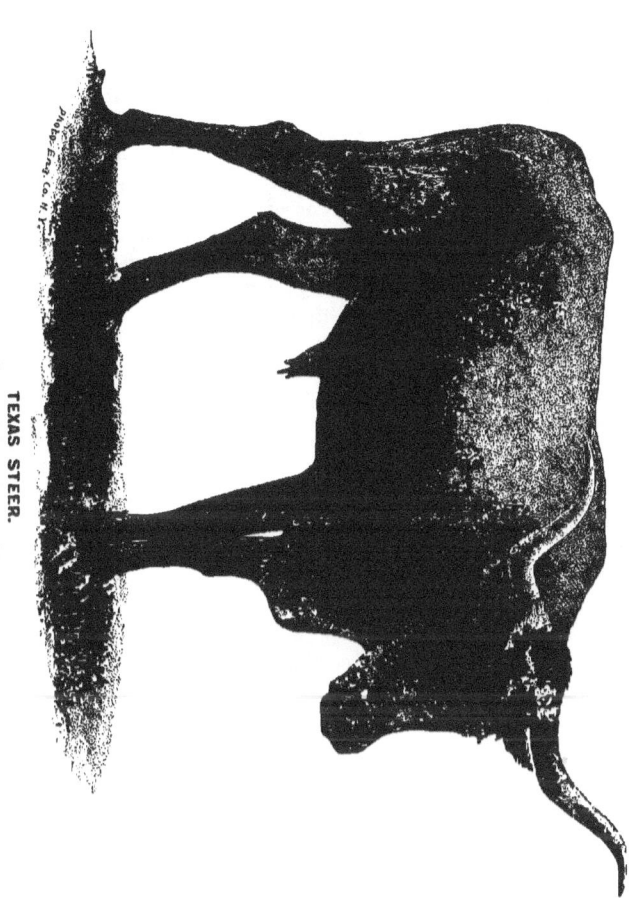

TEXAS STEER.
(Engraved from Photograph.)

for Texas cattle, the Southwest would wait long years before possessing many herds of improved varieties. It is wonderful what results obtain in a few years from a single improved bull, placed with Texas cows. There is no dying of such offspring by acclimating fever, and if the bull only survives until the cows are served, he has more than repaid his cost. It is this fact which has stimulated the demand for thoroughbred bulls during the last decade, and placed thousands upon thousands of Hereford, Aberdeen, Galloway, Shorthorn and other grades upon our ranges. The breed originally known as Texas Cattle will, before many years, be a thing of the past, but its descendants, combining the blood of improved varieties, will give a different character in the future to Texas cattle sold for eastern markets.

The engraving is an exact reproduction of a photograph taken under our immediate direction August 4, 1888, and may be accepted as a fair likeness of a native Texas ox. (The horns of the animal represented in the illustration measured—at time the photograph was taken—three feet five inches from tip to tip, and the animal—five years old—weighed about 1,000 lbs.)

Chapter XLVII.

HINTS ON SELECTION, CARE AND MANAGEMENT OF CATTLE.

As already noted in the summary of part second, we have considered the breeds of cattle under three heads—dairy, general-purpose and beef. Each of the known families of cattle must be classed under one of these divisions, and for whatever purpose bred, will all be subject to the same general principles of care and handling.

In these days of specialists and "experts," even the breeders of stock have caught the contagion, and lines are drawn so closely between dairy and beef types, that it is an absolute necessity to refer to some intermediate class the many breeds which are valuable in both extremes, but supreme in neither. Cattle are no longer chosen entirely with reference to size, weight and rounded contour; but the peculiar qualities of each animal are as carefully estimated, and for these qualities the animal as quickly appropriated to satisfy some taste or special judgment, as any other commodity, subject to the inevitable law of supply and demand. There is ample room for every improved breed of cattle, which has been, or in the future may be, established; and we have little patience with such narrow views as prompt a breeder to decry all other breeds but his. To advance one's interests by setting forth the good qualities of his wares is perfectly legitimate; but to attempt to advance one breed by tearing down another is pernicious, and will sooner or later destroy public confidence, not only in the men, but also in the breed they champion so unwisely.

In deciding the question as to which breed will prove most profitable, a man must be governed largely by: (1) The natural conditions of soil and climate; (2) nearness to market or shipping facilities; (3) the relative cost of outfits and materials for carrying on the different lines of work; (4) the cost and scarcity or abundance of competent labor; (5) the probabilities of fluctuation in market value, or the relative cost of holding over to meet a more favorable market; and (6), most important of all, the peculiar fitness of the man, either by natural ability, taste or education, for one of the special lines of work to which the various breeds are severally adapted.

It will thus be seen how impracticable it is to give advice on selection of the "best" breed, and how utterly worthless such advice must be unless given with intimate knowledge of all the peculiar conditions we have mentioned, and many others which will doubtless occur to the thinking reader. There are, however, certain points which may be given as an aid to individual selection, and of these we mention:

First.—The animal should be carefully studied, with reference to some standard description of the breed to which it belongs; such a description we have aimed to give in each Chapter devoted to a breed, and no animal should be selected for breeding purposes that does not show, in appearance or progeny, the dominant character of its particular breed.

Second.—If a cow desired for the dairy, she should have the typical milk wedge; that is, as seen either from above or from the side, a V-shaped outline, with the apex forward. The fore region may be rather light in appearance, but the barrel must gradually deepen to the flank, joining the udder in an almost continuous line, as though the entire body were a portion—as indeed it is—of the milk machine. As to shape and appearance of the udder, breed characteristics must largely govern, but we may say in general that a well-formed udder should be large only when distended with milk; when empty it should appear small, and will usually hang in loose folds or wrinkles. As a rule, those cows having broad udders close up to the body, but spreading well forward and back, may be expected to give a good quantity of milk, while the cows with rather narrow and longer udders—"bottle-shaped"—will usually give a better quality as to butter content. The so-called milk veins, running from the udder region on either side of the abdomen forward, should be irregular and puffy, rather than straight and even; a rich yellow colored skin is usually an excellent indication of value in the butter line, and a soft, glossy coat, is an invariable accompaniment of health.

The escutcheon or "milk mirror," consists of hair turned in a reverse direction from that grown on other parts of the body, and is found on the udder—spreading forward and backward, and between the thighs, covering a greater or less surface according to the milking capacity of the animal. As previously stated, we shall not undertake a description of the various classes and orders of escutcheons outlined by Guenon; the system is of sufficient importance to justify all the comment, favorable and otherwise, which it has provoked, and we can do no less than advise a careful study of the subject before deciding as to its practical utility. In our own experience, we have found the Guenon system of much value. The escutcheon cannot, in our opinion, be relied on as the only expression of good or bad milking quality, but if properly used in connection with other milk signs it furnishes a most valuable aid in the selection of dairy stock. Finally, and most important of all, be sure that the animal has a feminine look; a decided cowy appearance, especially of the head, not only indicates milking promise, but may also be accepted as a uniform sign of docility.

The typical outline for meat excellence should be sought in an animal full and even at all points, but expecially well rounded at the parts which carry beef of highest price and quality. Animals which lay on fat in bunches are objectionable, as are, also, those which carry an immense bony frame—too large to be ever fully loaded. To put the matter in a nut-shell: In selecting for beef, choose always the animal which will dress the largest amount of high-priced beef and the least proportion of low-priced beef and offal. The parts to be favored then, are: shoulders, fore ribs, loins, haunches and hams; and the parts to be curtailed as much as possible are: head, neck, legs and belly. Beef is the end— if not the aim—of all cattle, and on the great ranges of the West, until the fertile prairies are dotted with settlers' homes, the beef breeds will hold an undisputed sway.

Third.—Between these two extremes of milk and beef stands the general-purpose animal—the one of all others which must always play a prominent part in the economy of thousands of small farms throughout the United States. The small farmer demands a cow which will not only furnish a fair quantity of milk and butter, but also carry at the same time a frame of good size, and show a natural tendency to flesh when not in milk. Steers from such cows make profitable feeders, and the cows themselves when rendered unfit for breeding by any cause, as accident or age, may be fed for the butcher and turned into cash at minimum loss. To select such an animal, requires ability to discover and appreciate the good points, when partially hidden by others of perhaps equal worth, but opposite indications. With this perceptive ability, and a knowledge of the good points of both beef and dairy types, a man will experience little difficulty in selecting cattle for any desired purpose.

Concerning care and management for the herd, we are pleased to present the following letters from practical breeders in different portions of the United states:

Holstein-Friesians.

"LAKESIDE FARM, Syracuse, N. Y., July 24, 1888.

* * * * "The methods of feeding and caring for our stock are extremely simple. Calves are taken from dams when a day or two old and fed for a few weeks, new, full milk ; then, as the calf gets age and strength, we take away the full milk, and in its place give centrifugally separated skim-milk. We also give, dry, a small amount of ground oats and wheat bran, the amount of either food depending on the condition and assimilative powers of the animal. As the animal develops, we add to the amount of dry and liquid food given, as we think the calf will digest and assimilate it, until it reaches an age and development that warrants taking the milk away and supplying hay and grain. We always leave a little hay in manger, that the calf may eat *ad libitum*. In summer we send the females to pasture, and the males are kept in stable, but are given frequent exercise in open air yards or paddocks. We commence using the bulls at about a year old. We aim to breed the heifers, conditions being favorable, when about 15 to 16 months old, so that they will calve after two years old. As the time approaches for calving, the heifer is put in a box stall and carefully watched, and during calving if necessary, assistance is given. For the first few days after calving, very little grain food is given, and that largely bran; then, as she gains strength, we gradually add in quantity and quality of grain food, the amount depending entirely on the individual and its powers of digestion and assimilation, but in a mixture of two parts of wheat bran to one of ground oats and one-fourth of one part of oil meal, which is our mixture for cows, where quantity of milk is required, or, if feeding for butter, one part each of corn meal, ground oats and bran, and one-fourth of one part of oil meal, the amount per capita would be from 4 to 12 pounds per day.

"Our milch cows are milked two or three times a day, as circumstances dictate, and are fed at each milking, which is done in the stable, grain feed being fed dry. In summer, cows run in pasture; they are fed soiling foods, such as rye, clover, oats or corn in stable, when pastures are poor. In winter corn or clover ensilage is fed, with an alternate feeding of hay.

"The milk of each cow is carefully weighed separately, and the amount set down at the time on a blackboard conveniently placed, and each day transferred to a book made for the purpose; the milk is then taken to the creamery where it is thoroughly strained through a perforated tin strainer and four thicknesses of cheese-cloth into a large tank; from there it goes into a smaller tank, and thence into the De Laval Separator. The skim or separated milk is run into a tank, from which it is drawn as needed. The cream is put in large vessels and allowed to acidify, and then churned in a cubic churn propelled by steam power. When the butter is in the grain, the buttermilk is drawn off, and the butter thoroughly washed in clear, cold water; it is then taken to the butter-worker, and salt added, one ounce to the pound of butter, then packed away in a cold room, and next day taken out, worked and packed for market.

"We use no cotton-seed meal or concentrated or highly stimulating foods, nor any drink other than pure water. Scrupulous cleanliness is used in caring for both calves and cows, milk and butter.

"We keep our service bulls in stalls, and fasten them with chain from ring in the nose, and also from strap around the neck. They are so placed as to be able to see each other, and we think this tends to make them fearless of strangers and accustomed to company. These bulls we feed very sparingly of grain, and give hay and soiling foods in summer and ensilage in winter.

"Yours truly, SMITHS, POWELL & LAMB."

The above is an excellent type of well-planned, thorough system. Lakeside Farm has become very widely known for the high class of its stock and dairy products, and the success attained is explained by the above outline of actual methods pursued.

Jerseys.

MANOR, Tex., July 16, 1888.

"❦ ❦ ❦ ❦ My stock run in pasture in all except the very severest weather. Young things by themselves until old enough to breed, when they are turned into the large pasture with the others. The time of their breeding is noted. Unless in thin order, no feed is given to heifers or dry cows in the grass season. Cows giving milk are fed all the time on cotton-seed, shelled oats and crushed corn and cob meal, with hay or corn fodder as I happen to have. If a cow is to drop calf in winter, she is carefully watched, and stabled in roomy box stall well littered. If the weather is mild, she is left in pasture. (No mules in pasture). As soon as the calf is dropped, the cow is milked out clean.

" The calf is allowed to suck until it is three or four days old, when it is removed and afterwards never allowed to suck, but fed on whole milk fresh from the cow till it is four to six weeks old, when sweet skim milk is gradually substituted. At first the skim milk is slightly warmed, but afterwards, unless in exceeding cold weather, no warming is done. I have never had a case of milk fever or other trouble about calving, nor do my calves ever suffer from scours. If an animal appears constipated, a dose of salts or 'liver regulator' is given, but I doctor very little. In bad weather everything is sheltered and fed, the main food for everything being cotton-seed. In fact, except to cows in milk, cotton-seed, with access to straw stack and pasture, is the only feed.

"I have lost a few head from Black Leg, but believe it can be prevented—not cured if it is very far advanced. When an animal dies, all the young and susceptible animals are at once given a mild cathartic and antiseptic. Have used copperas, tablespoonful, with about as much of the dry powder Simmons' Liver Regulator, or one level teaspoonful salicylic acid and heaping teaspoonful of sulphite of soda ; in either case, the dose is repeated for two or three days. I have stopped three outbreaks—losing none after beginning treatment.

"In short, I follow nature as nearly as I can, depending on grass, good water and pure air for all. For about three months, stable ; remainder of time in open lots ; calves on grass from two weeks old.   Very truly, &c.,   L. B. GILES."

The above gives an idea of how the dairy herd is handled where cotton-seed is the main or staple food. While we are not of opinion that cotton-seed is the best food for cows in milk, yet there is no doubt that it and its product after extraction of the oil—cotton-seed meal—are the most valuable concentrated food-stuffs which the Southern dairyman can command. Fairly good—even excellent—butter is made from the milk of cows fed largely on cotton-seed meal, but its best effect is had when combined in smaller proportions with food-stuffs less rich in protein. Mr. Giles has certainly made an excellent showing in way of handling calves ; there are few herds where calves are reared by hand that do not occasionally suffer from attacks of the scours, and Mr. Giles' success in this respect is probably due to the fact that he makes accurate note of the animal's condition from the time it is born.

Devons.

NASHVILLE, TENN., July 19, 1888.

"* * * * As a breeder of Devons, having as the principal object in view the sale of young animals, it is necessary first that there should be absolute purity of blood ; this is secured by starting with pure bred cows and bulls, and as the bull is by much the largest part of the herd, extraordinary care is taken in his selection. No bull in my herd is inbred to his own calves, and although I do not part with a bull which I consider good, when his heifers come of age to be bred, another bull of different strain is bought to serve them. My heifers are bred not under two years old, and are placed with the bull in the month of July, so that the first calf of the heifer will be dropped in April or May, thus giving an opportunity for the udder to be expanded by the spring grazing. Of 16 heifers being bred this season, the youngest was dropped 2nd September, 1886, so that the youngest heifer will be at least 31 months old at calving, and most of them three years old. My object in this is to give stamina and constitution, both to the cows and their progeny, which I think are greatly impaired by the very early breeding practiced by some breeders, in the great desire to get quick returns. After the first calf is dropped, I do not consider it of much importance in our climate at what season the calf comes, so my bull runs with the herd of milk cows all the time, and calves are being dropped by my cows at all seasons of the year, the time between calves running from 10 to 12 months.

"The bull is driven to the cow-house regularly every night with the milk cows, and in my experience of twelve years as a breeder of Devons, buying a new bull about every two years, I have never had a vicious bull. This may be attributed in part to the docility of the breed, but I think it also partly attributable to the manner in which they are kept. All of my cows (twin calves or some rare cases excepted) are milked night and morning in order to protect and develop the milking habit, but not enough is taken from them to stint the calves, who finish the job and take what the milkman has left, and no great complaint is made about the quantity of the milk which goes to the dairy so long as the calves are fat.

"Calves are turned out to pasture every morning, and when weaned at six to eight months old, are put upon pasture. During the winter months the weaned calves have as much hay—red-top, timothy or clover—as they can eat, and once each day are fed with grain (cornmeal, coarsely ground) enough to keep them in good condition. Cows are milked in the cow-house in stall, with rope halter fastened around the neck, and are fed every time they are milked—during the summer very lightly, just a little being put in their troughs to keep them quiet; but in winter, all the finely-cut hay they can eat, and coarsely ground cornmeal as a grain ration. Except in extremely severe weather in winter, cows are turned out every day and night. Loose boxes about 10x20 feet are provided for cows which calve in the winter, and in summer small pastures near by, in which cows are put a few days before calving. Such is my system; the result: gentle bulls, healthy cows, breeding regularly up to the age of 18 or 20 years, and healthy calves, kept easily all the time in good growing condition, but never pampered until they look fat enough for prize beef. Truly,

"EDWARD D. HICKS"

Mr. Hicks knows how to handle Devons for profit. His plan of letting the bull run with the cows is one which must be carefully regulated as to number of cows admitted if the sire is to be kept in prime breeding shape; but, when so managed, is very satisfactory. It is the practice usually adopted by all breeders of range stock, certainly tends to render the bull more easily subject to control, and cannot fail to find plenty of advocates. His method of rearing calves will make fine beef animals, but, if continually practiced—one generation after another—will surely tend to destroy whatever capacity for large milk yield a breed may have originally possessed. As we have stated—"Nature" is all right in her way, but a considerable amount of "Art" has always been required to increase the dairy excellence of any breed. His practice is correct, inasmuch as it fills the demand for beauty of form, fattening propensity, and early maturity which a majority of Devon purchasers have created; but we confess to a feeling of disappointment that the Devon breed is not more strongly stimulated to bring into greater prominence its inherent dairy worth.

Red-Polled and Shorthorn Grades.

"TEMPLE, TEXAS August 20, 1888.

* * * *

"I begin with calves; pen everything each night; keep plenty of salt in the lot at all times; throw them a batch of shucks or cut corn—all of which has a tendency to make them gentle and docile. I breed them young, let the calves come at 24 and 30 months old, then feed well. I think that makes better milkers. It has, however, a tendency to dwarf the heifer—she never gets so large when so treated. My cattle are all 'muleys.' I can feed twelve head in a 12-foot trough and not crowd them. I use young bulls a little at one year old—say ten cows that year. I keep my bull up in day-time with calves all the spring, and turn him out at night; it makes him much gentler and more docile. I keep a ring in each bull's nose after one year old. I dehorn when calves, if they have horns at birth. I feed milk cows the year round—it pays. I use salt, sulphur and lime for my cattle; don't allow the ticks to accumulate on them. I have my cows milked at 6 A. M. and 6 P. M., as near as I can. I keep about 20 to 25 head of cattle, which are penned where the rain carries the washings from the pen on to the farm, hence the liquid manure is saved on the land without much work.

"Yours truly, W. A. CLARK."

Mr. Clark is a Texas farmer who has found money in the dairy business. He believes in dehorning, but thinks they should always be removed when the animal is very young.

American Holderness.

In answer to our request for statement as to methods practiced by him, Mr. T. A. Cole, of Solsville, Madison county, N. Y., originator of the American Holderness breed, sends a very interesting "write up," clipped from the *New York (Weekly) Sun*. We make the following extract:

"REARING CALVES.—As may be inferred, nearly all the calves are raised, and this is done in addition to the average annual yield per cow of 300 pounds of butter. At first they are fed exclusively on new milk, but gradually skimmed milk is added and the new milk is diminished, until, at the end of three or four weeks, nothing but skimmed milk is fed. To make up for the loss of cream, a little dry oil-meal is given them daily to lick. They are all shut up together on a floor 24x36 feet, which has been littered with the cobs from 500 or 600 bushels of corn. On these they caper and lie, the cobs absorbing all droppings, and the action of the calves keeping the cobs stirred up and clean. On these they are kept out of storm and sun until the room is wanted for storing hay. Then they are turned out to grass, but are given their sour milk rations until about the 1st of October. After this the sour milk, not wanted for the few pigs intended for the family pork, is given to the cows. The horses, all summer long, receive regularly a ration of buttermilk, which they appear to relish exceedingly. Care is taken that young animals shall continue in a healthy, thriving condition, but they are not permitted to become excessively fat, lest they acquire a tendency to put on fat rather than expend their energies in filling the milk pail. By in-breeding and this care, the cows are all remarkably uniform in their milk-producing qualities, both as to quantity and richness. Mr. Cole says this uniformity extends to the raising of the cream, and the time required to churn it—one cow's milk being as like another's as one-half a mess is like the other half. So completely does all the butter come at the same time, that he has tried in vain to get an additional yield of butter by churning the buttermilk. The separation appears to be complete at the end of the first churning."

The main point which we wish to mention in the practice of Mr. Cole, is the one of allowing the calves to bed on corn cobs. The idea is a good one, and if put in general practice among Western farmers would soon do away with the unhealthy odors too frequently found in the calf-pen. His practice of feeding back to the cows the surplus skim product from the dairy is rapidly growing in favor, and is giving excellent results.

Shorthorns.

"CENTRE GROVE FARM, DURANT, IOWA, July 28, 1888.

* * * *

"We are breeding Shorthorns for both milk and beef, so our methods may differ from those who bred exclusively for beef or exclusively for milk. Every breed has its office, and we believe the milking Shorthorn must fill a large demand made by the general farmer, who wants a good milch cow that will raise a good, easy-keeping, early maturing steer. To fill this now rapidly increasing demand, we are breeding and feeding the noble 'Red, White and Roan,' and the following are our methods:

"We keep our bulls in a separate pasture by themselves, where, if possible, no cows will be near them. Mature bulls will keep in good order on grass alone; growing bulls get a light ration of oats and bran twice a day. The breeding bulls get lots of exercise, even in winter, when they are turned out in tight yards on fine days. Ours are now tied in stalls at night, but we think running loose in box stalls would be preferable.

"Heifers, cows and calves are run in separate pastures as much as possible. Pastures are of mixed grasses, blue grass predominating. Water and plenty of shade complete the outfit, and for eight months of the year the cow is content. Green fodder, however, is sometimes given during August; this is relished as a change. Pumpkins are also thrown to them during this dry time. Rock salt in each pasture affords them a sure supply of that necessity.

"Cows are mated at the first 'heat' after the calf is dropped, unless in thin flesh, when more time is given. The first heat is surest to 'hold'. Heifers are bred at from 18 to 20 months, according to size and flesh. If getting too fat, we breed them younger, as excessive fat in a heifer is liable to produce barrenness. We try to prevent calves coming in July, August, January and February.

"Pregnant cows are handled much the same as the other cows. The calf should be weaned when its dam is five or six months pregnant, and the cow should be milked awhile and then dried off. The remaining three months of rest should enable the cow to put on flesh, and gain strength for the coming calf. If necessary, such cows are fed extra to produce this condition. We expect the calf on or about the 280th day, but watch closely from the 270th day. If on grass, keeping confined on light, loose food (bran and oilmeal, &c.,) for a week or more before and after calving, to prevent milk-fever, and to be present at parturition and save the calf. Great care is exercised to prevent pregnant cows from being chased by dogs, gored by other cattle, wading through deep mud, or eating mouldy or ergotized fodder. Sometimes feed a little flaxseed about the 270th day, to help her 'clean' well.

"When a cow begins to show signs of calving, the attendant stays near until all is safe, usually in the box stall with her. Some say that the cow prefers to be alone, but I think our cows like to have me there; they know I am there to help them. * *

As soon as the calf is delivered, I leave the cow and calf alone for a time, then feed her bran mashes (warm) and give tepid water. The cow is then milked three times a day for a few days, and twice a day for a few weeks (or months) till the calf can take all and not physic him.

"If the calf sucks and his bowels move once during the first six hours, he is fairly started on the road to market. We allow him to stay in a stall with his dam for a few days, and after that they are together only at night. During the daytime he plays with his mates, and early learns to eat oats, which are placed within his reach. This feeding is continued during the first year, and sometimes the second winter also. Calves run in a separate lot during the day, and after the cows have been partly milked the calves are put with them.

"At a very early age (two to four months), the bull calves are taken from among the heifers and placed in another lot. They are all weaned at from six to twelve months, according to the condition of the calf and cow, and the state of succeeding pregnancy. After the first year we expect them to keep in good condition on grass alone ; many will be ready for market at any time.

"Our grain ration for young stock bulls and suckling cows is three parts of oats, three of bran, three of corn and one of oil meal. This is varied very much, however, to suit the animal and the season. We very seldom feed corn alone ; often feed oats alone. Raise a few wurtzels to feed in winter as a change. Some corn-fodder is cut in early September and fed, ears and all, during cold snaps, besides the regular hay diet of stock cattle. Fine blue grass pastures are allowed to grow during the fall months, affording much nutritious food for stock during the warm winter days, when there is no snow.

"Such are about the methods now in use at Centre Grove Farm. Of course, something is learned each year to cause us to make some slight changes. When changes are made, however, we hope they are for the better.

"C. W. NORTON & SON, *per* OAK."

We should like to make a great many comments—mostly favorable —on the above, but space forbids mention of more than the main points suggested by the outline given. Our friend "Oak" is right—there is no doubt that the cows like to have him around at the "labor" period ; kindness to the brute creation is never thrown away, and cows brought up under such careful treatment as that pursued at Centre Grove Farm always crave and appreciate the attention given. The practice of separating the bull calves from the heifers at an early age should be emphasized— and the hints on breeding cows and heifers will bear reading twice. If they are breeding for both milk and beef, as noted, it is presumed that the calves are not allowed to do all the milking—and at irregular intervals, although it is not so stated—otherwise we should think the tendency would be more toward beef.

Another point we may notice briefly is the practice of keeping the bull entirely away from the cows except at time of immediate service. There is no doubt that—if mental condition at time of coupling has and effect on the offspring—that effect will be more strongly marked by such practice. We have tried both plans, and while many are in favor of permitting the cows and bulls to run at farthest in adjoining pastures, we believe—if separated at all—the separation should be complete. The only question that can be raised is one of disposition; it has been stated that bulls kept in sight of cows will be more easily managed, but in our own experience the reverse has been true, and we are pretty well satisfied that to keep a bull in good temper, he must either run with the cows and be handled with them, or be kept entirely separate except at time of service.

[On Saturday, September 21, 1889, Oak G. Norton died at his home, after a short period of intense suffering, from inflammation of the bowels. A young man's death is always sad, yet doubly so when he is blessed with such abundant power for good as rested in our strong young friend. Young as he was, his name was known throughout the West as that of a rising breeder of more than usual public and private worth, and in his death, while we have lost a friend in whom we had the utmost confidence, the world has lost much more—an honest, able man.]

Holstein-Friesians.

"WESTBURG FARM, JESUP, IA., August 29, 1888.

* * * *

"As to age of breeding, my practice at the outset was to breed so that each heifer would have her first calf at or near the age of three years. My own observations, and the milk records I have taken for five years, have not yet been sufficiently numerous to enable me to decide definitely. As to diminishing size by early breeding, I can only say that I have heifers which calved at two and two and one-quarter years, as large as those that calved at three and three and one-quarter years. As to milk flow, I am inclined to think early breeding is preferable. I prefer to breed as nearly as possible in December, January and February; just as good (if not better) calves can be raised in a warm barn through the winter as in summer. Milk being worth more in November, December, January and February, I find it more profitable to have them come at this time; in summer, milk is worth 45 to 60 cents per 100 lbs., and in winter 85 cents to $1.10 per 100 lbs. I avoid having cows come in during warm weather, as I think them more liable to have parturient apoplexy.

"I have practiced various ways of rearing calves; have seen little or no difference in size and constitution between feeding calves the fresh milk three times per day until they are six weeks old, and in allowing them to suck the cow to this time. My general practice is to allow them to suck at least seven or eight times. I have never taken a calf from the cow as soon as dropped. As far as milk flow and size are concerned, I am prepared to believe that calves reared on sweet skim-milk and oats for a time after they are four to six weeks old, make just as good cows as those allowed fresh milk for six months. I think that calves allowed to suck the cow for say five or six months, develop a habit of laying on fat, and do not generally make as valuable cows for milk on that account.

"My practice, in summer feeding of cows has been to give a small allowance of bran —say one to one and a-half lbs. at a feed—even while the pasture was good. It saves much of the labor in driving from the pasture, aside from contributing to the volume of the manure; it saves also time and muscle necessary in driving them in the barn prior to milking. For winter feeding, I aim to mix 50 lbs. of bran with 64 lbs. of ground oats and 56 lbs. of ground corn. Of this mixture I approximate the needs of different cows; have fed as high as 24 lbs. per day to a cow weighing 1,200 lbs., and giving 65 to 67 lbs. milk per day; have fed five to six lbs. at a feed to cows giving 30 to 35 lbs. per day. Have practiced mixing this ground feed on a small allowance of wet cut hay, and am confident, from the appearance of the excrement, that a great benefit resulted from this practice.

"I think that, as a general thing, twice a day is sufficient for milking. I have milked several cows that gave large messes three times a day, for at least one month after calving, and afterwards twice a day. Larger milk records can be made, of course, by milking three times a day throughout the year. A fresh cow, especially, should be milked quite regularly, while a cow that has given milk six months will not be affected very much by a little delay in milking. I aim to milk all cows regularly. When at the height of their flow in summer, I think they ought to be milked about 5 A. M. and 4:30 P. M. A heavy milker usually secretes the most milk from morning to night.

"I have practiced selling milk to creameries by the 100 lbs., receiving back at different times, the set skim and the separated skim-milk; have also set the milk at home in ice water, at 40 to 45 degrees Fahrenheit, for 12 hours, and sold the unsalted butter. As to separated skim-milk from creameries, that require the milk hauled but once a day, I have decided to my satisfaction that it is much less profitable than set skim-milk, either 36 hours or 12 hours old—just the relative difference I am not aware has ever been settled Calves fed on separated skim-milk, reared in this vicinity, are certainly not so thrifty and large as those raised a few years ago on set skim-milk.

"There is very great difference of opinion among men as to keeping cows in the barn during winter. My practice is to keep them in during all snow storms and blizzards, and all days when the thermometer is at zero or below. I turn them out two or three times a day for water, and as soon as they are through drinking put them back—cleaning out the stables while they are in. The temperature should be above 32 degrees Fahrenheit, when the cattle are in the barn. Truly yours,

"J. N. MUNCEY"

Mr. Muncey is one of our careful, accurate breeders, well qualified by taste and an extended education to solve some of the actual problems of the day. The point he mentions (difference in feeding value between "set-skim"—the skim-milk left when cream is removed, after setting milk away for a number of hours—and "separated skim-milk"—the product from centrifugal cream separators) is one of considerable interest. In the South, especially, the centrifugal process is of peculiar value, saving ice—a costly commodity—by reason of greatly decreased bulk in handling; and if, as Mr. Muncey suggests, the skim product from the machine is inferior to that from the set milk, some way must be found to remedy the defect. As a matter of fact, later experiments have shown that the addition of a small quantity of flaxseed tea, or oil meal gruel, to the separated skim milk effectually overcomes the objection mentioned by Mr. Muncey, and renders the separator product as valuable as the now old-fashioned set-skim milk was ever claimed to be for feeding calves.

1, Nose; 2, Face; 3, Fore-lock; 4, Ears; 5, Neck; 6, Shoulders; 7, Back; 8, Rump, or Quarter; 9, Tail; 10, Ham or Thigh; 11, Dock of the Tail; 12, Lower Thighs, or Legs; 13, Hock; 14, Shank or Hind Cannon; 15, Onglons, or False Hoofs; 16, Hoof or Foot; 17, Flank; 18, Side; 19, Girth, or Fore-flank; 20, Knee; 21, Front Cannon; 22, Pastern; 23, Fold, Dewlap, or Throat.

a, First quality wool, generally known as "refina" or "picklock; *b*, Second quality wool; *c*, Third quality wool; *d*, Fourth quality wool, generally known as "tags."

PART THIRD.

SHEEP.

SHORT-WOOLED BREEDS.

		PAGE
MERINOS . . . . Chapter XLVIII. 236		
Atwoods . . . . " " . 241		
Paulars . . . . " " 243		
Dickinsons . . . . " " . . 246		
Black-Tops . . . . " " 249		
Delaines . . . . " " 250		
HORNED DORSETS . . . . " XLIX 255		
CHEVIOTS . . . . " L 257		

MIDDLE-WOOLED BREEDS.

| SOUTHDOWNS . . . . Chapter LI . . . . 260 |
| SHROPSHIRES . . . . " LII . . . . 264 |
| HAMPSHIRES . . . . " LIII . . . . 267 |
| OXFORDSHIRES . . . . " LIV . . . . 271 |

LONG-WOOLED BREEDS.

| COTSWOLDS . . . . Chapter LV . . . . 274 |
| LEICESTERS . . . . " LVI . . . . 278 |
| LINCOLNS . . . . " LVII . . . . 282 |

HINTS ON SELECTION, CARE AND MANAGEMENT.

Chapter LVIII. 286

Chapter XLVIII.

MERINOS.

Youatt supposes the Merino sheep a derivation from the old Tarentine breed of Italy. In his book—"Youatt on Sheep"— he says:

"They were the Tarentine breed already described, and which had gradually spread from the coast of Syria and the Black Sea, and have now reached the western extremity of Europe. Many of them mingled with and improved the native breeds of Spain, while others continued to exist as a distinct race, and, meeting with a climate and herbage suited to them, retained their original character and value, and were the progenitors of the Merinos of the present day."

Low (1842) says:

"Upon the whole, although authentic documents on the subject are wanting, there is presumption that the sheep of Africa were employed to perfect the sheep of Spain with respect to the production of wool. The Merinos exhibit certain characters which seem to show them to have been derived from some country warmer than that in which they were naturalized, and it was during the dominion of the African possessors of the country that the wool of Spain arrived at its greatest excellence."

Stewart in his valuable work, "The Shepherd's Manual," says:

"The Spanish Merino existed as a distinct race 2,000 years ago, and the fine robes of the Roman Emperors were made from the wool of Spanish flocks. There is no history or tradition as to their origin which can be accepted as reasonable by any practical shepherd. It is probable, however, that the fine-wooled sheep which we read of in the ancient histories were rather the natural product of very favorable conditions of soil and climate, by which inferior races were greatly improved, than of any direct efforts to breed them up to a desired standard."

That the Tarentine sheep were taken to Spain at a very early day, is proved by the early writers; but there is little doubt that Spain received, at the same time, accessions of African blood from the fine-wooled flocks of the Barbary States on the other side of the Mediterranean.

Columella (an ancient rural economist and author of "De Re Rustica"—a copious treatise on agriculture, in twelve parts—who flourished about A. D. 20 to 40), informs us that his uncle (of the same name) took with him from Italy to Spain a considerable number of the Tarentine sheep, and that he also secured some African rams of singular beauty which had been exhibited at Rome.

Pliny the Younger refers to the "red fleece of Boetica"—an ancient district of Spain—in terms of the highest praise, but as the sheep of this district have always retained the "red fleece" of which he speaks, and as they always differed, and still differ materially, from the Merino breed, it is hardly probable that these sheep—supposed to be of Grecian nativity—had any important place in the immediate origin of the Merino.

To the American breeder a close, accurate account of the precise origin of Merino sheep would be of considerable interest; unless some as yet unfound history may be discovered, the precise origin of the Merino will remain a matter of deduction from circumstantial evidence. The Merino is certainly the oldest of surviving breeds, and as its authentic history is almost co-existent with the history of Spain, we may for all practical purposes, and without further question as to its remote origin, regard it as a creation of Spanish breeders, who used the finest sheep of Italy and Africa, and were further assisted in improving the then native flocks by the natural adaptation of Spanish soil and climate to the rearing of fine-wooled sheep.

When the flocks of Spain first came to be in great demand, there were found, then as now, two classes, known respectively as "*estantes*," or stationary, and "*transhumantes*," or migratory. The stationary flocks are those which remain in a certain district during the year; while the migratory class, on account of scarcity in food or water, make bi-yearly journeys in search of fresh pasture.

From the latter class—generally superior—most of the shipments to other countries have been made.

The French Merino originated from an importation of about 400 head of sheep, selected from the finest flocks of Spain, in 1786. A few had been imported to France nearly a century before this date by Jean Baptiste Colbert, Minister of Finance to Louis XIV., but they were not appreciated, and were soon lost sight of.

The importation of 400 head, mentioned above, was made by the French government during the reign of Louis XVI., and most of the sheep were placed on the Royal Farm at Rambouillet, where their improvement was carried on with considerable success; it was from this circumstance that they derived the name "Rambouillet" sheep, by which they have been commonly known. The Merinos under French management increased in size and weight of fleece, but lost to some degree the hardiness of their Spanish parents.

The fleece is fine—fully equal to Spanish wool—and carries a much smaller quantity of yolk. This character, in connection with their increased size, has made them quite popular in America, the small quantity of yolk rendering the fleece much less subject to loss of weight in washing; but the sheep have not found sufficient favor to push out the other smooth-skinned mutton Merinos, which we shall mention later as classed among the strictly American families. The wool is fine, beautifully crimped, usually white but sometimes buff, very compact, and opens in large layers.

The American Rambouillet Sheep Breeders' Association has been organized and Vol. I. of the Record published. S. D. Parsons, Iona, Michigan, is the present secretary.

The Saxon Merino originated from a flock of 300 Spanish Merinos of the Escurial family, sent in 1765, by King Louis XV., to Saxony, in response to the request of his brother-in-law, Prince Xavier. The Escurial family of Spanish Merinos had always been noted as bearing the finest wool of any in the kingdom ; and their Saxon breeders have carefully preserved this, the only really valuable feature of the breed. Saxon Merinos require great care and attention—being the least hardy of any of the modern Merinos—and, as they yield an average clip of not over two or three pounds, the higher price obtained for quality does not make up for the marked deficiency in weight of fleece.

The German or Silesian Merino is the only one (except the American) of the Spanish branches which may be called a success. It is the direct result of uniting the Infantado and Negretti families of Spanish Merinos, and is as purely Spanish in its nature as if really Spanish bred. The original importation to Silesia was made in 1811, by Ferdinand Fischer, of Wirchenblatt. This gentleman selected in person 100 Infantado ewes and four Negretti rams, and so carefully did he preserve the purity of the breed that the pedigree of every sheep since the foundation of the flock has been recorded, and no trace of outside blood can be found.

Silesian Merinos from Mr. Fischer's flock were first imported to the United States about 1850-60, by William Chamberlain, of Duchess Co., New York, in all some 250 head, and have since obtained considerable favor. The wool is finer than that of the Spanish Merino, and the carcass little if any smaller. They mature slowly, but are said to be hardy and fairly prolific.

From this brief account of the Merino in other countries, we may pass to consider more in detail the modern families which have attained popularity on this side of the Atlantic.

The American Merino.

The first importations of pure Spanish Merinos to the United States were soon lost sight of, through being mixed with other blood: but we give them in order, so far as possible, as being of interest to American breeders.

About 1791 four Spanish rams were shipped to the United States, and one of them was used in the vicinity of Wilmington, Delaware, until 1808. In 1793 Hon. William Foster, of Boston, imported from Cadiz two Merino ewes and one ram ; these sheep were presented to a friend, who, ignorant of their great value, killed and ate them. (Mr. Foster, it is said, afterwards caught this same unfortunate friend in the act of paying $1,000 for a Merino ram no better than the one he had eaten.)

In 1802, however, the first importation of importance was made by Col. David Humphreys, of Derby, Conn., then Minister to Spain, and from the flock then introduced the modern Atwoods, Dickinsons and Black-Tops have sprung.

MERINOS. 239

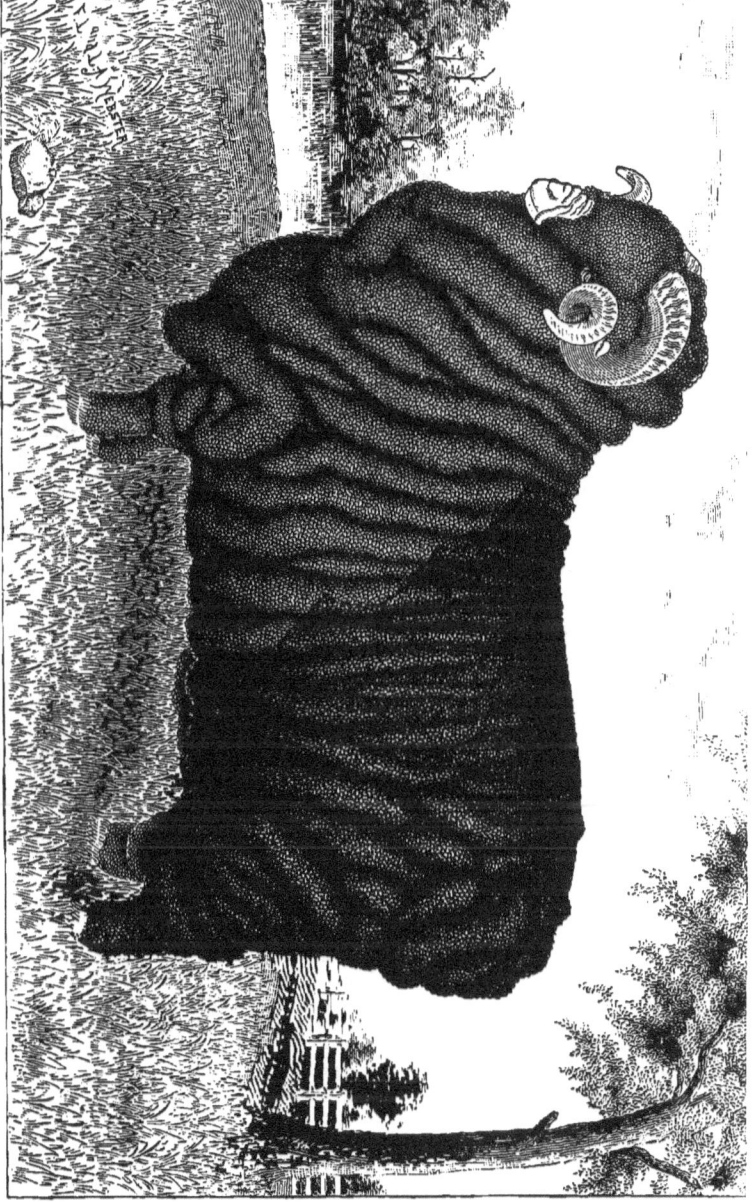

AMERICAN MERINO RAM, JOKER, 553.

(Mixed Atwood and Robinson blood.) Winner of 27 first prizes, and never beaten; weight of fleece 38½ lbs, the largest ever taken from a ram; property of L. E. Shattuck, Stanbeth, Mo.

Concerning this importation we quote from Vol. I. of the Atwood register:

"Col. Humphreys made a contract with a gentleman to deliver one hundred Spanish Merino sheep at Lisbon Ninety of these arrived at Derby, Conn., in the spring of 1802. In reference to this importation Col. Humphreys says, in his miscellaneous papers: 'Convinced as I was that this race of sheep, of which I believe not one had been brought to the United States until the importation by myself, might be introduced with great benefit to our country, I contracted with a person of most respectable character to deliver me at Lisbon one hundred, composed of twenty-five rams and seventy-five ewes, from one to two years old. They were conducted across the country of Portugal by three Spanish shepherds with proper passports, and escorted by a small guard of Portuguese soldiers. On the 10th of April they were embarked from the Tagus on board the ship *Perseverance*, of 250 tons, Caleb Coggeshall, Master. In about fifty days twenty-one rams and seventy ewes were landed at Derby, Conn., they having been shipped at New York on board a sloop destined to that river. The nine that died were principally killed in consequence of bruises received by the violent rolling of the vessel on the banks of Newfoundland.'"

The second importation of importance—and the one which, by reason of its magnitude, has done most to stamp the character of American Merinos—was made in 1809-10, by William Jarvis, of Vermont, then United States Consul at Lisbon.

Stewart ("Shepherds' Manual"), referring to the Jarvis importation, says:

"This consisted of 3,850 sheep of the flocks of Paulars, Negrettis, Aquierres and Montarcos of Spain. These flocks, consisting of 50,000 head, had been, for political reasons, confiscated and sold by the Spanish Government, with other property of the four grandees who had owned them. Of the imported sheep, 1,500 came to New York, 1,000 to Boston, and the remainder to Philadelphia, Baltimore, Alexandria, Norfolk, Richmond, Portland, Wiccasset and Portsmouth. Another shipment of 2,500 head followed in 1810, and were distributed between New York and Boston. These sheep were of the prime flocks of Spain, and Spain's loss was our gain."

From the importations made by these two gentlemen—Col. Humphreys and Mr. Jarvis—the American Merino, with its numerous subdivisions or families, has arisen.

From the United States Merino Sheep Register we take the following authoritative

DESCRIPTION AND CHARACTERISTICS.

"There must be a perfectly authenticated line of ancestry extending to one or more of the importations of Merino sheep from Spain, made prior to 1812, without admixture of any other blood. The constitution is indicated by a healthful countenance; expanded nostril; short, strong neck; deep chest; round barrel; strong, short back; strong loin; heavy bone of fine texture; muscle fine and firm, and skin thick, soft and of a pink color.

"Under the term fleece must be included quantity, quality and condition of the wool, as shown by the weight of fleece, the length and strength of staple, crimp, fineness and trueness of fibre, evenness throughout, freedom from gare, and the fluidity and amount of yolk.

"The term covering includes the extent and evenness of the fleece over the whole body, legs, belly, neck and head; the quality, lustre, crimp, density and length of wool, and the quantity and kind of oil or yolk. The shoulders should be well placed; back broad; quarters long and well filled up; head short; folds in the neck, elbow, flank, belly, thighs and tail.

"Rams at full growth, in breeding condition, should weigh 130 lbs. or upwards, and ewes about 100 lbs. The head should be of medium size; muzzle clear; nose (or face) covered with short, glossy, furry hair; eyes bright and placid; forehead broad; ears soft, thick and set wide apart; ewes hornless; horns on the ram well turned (set not too closely to the head and neck, nor yet standing out too wide), and free from black or dark colored streaks. The neck should be short on top and long below; strongly set to the head and shoulders, becoming deeper toward the shoulders; folds heavier underneath and extending up the sides of the neck, including heavy dewlap and apron. The legs should be short, straight, well spread apart, and bone heavy; hoofs clear in color and well shaped. General appearance should be bold and vigorous, with symmetrical form, and proper complexion of covering."

The following Scale of Points for American Merinos, should be used in connection with above:

Blood 20	Forward 81
Constitution 18	Head 6
Fleece 13	Neck 5
Covering 13	Legs and Feet 4
Form 9	General Appearance 4
Size 8	
Forward 81	Perfection 100

In the South, the Merinos are better known than any other breed of sheep; the fact of their continued breeding for centuries in the hot, dry climate of Spain, and the further fact—or perhaps we should say supposition—of a remote ancestry from the still warmer latitude of northern Africa, has fitted them especially for the warm, dry, elevated regions of the Southwest. It must be borne in mind, however, that the Merinos do not come in conflict, in any particular, with the heavier sheep of the Down and Long-wool tribes. The mission of the Merino is to furnish wool, and that, too, of the finest quality; and for this purpose he stands admittedly without a rival.

Of the more prominent strains of Merinos now known in the United States, we have thought best to give a short account, in order named, of the Atwoods, Paulars, Dickinsons, Black-Tops and Delaines. It will be remembered that we are not writing from the standpoint of a biased or partisan breeder; our statements are intended to do simple justice to each, and if we fail in this the blame cannot, at least, be imputed to any malicious purpose on the part of the author.

The Atwoods.

The origin of the Atwood family may be given, in brief, by the following quotation from Rules of Entry to the Register of the Vermont Atwood Merino Sheep Club:

"Descendants of sheep purchased from Stephen Atwood, or vouched for by him as pure descendants of the Humphreys importation, and no other, may be entered in the

Register on proving either ancestral purchase from Stephen Atwood, or their direct descent through the importations of W. S. and Edwin Hammond, R. P. Hall, W. R. Sanford, and C. B. Cook from his flock, to the satisfaction of the Executive Board."

The flock of Stephen Atwood was founded in 1813, when he purchased of John Riggs a six-year-old ewe, raised by Col. Humphreys, out of one of his imported ewes. Mr. Atwood's account of his sheep—which is attested by reliable gentlemen who were familiar with them—is given as follows in the Atwood Register :

"I bred the Riggs ewe and her progeny to rams I knew to be of pure Humphreys blood, till 1819," and at that time he states : "I bought from the Leman Stone flock, that he raised from Col. Humphrey's flock, five ewe lambs that I selected ; and with these five lambs and the ewe I bought first, I have raised my flock of sheep."

PURE-BRED ATWOOD MERINO RAM, CLINGSTONE 2d, 401.
Weight of third fleece, 30 lbs.; sold to South America, 1886; bred by GEORGE HAMMOND, Middlebury, Vt.

While Mr. Atwood was fortunate enough to preserve the blood in its original purity, to Edwin Hammond belongs the credit for most of the great improvement which the Atwood sheep have undergone.   Mr. Hammond was born in Middlebury, Vermont, May 20, 1801, and lived within a short distance of his birthplace until his death, December 31, 1870. He was a man of excellent judgment, and is placed by some on an equal footing with Bakewell (of Leicester fame) as an improver of sheep. The Hammond sheep are directly descended from the flocks of Stephen Atwood, and thus it happens that on proof of Hammond breeding, the purity of blood is at once accepted, and the animal admitted to record.

DESCRIPTION AND CHARACTERISTICS.

No authoritative scale of points or standard description has been adopted by the club, but the following points may be stated in brief, as distinctive of the Atwood sheep: They are large, round-bodied and strong-boned; very heavy shearers—a clip of 24 or 25 pounds for rams being not uncommon; the fleece is very dense, and although abundantly supplied with liquid yolk (natural oil) it exhibits little tendency to crust externally; when parted, the wavy crimps of the wool may be seen to the very tips of the fibre, and the coloring is a rich buff tint—one of the points for which Mr. Hammond bred in particular. The skin, as will be seen from the illustration, is strongly marked by folds ("wrinkly") at both neck and rump—a peculiarity even more strongly marked in the next family (Paulars). The sheep are hardy, and the rams have been extensively used for grading up the mixed flocks of Texas, New Mexico and Arizona.

The Paulars.

Concerning the history of the Paular Merino family, and its present status, as compared with the other recognized strains, we have thought best to give—without comment—the views of the acknowledged leader among Paular breeders in America, Mr. Jno. P. Ray, Hemlock Lake, N. Y. We have decided upon this course for several reasons, chief among which stands the fact that Mr. Ray is known to be a careful breeder, and, although undoubtedly somewhat partisan in his views, a thorough student of all literature bearing upon the history of sheep.

Replying to our request, he writes as follows:

"Probably the most noted of all the Spanish flocks were the Paulars, Infantados, Escurials, Guadaloupes, Negrettis, Montarcos and Aquierres. We have no authentic history to show how marked and well defined were the differences that existed between these families; there is a general belief among sheep men that the Escurials were the finest fleeced of all the Spanish flocks; the Negrettis the wrinkliest, and the Paulars the hardiest, best formed and heaviest folded in the neck. * * * * Col. David Humphreys [see Atwoods] left no records behind to show from what flock or flocks he obtained his sheep; Consul Jarvis, who went to Spain soon after, made a great effort to learn this fact, but without success. Stephen Atwood, the distinguished Connecticut breeder, who lived near Col. Humphreys, wrote Gen. Otto F. Marshal, Wheeler, N. Y., in 1884, that Col. Humphreys' sheep were of the Paular breed. That Edwin Hammond, the great improver of Merino sheep (Atwoods), was of the same opinion, the following certificates witness:

"'MIDDLEBURY, VT., September 23, 1847.

"'This may certify that I have this day sold to D. P. Pond, of Cornwall, state aforesaid, six full-blood Merino ewes—four of them being of the age of one year, and one of them bearing the age of two years. Said sheep are of the Paular breed, a part of them being purchased by myself and R. P. Hall of Stephen Atwood, of Connecticut, and the other portions of said sheep were raised by me and are precisely the same in pedigree as those purchased of Mr. Atwood. As I bred them pure from said Atwood sheep, I will here insert a certificate which I obtained of Mr. Atwood and reads as follows:

" 'WOODBURY, Litchfield County, Conn., January 27, 1844.

" 'This may certify that Edward Hammond and R. P. Hall, of Addison county, state of Vermont, have this day purchased of me three full-blood Merino bucks, and of me and others 27 full-blood Merino ewes, descendants from my flock of the Paular breed, which originated from the celebrated flock imported by Col. Humphreys, of Derby, New Haven county, state of Connecticut.

" '(Signed by Stephen Atwood.)

" 'EDWIN HAMMOND.'

("These certificates were published in the *Country Gentleman* of August 24, 1865; the original, given by Mr. Hammond, was carried to the *Country Gentleman* office by a deputation of Vermont breeders, of whom the venerable S. S. Rockwell, West Cornwall, was chairman.")

PURE-BRED PAULAR MERINO RAM.
Property of JNO. P. RAY, Hemlock Lake, N. Y.

"OTHER PAULAR BLOOD.—Consul Jarvis, hitherto mentioned, sent out from Spain 1,400 sheep of this breed. His flock, which he established at Wethersfield, Vermont, and bred in separate and distinct blood lines for several years and subsequently all mixed all together in breeding, was originally composed of about one-half Paulars, one-quarter Aquierres, and the other fourth Escurials, Negrettis and Montarcos.

"Andrew Cocks, Flushing, Long Island, purchased 800 head of sheep from the different cargoes sent in, and history and tradition sustain the fact that his purchases consisted of Paulars, which he selected with great care. He bred the flock pure down to 1823, when it was sold to Jehiel Beedle, on account of Leonard Beedle and Hon. Charles Rich, of Shoreham, Vermont. At the time of the sale to the Vermont parties, it is claimed that some of the imported sheep were still in the flock, and carried the original Spanish ear-marks. It would occupy too much space to reproduce the certificates given by Effingham Lawrence, John T. Rich, F. H. Jennison, Charles A. Hurlburt, Jasper Barnum and Levi Rockwood, all going to show that the Cocks flock were of the Paular family, and were certified to be such in the bill of sale given by Cocks to Beedle. We refer the reader to Moore's *Rural New-Yorker* of August 5, 1865, where the certificates may be found.

"The Rich branch of the Cocks sheep was bred for several years in the Cocks blood lines, then it was crossed to a ram bred by Consul Jarvis, and later still with the blood of Stephen Atwood's flock. From this flock was descended the celebrated flock of V. Rich, Richville, Vt., and the flocks of the late Tyler Stickney and Erastus Robinson, Shorebam, Vt., the blood of which is now widely dispersed throughout the country.

"About 1840, David and German Cutting purchased about 80 ewes and two rams that were bred by or descended from the flocks of David Buffum, Rense Potter, David I. Bailey and Geo. Irish, of Newport, Rhode Island. It is claimed that these sheep were descended from the importations of Paul Cuffe and Richard Crowincshield, and were without doubt consignments of Consul Jarvis. Messrs. Cutting bred these sheep to rams of Robinson and Rich and Atwood blood, and wherever this blood has found its way it has been crossed without reference to maintaining the original Rhode Island strains—hence but a small fraction of that blood remains in the Cutting blood-lines wherever found.

"In 1844, Jacob N. Blakeslee of Watertown, Conn., wrote a letter for publication in the *Cultivator*, published at Albany, N. Y., in which he claimed his sheep to be of Negretti, Montarco and Escurial blood.

"It may be assumed that our improved American Merino flocks are substantially, if not wholly, descended from the foregoing named blood-lines, with the Blakeslee blood, at most, in a very limited degree. For more than 40 years a class of our breeders have claimed a family of sheep descended purely from the flocks of the Atwoods of Connecticut, and have claimed a distinction in title and breeding. In view of this circumstance, and the fact that all other pure-bred Merinos partake largely of the Paular blood, they have been very generally alluded to as 'Improved Paulars,' 'Mixed Paulars,' and 'American Paulars,' which last name or title I hope will be generally adopted.

"The most successful breeders of these sheep have aimed to secure type and quality in their flocks, and have placed this above any special line of descent from importation, or from any one of the earlier flocks. In pursuing their course of breeding they have made use of the best specimens of the breed, and as a rule have avoided too close in-and-in breeding, and have achieved results unattained elsewhere when measured by high, sure weight of carcass, or weight of fleece—either gross or scoured. The aim has been to produce a well-formed and symmetrical animal, of constitutional vigor, carrying a dense, oily fleece of good quality throughout. Folds or wrinkles have been cultivated in a marked degree, and an amount of oil secured in the fleece that many have thought to be extravagant in the extreme; yet sheep of this class have made great improvement on the common wool-growing flocks—the wrinkles contributing toward density of fleece and covering, and the oil proving interchangeable with wool product.

"The accompanying Scale of Points will enable one to understand the points of excellence esteemed by breeders. A ram takes standard rank by making a score of 75 points, and a record at public shearing of 25 lbs. fleece and 110 lbs. carcass.

"SCALE OF POINTS FOR STOCK RAM.

"Bone 5
Physical development and general appearance 10
Head broad, nose wrinkly and face covered with soft, velvety coat 5
Neck short, broad, muscular, well set on shoulders 5

Forward 25

Forward	25
Shoulder massive as to depth and breadth	5
Back level, straight—Ribs, rotund	5
Hips broad and long	5
Fore legs straight, well set apart	3
Hind legs straight and set so as to give a perpendicular appearance to hind parts	5
Ear soft, thick and velvety	2
Color of nose, ears and hoofs pure white	5
Wrinkles on neck heavy, pendulous	5
Wrinkles across arm and point of shoulder on side and running well under	5
Tail, hip folds and flank	5
Density of fleece on neck	3
" " " " back	3
Density of fleece on side	3
" " " " hip and extending to flank	3
" " " " belly	3
Covering. { Crown of head or cap	3
Cheek	2
Fore leg	2
Arm-pits	2
Hind leg	2
Inside of flank	3
Connection between tag wool and belly	1
Fibre to indicate, as 'fine,' 'medium' and 'coarse.'	
Oil, as 'buff' and 'white.'	
Perfection	100

The illustration represents the ram "Prince Bismarck," a famous prize winner of the Paular family, that was never beaten in the show ring. In full fleece he weighed 200 lbs., and yielded a fleece, of one year's growth, of 35 lbs. 9½ ozs.

The Dickinsons.

Concerning the origin of this strain of Merino blood, we may say: Mr. Thos. Rotch purchased from Col. Humphreys (Derby, Connecticut) some of the latter's pure-bred Spanish Merinos, imported in 1802, and took them to Stark county, Ohio, about the year 1810. W. R. Dickinson—from whom the family takes its name—lived at Steubenville, Ohio, but had large landed possessions in Stark county, and soon secured the entire flock of pure-bred Merinos as his own. The sheep were bred with scrupulous care as to purity of blood, and under Mr. Dickinson's skillful management soon reached a high state of improvement. After the death of Mr. Dickinson (1831), Adam Heldenbrand became the owner of all the pure-bred Humphreys sheep which Mr. Dickinson had bred, and from him was secured the nucleus which formed the flock of James McDowell.

As we shall mention under the next topic an apparent conflict of statements between breeders of Dickinson and Black-Tops, it may be well to make the following extract from a published letter, written by

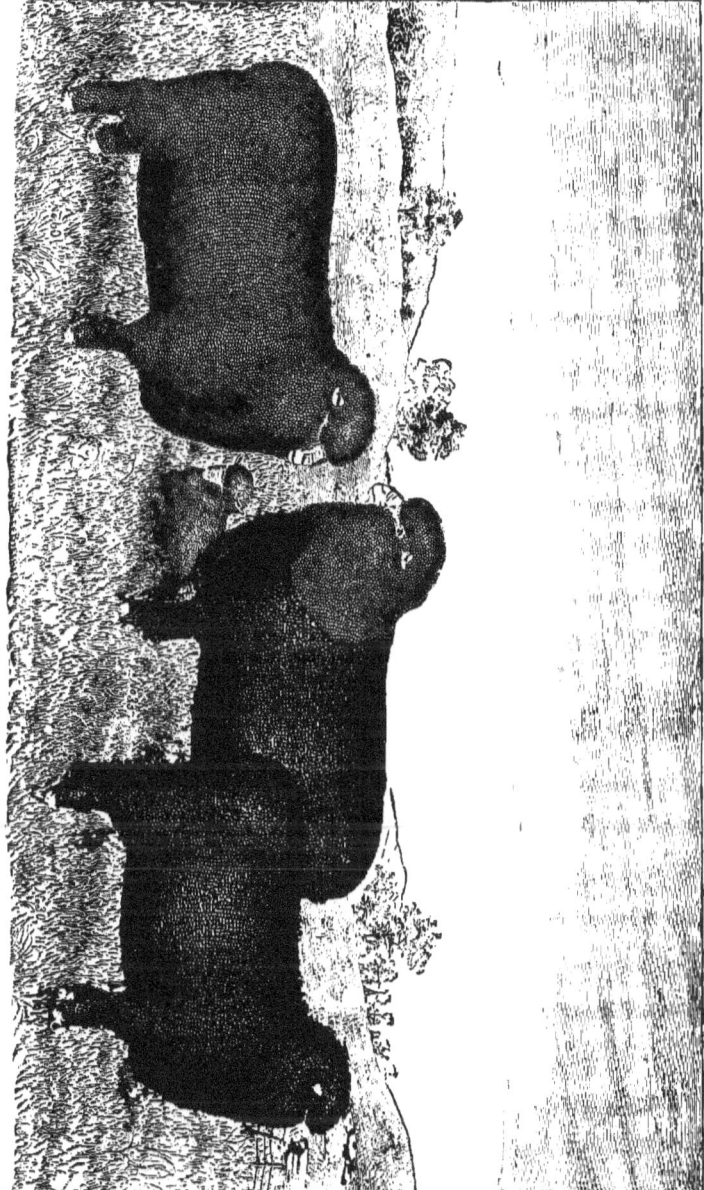

PURE-BRED DICKINSON MERINO EWES.
Property of H. G. McDowell, Canton, Ohio.

James McDowell in 1884, in which Dickinson breeders find their authority to deny a Humphreys origin for the Black-Top sheep; the last statement is the one refered to:

"W. R. Dickinson, of Steubenville, Jefferson county, O., in the early part of this century, commenced the breeding of a small flock of pure Merino sheep that were imported from Spain in the year 1802 by Col. David Humphreys, of Derby, New Haven county, Connecticut. These he secured through the agency of Thomas Rotch, an eminent and enterprising citizen of Connecticut, who migrated from that state to Stark county, O., in the early part of this century, bringing with him the first large flock of Spanish Merinos into Ohio.

"These sheep were bought direct of Col. Humphreys, which was learned by my personal acquaintance with Mr. Dickinson, Thomas Rotch and his shepherd, John Hall, who brought the sheep from Connecticut to Ohio.

"The sheep which Mr. Dickinson secured were kept at Steubenville, O., for a few years, and were the origin of his entirely pure-bred Merinos, descended directly from sheep imported by Col. Humphreys from Spain in 1802.

"These were distinctly marked, and separately kept. Mr. Dickinson stated in the latter years of his life that he never sold any of the ewes descended from his own pure-bred flock, his sales being of ewes purchased throughout the country—a grade of well-bred Merino flocks or those descended therefrom, in which he dealt extensively."

Dickinson Merinos, eligible to entry in the Dickinson Merino Sheep Record, must trace their descent to the standard-bred flock of James McDowell, Canton, Stark county, Ohio (without admixture of impure blood), which flock, as we have already mentioned, was directly descended from the Humphreys importation of 1802, through the famous flock of W. R. Dickinson.

The following, adopted by the Association, may be accepted as a standard

DESCRIPTION.

"Body deep, round, wide and long, showing mutton capacity, good feeding and thriving qualities, heavy, thick flesh, straight under and top lines, well proportioned, filling every part of its skin when fully matured. Skin thick, soft, not raised in corrugations, pink red. Head small, carried high. Quiet, placid eye. Nose white, not mottled, covered with fine, soft white hair, wide and slightly arched. Ears, short, thick, covered with fine, glossy hair. Horns small, neatly curved, light yellow color; better without any horns. Neck short, arched in under and on top, the base very strong. Shoulders, wide, deep, rounded, breast bone projecting forward of front limb. Back straight, wide, ribs extending out horizontally from spinal column, rounding in line with shoulders, extending close back to hips. Loins strong, wide. Hips wide, long. Thighs wide, thick flesh extending close down to hock joints. Limbs short, bone heavy, joints smooth and flat, the contour of, to show perpendicular lines from elbow and stifle joints to center of hoofs, and from base of tail to center of a straight line drawn horizontally from caps of hock joints, when standing erect on limbs. Hoofs deep, thin, white; texture tough and elastic. Fleece smooth, even, dense, soft to the touch. Staple three to five inches, fibres glossy, crimped. Quality XX., XXX. or above, fine. Quantity, rams 15 to 25 lbs, ewes 10 to 15 lbs. unwashed wool, covering entire body with even length and grade, except parts injuring thrift and comfort of sheep, entirely free from gum and hair. Oil very fluid, white or nearly so, enough to preserve the wool and rising to outer ends of fibres. Size of full grown rams 200 lbs., and ewes 150 lbs. Internal organs strong. Mature early, $2\frac{1}{2}$ years."

The following Scale of Points—also adopted by the Association—should be used in connection with the above description:

Skin	4	Forward	49
Head	4	Hoofs	4
Nose	3	Smoothness of fleece	6
Ears	3	Staple	4
Horns	3	Quality of fleece	6
Neck	4	Quantity of fleece	6
Shoulders	5	Covering	8
Back	8	Oil	5
Loins	3	Size of animal	5
Hips	3	Internal organs	4
Thighs	4	Maturity	3
Legs	5		
Forward	49	Perfection	100

Dickinson Merinos are now favorably known in many parts of the United States. The Record Association was organized in May, 1884. Mr. H. G. McDowell, son of James McDowell, is the present active and efficient secretary.

The Black-Tops.

This family, if the claims of its breeders are correct, furnishes a good example of change wrought by slow, steady purpose in one direction—the Black-Top Merinos being placed before the public as lineal descendants of the Dickinsons—just described—and through them of the original Humphreys importation in 1802. Referring to preceding topic, will be found the Dickinson breeders' claim that W. R. Dickinson never sold any of his Humphreys sheep. If this can be proved, it will leave the Black-Tops with a broken link in their chain of genealogy. We do not undertake to decide the case, but give both statements, and invite the reader to draw his own conclusions, or investigate further on his own responsibility.

Concerning the change, or, as the breeders of Black-Tops have it—improvement in these sheep of Dickinson descent, we may say: In 1821 Wm. Berry, of Washington county, Pa., purchased a choice ram and a number of ewes from W. R. Dickinson's flock; and, according to Vol. I. of the Black-Top Register, Mr. Berry was assured and satisfied that these sheep were directly descended from the original Humphreys importation made in 1802. Without discussing this question further, it is certain that Mr. Berry strictly carried out his purpose to breed within the flock and make all improvement by selection and care. In 1847 he rented his farm and sold his flock to his two sons—William and Matthew—himself moving to Canonsburg, Pa., where he remained until his death, Dec. 26th, 1866. In the experience of both Mr. Berry and his sons, it was noticed that the sheep with darkest "tops" were the largest and made the best records in shearing. They also found that the darker sheep were more hardy, and better able to endure the rough winter weather of that latitude than were those of lighter cast. It is believed that Mr. Berry was the first to apply the name "Black-Tops," and that he did so to distinguish them from the light colored, delicate Saxon Merinos, which for a time were bred in the vicinity.

By permission of the secretary, W. G. Berry, of Houstonville, Pa., we make the following authoritative extracts from Vol. I. of the Black-Top Spanish Merino Sheep Register:

DESCRIPTION AND CHARACTERISTICS.

"Constitution indicated by physical development; deep and large in the breast and through the heart; broad back; very heavy, square quarters; skin of fine texture and pinkish in color; expansive nostril; brilliant eye; healthful countenance, and good feeders.

"In good condition, with fleece of five months' growth, full grown rams should weigh not lesss than 175 pounds, and ewes not less than 125 pounds.

"Head carried well up; standing squarely on feet and legs; well rounded body, showing in all points symmetry of form; body throughout heavy boned, well proportioned in length; smooth joints, ribs starting horizontally from the back bone, and well around to breast bone; breast bone wide, strong and prominent in front; strong, straight, and heavy back bone; heavy, muscular quarters; shoulders broad and flat; muscles firm and heavy, and body entirely free from folds. There may be a slight throatiness, and a small dewlap—smaller on the ewes than on the rams.

"The head should be wide, with clear, bright eyes and prominent ears. Ewes should give no appearance of horns, while upon the rams the horns should be well developed, clear in color, and symmetrically curved.

"Neck very heavy, especially with the rams, deepening towards the shoulder. Legs medium in length, set well apart, with well-shaped, medium-sized feet. The body and legs to the knees covered with medium or fine wool, extending well forward between the eyes. Fleece should be compact, but should open freely—showing a length (at twelve months growth) of not less than three inches, and the oil (yolk) must be white, flowing freely from skin to surface, and form on the exterior a uniform dark coating."

The following standard Scale of Points should be used in connection with the above:

"Constitution	15	Forward,	64
Size	12	Covering	8
General appearance	3	Quality of fleece	7
Body	15	Density of fleece	7
Head	5	Length of staple	8
Neck	4	Oil	6
Legs and feet	10		
Forward	64	Perfection	100"

The Delaines.

The origin of this family is of recent date, and has grown out of a continued and steady demand for what is known as *Delaine* wools. Just what constitutes Delaine wool is rather hard to define, but the process of manufacture requires combing instead of carding—the fibers being laid

MERINOS. 251

PURE-BRED BLACK-TOP MERINO EWES.
Bred and owned by Jno. M. Berry, Eighty-Four, Pa.

parallel with each other, and spun at full length in the yarn. To Mr. E. R. Mudge, of Boston, Mass.—now deceased—belongs most of the credit for founding this branch of textile industry, and to the breeders who aimed to supply the demand thus created we turn to find the origin of the Delaine Merino Sheep. It is claimed that no deep in-breeding has been practiced, and that the sheep are, therefore, free from all taint of weakness so frequently traced to incestuous breeding. On the other hand it is stated, that nothing but the purest Merino blood has ever been introduced, and to explain the seeming contradiction, we may say in brief, that the Delaine Merino has been produced by a careful system of crossing the pure Spanish with the American Black-Top Merino. The original Spanish foundation for the Delaines was largely made up of sheep descended from an importation made in 1820, by Richard W. Meade—at that time Minister to Spain. These sheep were first stationed near Philadelphia, but were afterwards sent to Washington county, Pa., where their choicest descendants have since been bred.

DESCRIPTION AND CHARACTERISTICS.

The fleece presents a uniformly smooth surface, dark on the outer end of wool, but a "black-top"—caused by excess or sticky character of yolk, and consequent clogging up with dirt to form an outer crust—is considered a great objection. The natural oil or yolk should be freely liquid, not gummy, showing an even white color and rising to the top of the dense, fine covering. The staple (fiber) is of good length, averaging from two and a-half to three inches in wool of one year's growth, covering the body and legs to the knees. The animal is of good size, mature rams weighing about 150 pounds, and ewes about 100 pounds—with a vigorous constitution and a carcass for mutton which, in a fine wool sheep, is surprising. To illustrate their mutton capacity, we clip the following from the issue of April, 1884, *National Stockman*, published at East Liberty, Pa.:

"Among the sheep sold here this week, there was a car-load of fine wool wethers, something under three years old, averaging 114½ pounds. They were of the Delaine Merino family, were raised and fed by James McClelland, of Canonsburg, Pa., and brought seven cents per pound, a price which shows that they found high favor among the butchers."

The following Scale of Points, condensed from the *National Delaine Merino Register*, has been adopted by the association, and is now in use by its members:

Constitution	10	Forward	27
Heavy round heart	6	Back	8
Neck	6	Ribs	5
Dewlap	5	Legs	6
Forward	27	Forward	46

MERINOS. 253

PURE-BRED DELAINE MERINOS.
Bred by J. C. McNary, Houstonville, Pa.

Forward	46	Forward	80
Bone	8	Darkish cast on top	5
Foot	10	Opening up white	5
Length of staple	8	Good flow of white oil	5
Density of fleece	8	Good crimp in staple	5
Forward	80	Perfection	100

The Delaines, as well as the Black-Tops and Dickinsons (see illustrations), are smooth, no folds, only a fullness at the throat being permitted. Their breeders make no pretense of "line-pure" descent from a single sheep or a single flock, but on the contrary, are rather proud of having secured in combination the blood of the best (in their judgment) flocks in America and Spain.

Chapter XLIX.

HORNED DORSETS.

As far back as we have any record this breed of sheep has existed in the shire of Dorset, England. From the fact that the old Dorset resembled the old Spanish Merino, it has been thought that the former may have descended from the latter. The resemblance, however, was only in form and external appearance—the properties of the two breeds being entirely different. In this connection we quote Prof. Low (1842):

"While the Merinos are bad nurses, the Dorsets are the most productive of milk of any of our races of sheep. In the broad loins of this race we have the same external character which, in the case of the cow, indicates the faculty of yielding abundant milk. The remarkable fecundity of these sheep has given rise to the supposition that they are derived from some warmer country where the females bring forth twice in the year. We have, however no evidence of this fact, and may accordingly believe that the property is one which is due to situation, although the peculiar circumstances, whether of climate or food, which gave rise to it may escape our observation."

The breed is not well known in America, but there are several breeders of considerable prominence, both in the United States and Canada; and during the last five or six years they have pushed forward the Dorset with great success. We do not know of any Dorsets in the South, but see no reason why they would not prove of value, especially in the higher portions of the Texas "Panhandle" region.

DESCRIPTION AND CHARACTERISTICS.

Color of face and legs white; head fine, rather long, and supplied with horns in both male and female; nose and lips black. The shoulders are low but broad; chest deep, with low brisket; back straight, and loins unusually broad and strong. The bone is light, and the legs rather long, but the general make-up indicates good breeding and hardiness. In size they are above medium—fat two-year-old wethers reaching as high as 230 to 250 lbs., and mature breeding rams weighing 175 to 200 lbs. The fleece is short, of above medium fineness, and high-class flocks yield an average clip of six to eight pounds. The peculiar characteristics which distinguish the Dorsets from all other sheep are their early and prolific breeding, rapidity of fattening and early maturity. They surpass all other breeds in general fecundity—as a rule breeding twice a year, and freqently bearing twins and triplets. For the production of early market lambs no sheep can rival them, unless it be the cross-bred produce of Southdown rams on Dorset ewes, which have been most popular with English breeders.

The illustration represents a group from Mr. Fuller's excellent flock, Hamilton, Ontario, Canada.

HORNED DORSETS.
Property of Valancy E. Fuller, Hamilton, Ontario, Canada

Chapter L.

CHEVIOTS.

The Cheviot breed of sheep had its origin in the Cheviot Hills or mountains, situated in the north of England and extending into Scotland. The hills are mostly conical, and are separated by very narrow valleys. On one side of the range of mountains lies the "heather" country, the home of the old Black-Faced Heath Breed—and on the other is a rich, cultivated tract.

This district, according to Low, "has produced from time immemorial a race of sheep entirely distinct in its characters from the wild heath breed of the elevated moors adjoining."

There is a fanciful sort of tradition to the effect that at the time of the attempted invasion by the Spanish Armada (1588), and the consequent wreck of the formidable fleet upon the stormy British coast, some of the sheep with which the ships were provided swam ashore and escaped to the Cheviot Hills, where they have since bred and multiplied.

Cheviot sheep have gradually extended over the entire mountainous portion of Scotland; and during the past century have been greatly improved by a class of breeders second to none in the world.

They were imported to America about 1840, but have been in only a few localities—mainly in the state of New York—and are still comparatively unknown.

We are not aware that any Cheviot sheep can be found in the Gulf States at present writing; nor is it probable that they will ever be extensively introduced.

DESCRIPTION AND CHARACTERISTICS.

Color of face and legs white—rarely tinted or speckled; the head is of good size, strictly hornless; face broad, and especially full at forehead; ears wide apart and of good size; eyes prominent and lively—all combining to make up a peculiarly intelligent, strong-featured expression, well suited to an independent mountain breed. The shoulders are rather light, as in all mountain breeds of sheep; but the body is long, deep, and remarkably well filled at the loin and quarters. The fleece is short and of medium fineness, and makes up the great bulk of the genuine Scotch tweeds and Cheviot cloths.

As compared with other breeds in respect to fleece they do not show to advantage, since their wool is too coarse for carding and too

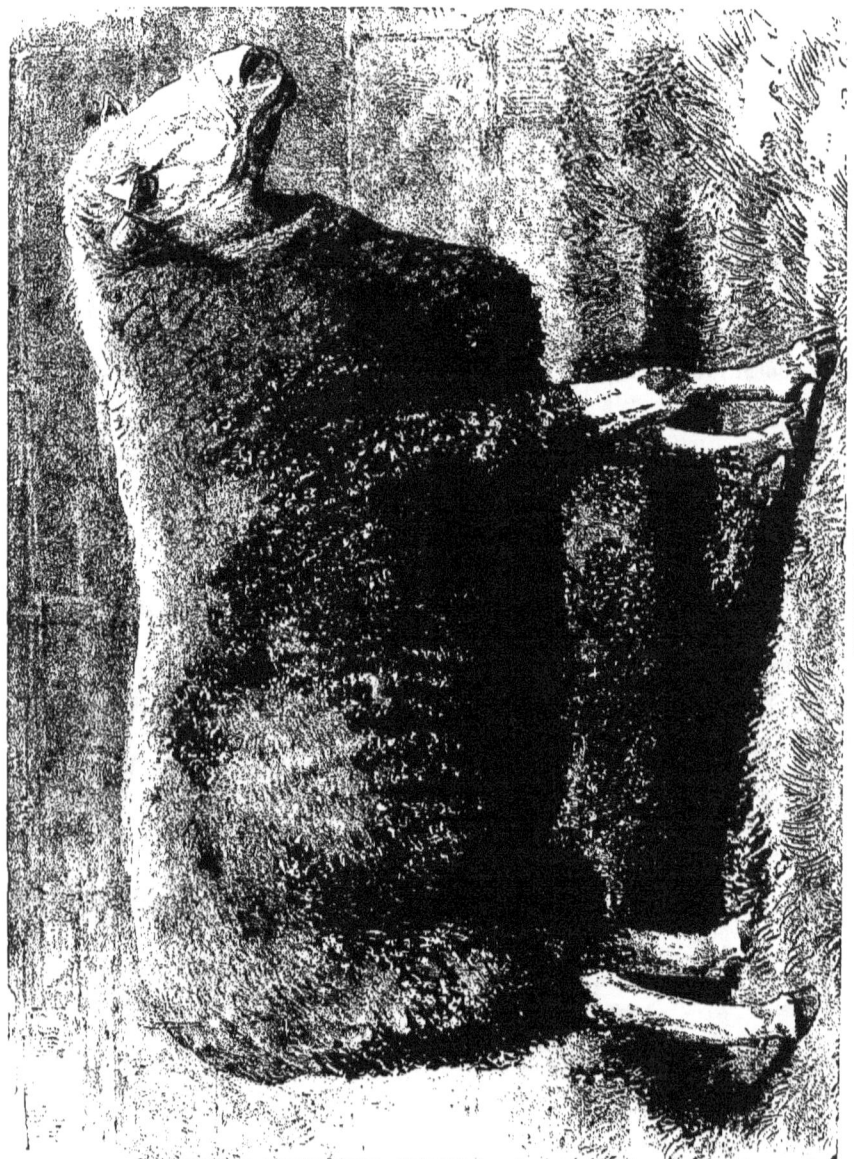

CHEVIOT RAM.

short for combing; and high-class flocks yield an annual clip of not over three to five pounds per head.

In size the Cheviots rank as medium; two-year-old wethers can be made to weigh 180 to 200 lbs., and breeding rams at maturity should scale about 175 lbs. They fatten quickly on root-crops, after pasture, without grain. The ewes are good mothers, although not so prolific as some other breeds, and the lambs very hardy.

For western and northern ranges, especially those in the mountainous regions of Montana, Idaho and Wyoming, the Cheviot should prove an excellent breed.

The pure bloods are, perhaps, not so valuable, but they furnish an admirable basis for crossing with Cotswold and Leicester rams, increasing thereby length of staple and size of carcass, while retaining the hardy mountain instincts of the Cheviot race.

Chapter LI.

SOUTHDOWNS.

The Southdown heads the list of middle-wool mutton sheep; both from its acknowledged superiority, and from the fact that nearly, if not quite all, of the other "Downs" are indebted to it for much of their present excellence. The breed takes its name from the slopes of the Chalk Hills of England, called "Downs."

Referring to this place of their origin, Professor Low (1842) says:

"The Scotch Downs of Sussex consist of a range of low chalky hills, are five or six miles in breadth, stretching along the coast upwards of sixty miles, and passing into the chalky lands of Hants on the west. In contact with this range of hills is a tract of low cultivated ground, which is usually connected with the Down farms, although many of the latter have no vale or flat land attached. The herbage of these hills is short, but well adapted for the keeping of sheep, of which vast numbers have, in every known period, occupied the pastures. Whilst the dryness of the air, the moderate elevation of the land, and consequent mildness of the climate, are all eminently favorable to the rearing of a race of Downs or mountain sheep, the contact of the cultivated country affords the means of supplying artificial food. It is this combination of favorable circumstances which has rendered these calcareous hills capable of supporting a greater number of sheep than perhaps any tract of similar fertility in the country, and has afforded the means to the breeders of applying the resources of artificial feeding to their improvement.

"The original breed of the Sussex Downs was not superior to that of many other districts of the chalk formation; but the means of supplying the animal with artificial food, which the geographical situation of this long and narrow chain of hills in contact with the richer country afforded, aided the breeder in applying to the improvement of the race a system of breeding and feeding which has rendered the Southdown breed the most esteemed in the countries suited to it, of all the short-wooled sheep of England."

From this it will be seen that the Southdown was a natural outgrowth of circumstances, and really "native" to the locality from which it takes its name.

Improvement of the breed began about 1775-80, but received its greatest impulse about the beginning of the present century, since which time it has been constantly active and progressive.

To Mr. John Ellman, of the Glynde farm, near Lewis, in Sussexshire, is universally accorded first place among the improvers of Southdowns.

He began about 1780, and devoted the remainder of his life—some 52 years—to careful, unselfish work in advancing his favorite breed of sheep.

While Mr. Bakewell was fully his equal in point of skill as a

SOUTHDOWNS.

breeder, perhaps his superior, he was inclined to keep his methods closely concealed, incurring thereby a rather general disfavor. Mr. Ellman, on the other hand, freely communicated the results of his experiments, and showed himself to be entirely free from all illiberal prejudice. His aim was to produce a sheep which should combine the points most desirable, in his judgment, for the locality in which he lived; and with him it was—first, health and constitution; second, fixedness of type. He, therefore, did not in-breed so closely as did Bakewell, but purchased freely from his contemporaries in order to infuse fresh blood and retain the vigor of his flock.

Since Mr. Ellman's death (1832), there have been many careful breeders to carry forward the work, and keep up the popularity and excellence of the Southdown breed, among them Mr. Jonas Webb, of Suffolk, who may be called his immediate successor.

The Southdown, next to the Merino, is the most widely known of all the breeds of sheep at present in the United States; and in the Western and Middle States finds its greatest popularity.

In the South the Merino has the preference, but many Southdowns are being shipped in for use in grading up on flocks of Merino basis, and are reported to acclimate readily and produce a desirable grade.

DESCRIPTION AND CHARACTERISTICS.

Color of face and legs a uniform tint of brown, gray or mouse (formerly speckled faces were admitted, but later breeders aim to exclude all except the colors mentioned); head medium in size, hornless, forehead and cheeks well covered with wool; ears rather small, wide apart and lively; eyes bright and full; neck short, fine at head, but well set on to broad, full shoulders. The chest is wide and deep; back and loin broad; ribs well arched; hips wide and close to floating ribs; thigh fleshed low down, and legs fine-boned, short, and wooled to knee and hock. The belly is straight and well covered with wool; general appearance smooth—with no trace of coarseness—spirited and attractive.

The fleece is white, compact, moderately long and close, and carrying some yolk. They are fair, not heavy, shearers—running some four to six or seven pounds per fleece in high-class flocks; but their mutton is unexcelled, and has always commanded the top of the English market.

The ewes are prolific, make excellent mothers, and their lambs are uniformly hardy and vigorous.

In size they are above medium—two-year-old fat wethers weighing as high as 200 to 225 lbs., and mature breeding rams about 170 to 190 lbs.

Where a sheep is wanted to produce mutton as a prime object, with wool as a secondary, but if possible paying accompaniment, we know of no breed which more completely fills the requirements than this.

The following Scale of Points—to be used with description—for judging at fairs, is clipped from the American Southdown Record, Mr. S. E. Prather, of Springfield, Ill., secretary:

Head	5	Forward	47
Lips	1	Hips	6
Ears	2	Thighs	6
Eyes	3	Legs	3
Face	3	Fore Legs	2
Neck	4	Hind Legs	2
Shoulders	5	Belly	5
Breast	5	Fleece	12
Back and Loin	7	Form	9
Ribs	6	General appearance	8
Rump	6		
Forward	47	Perfection	100

Four volumes of the Record have been published, comprising 5,000 entries, and the secretary writes under date December 22, 1892:

"* * Entries for Volume V. are coming in more rapidly than ever before * *."

The illustration of a group from Mr. Harvey's flock fairly represents the breed in all particulars.

Chapter LII.

SHROPSHIRES.

This breed—long and favorably known in England—is, in America, comparatively new. The first importation of any note was made in 1855, Virginia claiming the honor, but it is only within the last eight or ten years that Shropshire sheep have attracted any marked attention from breeders on this side of the Atlantic.

The origin of the breed may be traced almost directly to the polled sheep of Cannock Heath, and the old black, or spotted-faced breed of Morfe Common. In Volume XVI., Journal of the Royal Agricultural Society, there is given this fragment of a report from the Bristol Wool Society (1792) regarding the breed last referred to:

"On Morfe Common, near Bridgnorth, there are about 10,000 sheep kept during the summer months, which produce wool of a superior quality They are considered a native breed, are black-faced or brown, or spotted-faced horned sheep, little subject to either rot or scab."

The sheep of Cannock Heath were hornless, with grayish faces and legs, and are described by Youatt as attaining great weight. From these two hardy native breeds the Shropshire has been gradually improved—whether within itself or by further out-crossing with other breeds is difficult to determine—until it stands at least the acknowledged rival of any of our modern middle-wool breeds.

From Volume I. of the American Shropshire Record we quote:

"In England, the turning point with Shropshire sheep was in the Royal Show Yard at Gloucester, in 1853, when their superiority was recognized.* * * In the year 1859, the breed was awarded a place on the prize sheet of the Royal Agricultural Society, as a recognized and distinct breed, at which time 192 Shropshires were exhibited with marked success."

In America they have not hidden their light under a bushel by any means. In 1884, at the Chicago Fat Stock Show,

"A Shropshire took first prize in the class between two and three years old—competing with Hampshires and Oxfords ; sweepstakes for best sheep any breed between two and three years ; grand sweepstakes, as best sheep any age and any breed ; heaviest fat sheep and best dressed carcass."—*From an address by J. L. Stone, before the Pennsylvania Board of Agriculture, June 17, 1886.*

DESCRIPTION.

The face is dark grayish or brown, wool coming well down to the eyes, and with no trace of horns. The legs are darker than face—almost black; head longer than in the Southdown and ears larger, while the

SHROPSHIRES.
Property of John R. Campbell, Jr., Woodville, Ontario, Canada.

wool is close set, finer and longer in staple. In addition to this brief outline, we give place to the complete description of a typical animal, adopted in connection with Scale of Points by the American Shropshire Association (Mortimer Levering of Lafayette, Ind., secretary), and appearing in Volume I. of the American Shropshire Record:

"Constitution and quality, indicated by form of body; deep and large in breast and through the heart; back wide, straight, and well covered with lean meat or muscle; wide and full in the thigh; deep in flank; skin thick but soft and of a pink color; prominent, brilliant eyes and healthful countenance.

"In fair condition when fully matured, rams should weigh not less than 225 pounds and ewes not less than 175 pounds.

"General appearance and character: Good carriage; head well up; elastic movement, showing great symmetry of form and uniformity of character throughout.

"Body well proportioned, medium bones, great scale and length, well finished hind quarters, thick back and loins, twist deep and full, standing with legs well placed outside, breast wide and extending well forward.

"Head short and broad; wide between ears and between eyes; short from top of head to tip of nose; ears short, of medium size; eyes expressive; head should be well covered with wool to a point even with the eyes, without any appearance of horns; color of face, dark brown.

"Neck—Medium length, good bone and muscular development, and especially with he rams, heavier toward the shoulders, well set high up, and rising from that point to th back of the head.

"Legs—Broad, short, straight, well set apart, well shaped, color dark brown, and well wooled to the knees.

"Body, head, belly and legs to knees well covered with fleece of even length and quality; scrotum of rams well covered with wool.

"Wool medium, such as known in our markets as 'medium delaine' and 'half combing wool,' strong, fine, lustrous fiber, without tendency to mat or felt together, and at one year's growth not less than three and one-half inches in length."

Scale of Points for Shropshires, to be used in connection with above description:

Constitution	25	Forward	70
Size	10	Neck	5
General appearance	10	Legs and Feet	10
Body	10	Fleece	10
Head	15	Quality of Wool	5
Forward	70	Perfection	100

The association has already published eight volumes of the Record, comprising a total of 52,000 individual animals, and representing 1,050 owners and active members of the association.

The Shopshires are especially fitted, by conditions under which they have been reared, for moist or even wet localities. That they will do remarkably well on the dry range of the Southwest we are constrained to doubt, but Shropshire rams for use in grading up the middle wools already on the range are giving satisfaction. What more could be asked?

Chapter LIII.

HAMPSHIRES.

This breed originated in the Chalks of Hampshire, England, from which locality it takes its name. It is supposed to be the result of mixing the blood of the old Wiltshire and native, or old Hampshire sheep, with the Southdown. It is stated, also, that the Cotswold, and possibly the Leicester, may have had some place in the make-up of the modern Hampshire breed, but this is disputed by those who may be called good authority. In this connection we give place to the following interesting communication from that veteran breeder and importer of Hampshires, now president of the Hampshire Association, Mr. James Wood, Mount Kisco, N. Y.:

"The statements made by a number of writers on Hampshires, that they carry Cotswold and perhaps Leicester blood, are all based upon a supposition of Spooner in a paper on 'Cross Breeding,' published in the Journal of the Royal Agricultural Society

HAMPSHIRE RAM, CYCLONE.
Imported by JAMES WOOD, Mt. Kisco, New York.

in 1859, which I have. In the main, it is an admirable paper. He does not say it is a fact, or that there is sufficient evidence to prove it, but he supposes there may have been an infusion of such blood.

"All independent authorities are against it. Youatt is the oldest author who mentions Hampshires, and he states that they had their origin in the original Wiltshire and Berkshire sheep crossed with the Southdown. Prof. Wilson—a very high authority—states that no other blood was used. John Coleman, professor in the Royal Agricultural College, Cirencester, and late editor of *The Field*, denies the Cotswold theory. Squarey, in Coleman's 'Sheep of Great Britain,' says only the old Chalk breeds and

Southdowns were used. Armitage, in 'The Sheep,' makes no mention of Cotswold blood or Leicester. Scott, in 'The Practice of Sheep Farming'—the last English book on sheep - makes no mention of such blood. Alexander Macdonald, in the *Mark Lane Express* of May 7, 1888, gives their origin 'from the crossing of Wilts and Hants sheep, embellished by an infusion of Southdown blood.'

"Every author who has not copied from Spooner is clear upon this point. I consider the matter to be of considerable importance, as upon the fact of the local origin of the breed rests the explanation of the remarkable prepotency of the Hampshire, when used in cross-breeding. Spooner states that they have extraordinary power in cross-breeding, and this is illustrated by the fact that the prizes for cross-bred sheep at the great English shows almost always go to sheep with a Hampshire parentage."

HAMPSHIRE RAM, BARON.
One year old; Imported by JAMES WOOD, Mt. Kisco, N. Y.

Mr. Wood further states that the average weight of breeding rams in his own flock, and others with which he is familiar, might be safely placed at 250 to 275 lbs., and that his breeding ewes shear an average clip of seven to eight pounds.

The Hampshire is the largest of the Downs families proper, and has the Downs characteristics—dark face and legs, and no horns.

Although the breed has been known since near the beginning of the present century, it has been only of late years that it has taken a prominent place in public favor. Introduction into the United States occurred some time previous to the Civil War, and the largest and finest flocks were found in the South. During the war, however (1860-65), the great bulk of the Hampshire Down flocks in the South were destroyed, and the breed practically exterminated in this section. Within the past decade they have been quite extensively imported to various parts of the South and Southwest, and are said to surpass their progenitors—the Southdowns—in the readiness with which they acclimate and adapt themselves to our peculiar conditions.

DESCRIPTION AND CHARACTERISTICS.

Color of face and legs dark brown, almost black; the ears are of good size, and more pointed than those of the Southdown; the head

HAMPSHIRE EWES.
Imported by JAMES WOOD, Mt. Kisco, N. Y. (*By courtesy of* "*Country Gentleman,*" *Albany, N. Y.*)

is large and the nose decidedly Roman; the back is straight, and broader than in either the Southdown or Shropshire. As already noted, it is the largest of the Downs families proper, about equaling the Oxfordshire (which latter, although classed as a Down, should be placed in a class intermediate between Downs and Longwools), fat two-year-old wethers weighing as high as 275 to 300 pounds, and mature breeding rams scaling an average say between 200 and 225 pounds. Although heavier than Shropshires, they are hardly so symmetrical, being longer in the legs and somewhat lighter underneath, but the back at the loin is remarkably padded with an excellent quality of mutton. The fleece is longer than that of the Southdown, and of a quality somewhat coarser; but as a rule, considering the greater size of the breed, the Hampshire Downs do not shear so heavy a fleece; an average clip for high-class flocks might be placed at five to seven pounds.

The prominent characteristic of the Hampshire breed lies in the remarkable precocity of the lambs, which frequently increase from 15 or 16 pounds at birth to 140 or 150 pounds at seven or eight months; and their excellence in this respect has led to the use of Hampshire rams in producing early lambs for city market.

The Hampshire Down Breeders' Association of America—John I. Gordon, secretary, Mercer, Pa.—has adopted the following Scale of Points:

```
Head—size and shape, 5; ears and eyes, 2; color, 5; legs and feet, 3 . . . . . . . 15
Neck shoulders and breast—neck, 5; shoulders, 10; chest and breast, 15 . . . . 30
Body—back and loin, 15; ribs, 5 . . . . . . . . . . . . . . . . . . . . . . . 20
Quarters—length, 10; width, 10; twist, 5 . . . . . . . . . . . . . . . . . . 25
Wool—forehead and cheeks, 2; belly, well covered, 3; quality, 5 . . . . . . . . 10
                                                                              ___
            Perfection . . . . . . . . . . . . . . . . . . . . . . . . . . 100
```

Secretary Gordon writes that "Vol. II. Flock Record will be published in January, 1893, and will contain the pedigrees of something over 1,200 animals."

Chapter LIV.

OXFORDSHIRES.

The Oxfords should stand between the "Downs" and "Longwools" in their classification, the tendency being more toward the latter. They originated about 1830, by crossing the improved Cotswold with the Hampshire. Probably the Southdown was used in the mixture, to some small extent, but the two breeds first mentioned may be looked upon as the parent stock. The wool is more marked by the Cotswold's combing quality, while the dark faces and legs show unmistakable evidence of the Hampshire blood.

The Oxfordshire breed first came into public notice about 1850 to 1860, during which time the best flocks were found in the shire of Oxford. Since that date, their excellent qualities have given them a foothold in almost every county of England. In America, they are not so widely known as some other breeds, but a Register has been established, and the breed has been pushed forward rapidly. We understand, also, that a number of Oxfords have been brought to the Southwest, and that they are giving excellent satisfaction.

DESCRIPTION.

Color of face and legs dark brown, with a grayish tinge, inclining to drab: head medium to large, with a tuft of wool at the forehead, standing out more from the head and not so long as in the Cotswold; the forehead is very broad and full; ears set low and well back; eyes large, and muzzle finely pointed. The fleece is not so long as that of the Cotswold—being about five to seven inches—but is closer and finer, with much the same tendency to curl, and stands well out from the body.

The following Scale of Points has been adopted by the Oxford Down Record Association:

Head	8	Forward	37
Face	4	Breast	10
Nostrils	1	Fore Flank	5
Eyes	2	Back and Loin	12
Ears	4	Belly	3
Collar	6	Quarters	8
Shoulder	8	Hock	2
Fore Legs	4	Twist or junction	6
		Fleece	17
Forward	37		
		Perfection	100

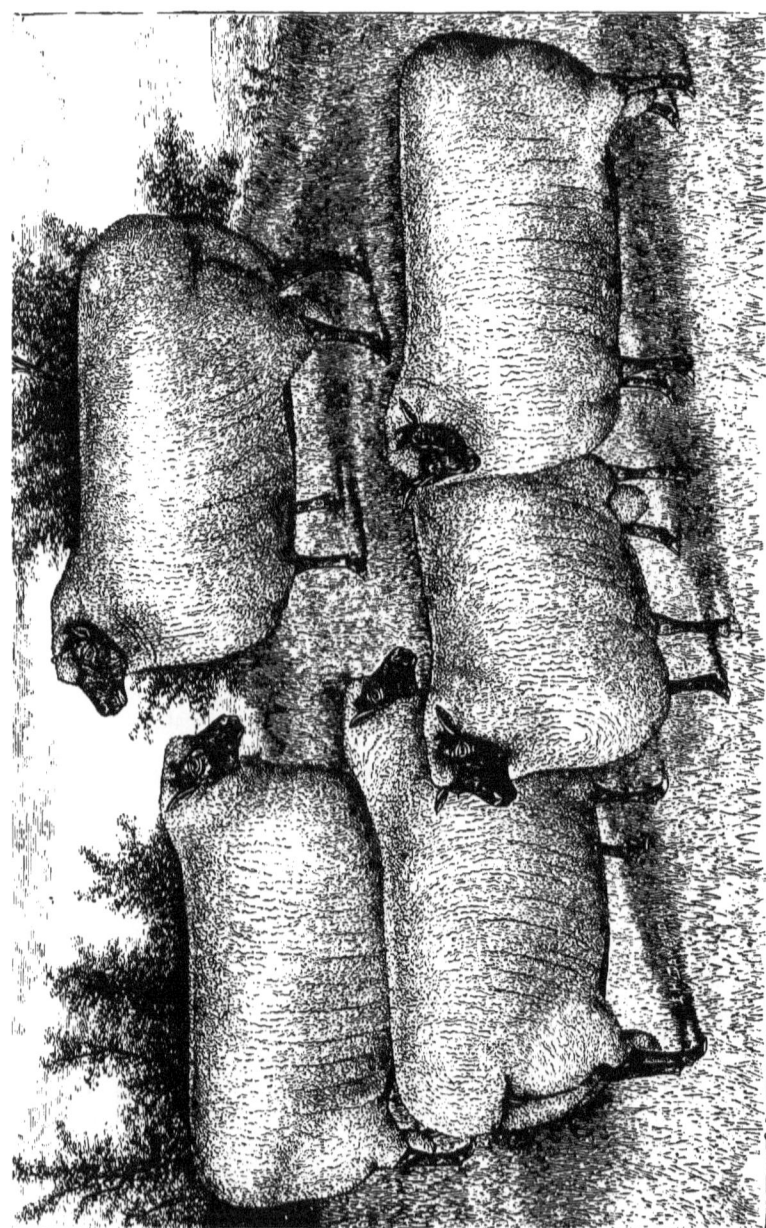

OXFORD RAM, FREELAND, 220, AND FOUR SONS.
Owned by W. A. Shafor, Middletown, Ohio.

The Oxfordshire is a well made, round bodied, short legged, mutton and wool combined sheep. In size it about equals the Hampshire; an average weight for mature breeding rams might be placed between 200 and 225 pounds, while two-year-old fat wethers are frequently found weighing upwards of 275 to 300 pounds. The Oxford is said to stand herding upon wet or spongy range better than any other breed of sheep, and from the fact that its original home at the base of the Cotswold Hills was just such a wet, springy locality, we are inclined to credit the statement.

We are pleased to present the excellent portrait from life of the ram Freeland, 220, and four of his sons, kindly furnished us by Mr. W. A. Shafor, of Middletown, Ohio, a breeder of Oxfords, and secretary of the American Oxford Down Record, to whom we are indebted for many favors. Freeland was bred by Mr. Milton Druse, of Fyfield, England, and at two years of age —when imported by T. S. Cooper, of Corpersburg, Pa.—weighed 425 pounds.

Chapter LV.

COTSWOLDS.

The Cotswold breed is very old and firmly fixed in its characteristics. It is said to have been introduced into England from Spain in the Twelfth Century; the statement is only a supposition, however, probably based on the fact that Spain possesses a breed of Longwools not unlike the old unimproved Cotswolds. Certain it is that in the Thirteenth Century Cotswold wool was known and valued in England, and found a place as such in wool quotations. In 1467, permission was granted as a royal favor by the King, Henry IV., to export some of these sheep to Spain, a fact which illustrates the high favor Cotswolds had obtained at that date.

Improvement of the breed was mainly effected after Bakewell's time, by using the Leicester as a cross; this gave a greater aptitude to fatten, smoothness, quality and appearance, without injuring the hardy constitution of the old Cotswold breed. In America the breed has become widely known, and is in general favor as a combined wool and mutton sheep.

Probably the first large importation was made about 1840, at which time some 70 or 80 head were brought over; since that date numerous flocks have been founded, and the original excellence of imported animals has been fully sustained by American breeders.

DESCRIPTION AND CHARACTERISTICS.

Color of face and legs white or light grayish; fleece (combing) eight to 10 inches long, pure white, and weighing from 10 to 16 pounds for an average clip. In size the Cotswold ranks among the large breeds, ranging from 250 to 275 pounds, and occasionally a specimen dressing over 300 pounds. The head is strong and large, with a somewhat "Roman" nose, no horns, and a characteristic forelock of long curling wool hanging over the forehead; the back is broad and flat, and the wool falls away, naturally parted, from the center; the legs are of medium length, with rather heavy bone, but clean and trim withal, and the feet are sound and said to be not subject to foot diseases. The Cotswolds are large, handsome, long-wooled sheep—prime for mutton and furnishing an excellent quality of combing wool. They have been extensively used in crosses, and have already figured in the origin of several well-known

COTSWOLD EWES.
Bred by T. L. Miller, Beecher, Ill.

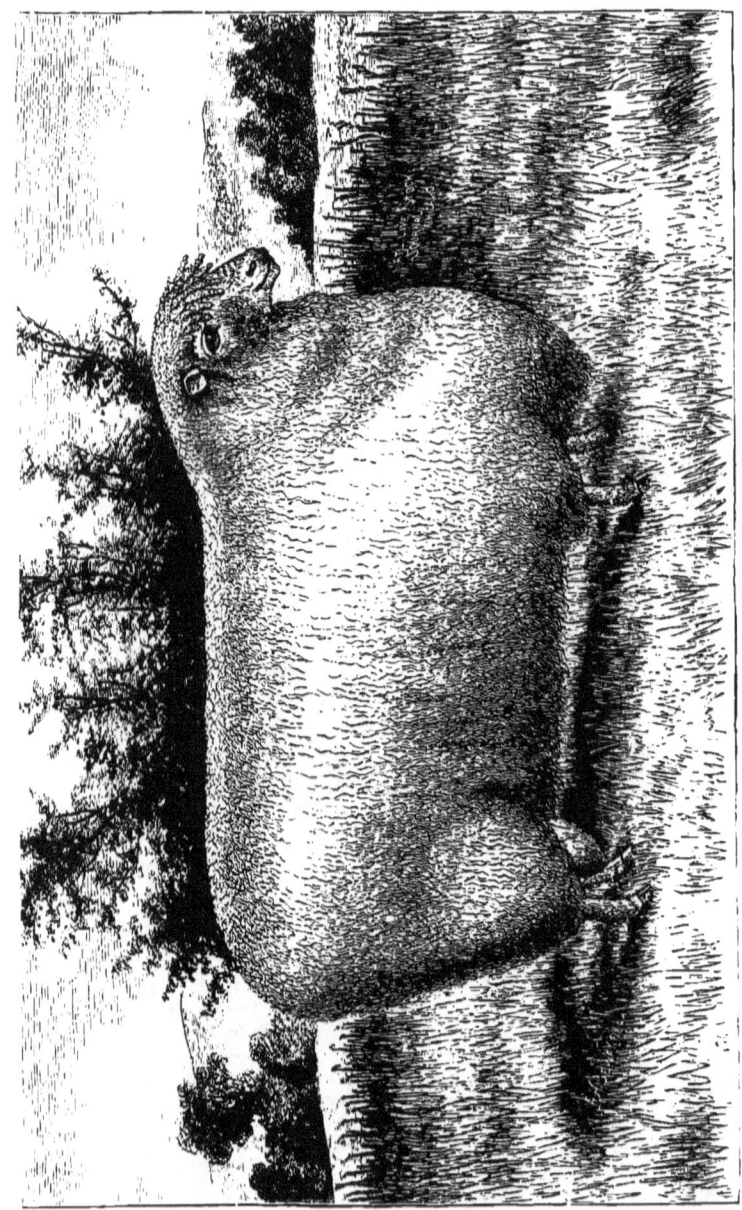

COTSWOLD RAM, STANDARD.
Bred by T. L. MILLER, Beecher, Ill.

breeds. They are not so prolific as some other varieties, but the ewes are good mothers, and the flock will thrive with ordinary management.

The following Scale of Points, to be used in connection with description given, is taken from Volume III. of the American Cotswold Record, George Harding, Waukesha, Wis., secretary:

EWE.		RAM.
8	Head	8
4	Face	4
1	Nostrils	1
2	Eyes	2
4	Ears	4
5	Collar	6
8	Shoulders	8
4	Fore Legs	4
10	Breast	10
4	Fore Flank	5
12	Back and Loin	12
5	Belly	3
8	Quarters	8
2	Hock	2
5	Twist	5
18	Fleece	18
100	Perfection	100

The animals represented in illustrations are from the flock of T. L. Miller, Beecher, Ill. Mr. Miller requests us to say, however, that he is not now breeding Cotswolds, his entire time being devoted to Hereford cattle.

Chapter LVI.

LEICESTERS.

The improved Leicester is peculiarly the result of Mr. Bakewell's wonderful skill as a breeder, and its origin and improvement may be best studied by a short review of Bakewell's methods as employed in improving and fixing the type of the Leicester breed. Mr. Bakewell lived at Dishley, in Leicestershire, England, and about 1750 began to apply himself to the improvement of sheep in his locality. His plan was to select from different flocks, without regard to size, the sheep which showed greatest aptitude to fatten with least appearance of excess of bone and offal, and he regarded the fleece as of secondary importance.

From Youatt "On Sheep" we quote:

"The sort of sheep, therefore, which Mr. Bakewell selected were those possessed of the most perfect symmetry with the greatest aptitude to fatten, and rather smaller in size than the sheep then generally bred. Having formed his stock from sheep so selected, he carefully attended to the peculiarities of the individuals from which he bred; and, it appears, did not object to breeding from near relatives, when, by so doing, he put together animals likely to produce a progeny possessing the characteristics that he wished to obtain. Mr. Bakewell has been supposed by some persons to have formed the New Leicester variety by crossing different sorts of sheep; but there does not appear to be any reason for believing this; and the circumstance of the New Leicesters varying in their appearance and qualities so much as they do from the other varieties of long-wooled sheep can by no means be considered as proving that such was the system which he adopted."

It has been stated, however, that Mr. Bakewell used sheep of six or seven different breeds, and that at one time, a magnificent black ram was found hidden away in a pen at his place. We are inclined to believe that the general reticence as to his methods—amounting almost to apparent selfishness—which he observed, led to a great deal of unwarranted suspicion and surmising. The account given by Youatt seems more reasonable, and especially so, since it is a now well-known principle of breeding, that judicious selection, combined with proper care of breeding animals, may—without admixture of other blood—entirely change the appearance and character of a breed.

Having thus far established his flock, Mr. Bakewell pursued the plan of hiring out rams to the neighboring breeders—a plan, by the way, which was beneficial to himself in permitting a wider range for selection of his breeding stock, and to the farmers, by permitting a change of rams at minimum expense—and in this way continued until the Lei-

LEICESTER EWE.
(English Engraving.)

LEICESTERS.
Bred at Experimental Farm, Guelph, Ontario, Canada.

cester breed was firmly fixed, both in character and popularity. Whatever may be said of Mr. Bakewell's selfish reserve regarding his plan of breeding, it cannot be denied that he has done great good in improving the modern breeds of sheep—a statement more easily believed when we realize that the New or Improved Leicester has had much to do in improving nearly all of the modern mutton breeds.

In America the Leicesters have not been extensively bred and advertised, although in Canada they are much better known and appreciated than in the United States. The first importation of which we have any record was made by Christopher Dunn, of Albany, New York, in 1812, and there are, perhaps, not over a score of breeders—on anything like an extensive scale—in the United States to-day, and none, at least to our knowledge, in the South. An American Leicester Breeders' Association has been organized, with A. J. Temple, of Cameron. Ill., secretary

DESCRIPTION AND CHARACTERISTICS.

Color of face and legs white; head small and clean, with tuft of wool at forehead (not so long as in case of Cotswold); the eyes are bright; ears of good size, placed well back; neck and shoulders square and deep; back straight, with deep carcass; hind quarters not so full and square as in the Cotswold, but fairly well padded, and legs clean and fine-boned. Mr. Wm. Rivers, a prominent breeder of both Leicesters and Southdowns in Canada, writes us under date July 2, 1888, as follows:

"The flesh (of the Leicester) is juicy, but of moderate quality, and is remarkable for the amount of outside fat it carries. They are not considered so hardy as other large breeds, and require shelter and good keep. We have found the ewes to be prolific and good mothers, but the young lambs require more attention than those of the Southdown. Early maturity and aptitude to fatten are the principal characteristics of the breed"

We may add that some other breeders have not found the Leicesters prolific, and it is generally believed that prolificacy is not one of the Leicester's strong claims.

The Leicester fleece is classed with the long wools (combing)—showing a staple of from six to ten inches, and high-class flocks shearing an average of eight or nine pounds. In size, they are among the large breeds—fat two-year-old wethers weighing from 230 to 260 pounds, and mature breeding rams about 190 to 215 pounds.

Of our illustrations, one represents a group of Canada-bred sheep, engraved after a sketch from life; the other represents a ewe, bred and raised in England.

Chapter LVII.

LINCOLNS.

Like the Leicester, this breed is a very old one, made over. The old native sheep of Lincolnshire, England, was a big, gaunt, raw-boned animal—capable of feeding to enormous weight, but requiring a large amount of food, and a long time to accomplish it. After Bakewell's time, Lincoln breeders began to use Leicester rams to improve their flocks, with the result of decreasing size and length of time required to mature; increasing at the same time quality of flesh and wool, and aptitude to fatten.

So excellent was the basis and so great the improvement, that from 1860 (at which date the Lincoln breed was first given a separate class) to 1870, the majority of prizes for long-wooled sheep at English fairs were taken by the Lincolns. In America they have long been bred in a small way, but there are as yet few breeders of any prominence. Canada leads the United States in numbers of both Lincolns and Leicesters, and most of the flocks now in the United States are descended from Canada bred or Canada imported stock. Geary Brothers have a fine flock of Lincolns at London, Ontario, Canada, and as they also have a farm at Brookfield, Missouri—where their large Aberdeen-Angus and English shire interests are located—it is presumable that the Lincoln sheep will eventually become pretty well scattered and favorably known, at least in Missouri. There are also flocks of some size in Minnesota, Ohio, Iowa, Wisconsin and Kansas. An American Association has been organized, with L. C. Graham, of Cameron, Illinois, secretary.

DESCRIPTION AND CHARACTERISTICS.

Color of face and legs white; head large and conspicuously free from wool at the forehead, which narrows somewhat sharply backward. The neck is of medium length, well set on to deep shoulders; back straight and full, but not so broad as in the Cotswold; legs rather long, firm, large boned; and general appearance, if not sprightly, at least strong and vigorous. The fleece is the longest of the long wools (combing), lustrous in character, and showing a staple from nine to twelve inches in length. High-class flocks yield an annual clip of from nine to fifteen pounds the fleece.

LINCOLN RAM, LORD PRESTON.
(English Engraving.)

LINCOLNS.

Property of G. & J. Geary, Bruckfield, Mic., and London, Ontario, Canada.

In size, the Lincolns are classed as the largest of modern breeds—fat two-year-old wethers frequently weighing upwards of 300 pounds, and mature breeding rams from 225 to 250 pounds. From Consul General Merritt's Report, dated at London, England, March 25, 1884, we clip the following in reference to Lincoln sheep:

"Being very broad, deep and compact in form, they generally outstrip the Cotswolds in weight at the Smithfield Club Shows, and last December, the heaviest pen [three animals of a kind taken collectively] of sheep in the Agricultural Hall was that of Mr. John Pears, which took first prize in the Ewe Class, the animals weighing nine cwt., two quarters, twenty-four pounds."

An average of 323⅔ pounds per head.

The Lincoln requires rich food and plenty of it, but when the proper conditions are given, it would be hard to find a more profitable sheep. For the South, we would hardly consider them valuable—although it must be admitted that the opinion is purely theoretical, since we have no knowledge of any Lincoln flocks in the Gulf states.

The large illustration represents the ram Rescue, winner of nine first and four second prizes in England and Canada; and the two shearling ewes Daisy and Ermine, winners of the first and second prizes respectively at no less than five fairs or exhibitions on the Canada side; all imported in 1883, by Geary Bros., London, Ontario, Canada, and Brookfield, Mo., U. S. A.

The ram, Lord Preston, was bred and raised in England, and the engraving is the work of English artists.

Chapter LVIII.

HINTS ON SELECTION, CARE AND MANAGEMENT OF SHEEP.

The selection of sheep—more than any other race of domestic animals—requires strict regard to the purpose for which they are desired. In the chapters under Part Third we have tried to give an accurate description of each of the modern breeds, and have stated in brief the peculiar conditions under which each breed will give best returns. With these hints already before us, it is unnecessary to treat further of selection of breed than to say: Each party must first determine the purpose for which he desires sheep—whether for mutton or for wool, or for both combined—by a careful study of his market facilities, both as to relative demand and price for mutton and wool, and also as to relative shipping charges in transporting either to market. Having once reached a decision on above, and after carefully studying the characteristics of the different breeds of sheep, and comparing the needs of each with the conditions of climate, soil and food which obtain in his immediate locality, he is then ready to select *the breed* with something like an intelligent judgment.

The man who tries raising sheep because he thinks "sheep are not worth much anyway, and if a few die it is no great loss," had best obtain more sense before investing his dollars. There is nothing in the live stock line which demands such close calculation, and such an intimate knowledge of the business, as the breeding and handling of sheep. It is a common saying that *"the ram is half the flock,"* and it might be stated with equal force that *the shepherd is the other half.* It is really of great importance that the shepherd in charge of the flock be a man who thoroughly understands his work, and such a man must be sought among those who have "grown up in the sheep pen." To graduate in the School of Experience requires many years, but the course, when completed, is of incalculable value. It is not every man that can have the advantage of early boyhood training in this direction, but if a practical shepherd can be secured, he may still be able to handle sheep with reasonable success.

In selecting service rams, the breeder should aim to secure perfection in shape and fleece, rather than excess of weight. An unusually large ram may produce some very large lambs, but he will also produce very many small ones; while, on the other hand, a short-coupled, close made, smooth and even, but smaller ram will breed with much greater uniformity. The head of the stock ram should always be small in proportion to the body; the legs firm but not large; the back and loin well padded with mutton and covered densely with wool of even length, and the general appearance and style should be brisk and sprightly—a lazy looking, "droopy" ram, as a rule, is not a strong breeder. Light but strong bones are much to be desired in a sheep, and large bones are always objectionable. If the head is too large—unless bred to ewes unusually broad and deep in the pelvic region—much trouble will result at lambing time, and considerable loss may be incurred.

The ewe should be selected with reference to type of the breed to which she belongs, and, especially if bred to produce a certain result, should exhibit the peculiar characteristics which the breeder aims to secure. The primary purpose of the ewe being that of a mother, she should be chosen with especial reference to her capacity to carry and nourish the fœtus, and produce milk for the lamb. Ewes are like cows some are good milkers, but many are poor in this respect, and the external signs of milking excellence are much the same in both. A feminine appearance of the head, wide, open pelvis, and body deep at the flank, and marks which should always guide in selection of the ewe.

We are not of opinion that the ordinary sheep farmer will have very great success with thoroughbred flocks of any breed; but we cannot urge too strongly the use of thoroughbred rams in grading up the hardy native or mixed-bred sheep common to different sections of the country. Mixed-bred flocks receive very kindly the blood of any of the improved breeds, and it is only a question of result desired as to what breed of ram should be selected. As a rule, wherever dry, scant ranges are found— especially in warm climates—wool will be more profitable than mutton, and no sheep will succeed better than the Merino. Where land is more fertile, and food in consequence more abundant, a combination of mutton and wool may be found more profitable; for such conditions as are found in the upper portion of the Mississippi Valley, the "middle-wools" have held the field against all others; and in the same section it has been found profitable, when flocks of short-wool basis were already present, to use compact rams of the long-wool breeds—combining in this way the hardy characters of the former with the size and mutton capacity of the latter, and producing a middle-wool flock with least expenditure of time and money.

To improve a flock requires, primarily, an accurate knowledge of the type desired. The improver must carry in his mind's eye, a picture of the sheep he wishes to produce, and every animal of either sex which he employs to accomplish his purpose must be selected by comparison with this ideal type. He must remember that it takes time to accomplish much in the way of improvement, and that he cannot expect to secure in any two, or even three or four animals, all the points—in perfection—which he wishes combined in one individual. Above all, let it be remembered that the most careful and judicious selection may be set at naught by ignorant or careless management of the breeding flock; sheep are delicate property, and while with breeders of any race of domestic animals careful attention is a paying investment, with the breeder of sheep it becomes a most essential factor of success.

The student will find it profitable to make a careful study of the actual methods employed by successful breeders in different parts of the country, and to this end we invite attention to the following letters:

Shropshires.

"FAIRVIEW FARM, WOODVILLE, ONT., July 25, 1888.

* * * *

"Ewes, if at all low in condition, are prepared for turning to the ram by feeding a little mixed grain—two-thirds oats and one-third peas—once daily. It is thought by many practical flock owners that ewes gaining in flesh when being served give a larger number of twins. The bucks are usually let to them about the first of September for early lambs, and in October for a later lot. As my flocks are all pure-bred Shropshires, the object in having lambs dropped so early is to have them well forward for exhibiting in the fall, but it is also the most profitable way of raising market lambs, as about Easter good ones bring double the price of those marketed two months later. During the late fall the flock is allowed into its winter quarters at night, but is not kept yarded until the snow covers the ground.

"The winter feeding until lambing time is as follows: Pea-straw from peas cut before being fully ripe is fed in the morning, three pounds of turnips per ewe at noon, and a full feed of clover hay at night, with abundance of good, clean water. No grain is fed at this period except a small daily allowance of mixed oats and bran to thin ewes. During the winter they are not closely housed, but have an open shed to shelter them from storms and wet, with yards attached for exercise, but separate from all other stock.

"During our cold winter weather warm quarters are necessary for lambing, but when the lambs are two weeks old, they run into the sheds and yards. After the lambs are dropped, the ewes are carefully tended; warm drinks of water, bran and a sprinkle of salt are given thrice daily, and clover hay. The third day, oat and pea meals are added to the bran, when the water used for moistening may be cool (but not too cool), and three pounds of mangel-wurzel are given daily. The slop is increased in quantity, until all that is eaten at once is fed morning and night, and the roots are increased to six pounds for a noon feed, with a full supply of clover hay and water. This liberal feeding induces a heavy flow of milk, just what is required to make the lambs grow rapidly at that stage, and the ewes, as well, will often gain in condition. When the lambs are three weeks old, a separate division is provided for them to run in at will, where a mixture of ground oats, peas, and also bran, with oil cake [linseed] added later on, is fed. When turned to grass, the ewes are given some dry grain for a week or two, and when early forward lambs are wanted, the mixture is continued all summer. Whether pre-maturity is wanted or not, all lambs are given an allowance of grain after weaning, about the 15th of July or August 1. By this system, Fairview flock has produced yearly averages per ewe of $1\frac{1}{2}$ to $1\frac{3}{4}$ lambs, some weighing, year after year in September, 130 pounds, and in 1883, a ram lamb, dropped in February, was exhibited from this flock at the Industrial Exhibition, Toronto, Canada, which weighed 175 pounds in September.

"As a rule, ram lambs are not used, though no doubt an early, well developed one is quite capable of serving a dozen to twenty ewes without hurt, and with good results. When used on a large flock—40 to 60 ewes—he is not allowed constantly with them; is kept apart, fed whole oats and peas, with bran added, and turned to the flock a short time each evening. With half the number a mature buck is run the whole day with the flock, kept separate at night, and fed grain.

"The winter care of rams is similar to that given ewes before lambing, with the exception of double the quantity of roots being fed; and also some grain, if more than ordinary condition is required, as for show purposes, or for pushing on lambs to earlier maturity as shearlings.

"Shearing is generally'done before the sheep are turned to grass, in the beginning of May, though sometimes, if the weather is favorable, the wool is taken off a month earlier than that date. To keep the wool in good condition and prevent its being pulled, because of ticks or skin disease, the flock is dipped with tobacco water, or one of the patent sheep dips, early in the fall, while the weather is mild. The lambs are dipped previously in May, when tobacco water is preferred, as it does not injure the tender skin, which the others are apt to do. After shearing, each fleece is carefully spread on a table, skin side downwards, all tags removed, and the sides folded toward the center until about 18 inches in width, when it is tightly rolled from the tail end, and a rope twisted from the neck end, with which the fleece is tied up. When tidily done, it can be handled without breaking, and the manufacturer can sort at will.

"Very truly,   JOHN R. CAMPBELL, JR."

In Mr. Campbell's letter we have a clear exposition of the manner of handling sheep in a cold country, and one which cannot fail to be of value, not only to the breeders of sheep in a similar climate, but to breeders in any latitude. The object in breeding sheep is to make money, and the point with mutton producers is to secure great weight at an early age; Mr. Campbell explains very clearly the double advantage he derives from this early forcing process and shows a close acquaintance with the profit side of sheep account.

American Merinos.

STANBERRY, Mo., July 23, 1888.

* * * *

"Commencing at breeding time, when the ewes are supposed to be in lamb, the rams are separated from the ewes, generally keeping all the rams in one fold, and in good thriving condition; never allowing any to get thin in flesh, usually feeding regularly on the best of clover and timothy hay whenever they desire to eat it; if this and the pasturage—which should be of the best, and always with pure water, easily accessible—is insufficient for the growth of flesh, we give at least once per day a feed of grain, about one gill to half pint each—a mixture of three parts oats and one wheat.

"Through the breeding season, such feeding ought to be nearly, if not quite, doubled for rams. A remunerative plan is to separate the rams at night from the sight of the ewes, and to these as to all other sheep, give thin feed, of a wholesome quality, and in a strictly clean place, with ample room for all to feed without crowding. None of the brute creation is naturally more cleanly, and consequently for profit such rules must be adhered to.

"With the ram, constitution and vitality cover 60 out of the 100 points, and from the lot the most vigorous and strong (other things being equal) are selected for service. Ewes, after having been bred, are allowed or required to take more of gentle exercise, with an abundant amount of nutritious pasture, and are supplied with well cured and timely prepared roughness, from grass, corn fodder, small grain straw, etc., to supply any deficiency caused by frosts or drouth ; if necessary to keep or put into good, strong flesh, be sure to add a grain feed, proportionate to the needs; 300 well kept ewes will shear annually more wool and raise more lambs than 500 half starved. Especially at the approach of the lambing season do the ewes need extra care and feed. When the herdsman says ' the ewes do not own the lambs,' he ought to be informed that the flock-master does not own his sheep, for ' tis the full udder that calls for the lamb,' and the dam can only supply to her offspring from what has first been given her. In proportion to the desire for the growth of the lambs should be the food supply to the ewes. If the lambs are intended for mutton, they ought to be encouraged to eat of grain as young as possible, say from eight to twelve weeks old, and all lambs will grow and thrive best that are weaned at about five or six months of age. They should be separated from their dams, and put on the most succulent pasture, and fed partially on grain for the first winter—for stock sheep, an amount sufficient for good thrift and growth; for the block or shambles, as much as is readily consumed till the butcher wishes them, let it be three months or three years.

"Shearing and marketing of wool is an important part of this industry, and as a rule, from one to three cents per pound can be gained or lost in the way wool is handled, and as a rule from 10 to 20 per cent. in the time of year this is done. Sheep ought to be shorn earlier in the season than is generally practiced, from which two great advantages arise : one is, that in the fall of the year, or when inclement weather comes on, the earlier shorn has more protection ; and the other is, the earlier shorn will give annually a larger fleece for several reasons, among them : (1) that a large amount of wool, which some sheep naturally shed, is saved ; and (2) being clipped, prevents the habit of shedding. I always shear as early as the weather will permit, not minding the month except for the show sheep, which according to the rules of our associations, put the limit not earlier than April 1st. I have never known any losses to newly shorn sheep except from their being exposed to wet, and have known more in June than in March. At shearing, all impurities should be clipped from the fleece, which should be carefully handled, not torn, and being turned flesh side out on a clean table, folded together and rolled up, and tied with specially prepared twine, sufficient, and only so, to keep in place, after which keep the wool clean from dust, straw or other things, and if one has a desirable lot of wool with an attractive appearance, the commission man will find it, and the grower can sell at home, and know what he gets for it. This I have always done.

"Most truly,   L. E. SHATTUCK."

Mr. Shattuck believes in early shearing—a point on which we think he is quite correct. If sheep are to be shorn for a record it is, of course, necessary that some system prevail, by which uniformity may be secured ; but if a man is breeding for dollars and cents, and without regard to association rules, we see no reason why the shearing cannot be done at least a week earlier than is generally practiced. We are glad to note this point regarding milking quality in the ewe ; too many overlook this, and seem to regard the ewe as an unchangeable machine—capable of just so much and no more in this direction. There is as much difference among ewes in milking quality as among cows ; no one would make the mistake of breeding cows that could not support their calves, and yet this very thing is overlooked by one-half of the modern breeders of sheep. Mr. Shattuck is one of our most successful wool men, and his hints on handling the fleece and marketing the wool may be read with profit.

American Merinos.

SOWERS, TEXAS, July 31, 1888.

"I have 300 acres of land located on Grapevine Prairie ; the land is high and quite undulating. Soil mostly gravelly mesquite land ; all fenced sheep proof, five wires—three barbed and two smooth—beginning with barbed at top and bottom ; posts 16 feet apart. I began in the spring of 1885 with 175 head Michigan-bred ewes and five rams. On the 20th, October I begin breeding the ewes. To every 100 head I turn in one ram in the morning, and take him out at night. On the second day after, I return ram to the flock, or a fresh one in his stead. I continue in this way until all the ewes, or nearly all, are with lamb, then I allow one or more of my best rams to remain with the flock until about Christmas, when I remove all the rams from the ewe flock until the following October. My land is divided into five pastures, all well shaded and watered. I do not allow my flock to run more than a month in one pasture before changing them around.

"My flock is divided into three flocks—breeding ewes, rams and lambs, and are kept thus separated the whole year round. I begin feeding as early in the winter as weather and condition of flocks demand, on sorghum, corn fodder, prairie hay, corn, cotton seed and sheaf oats. I limit myself to no given amount per head, but feed, according to the mildness or severity of the weather, about what I think they require and will eat up clean. During the cold and all of the wet weather of the year, I keep them housed in well-built sheds. My lambs begin coming March 20th, and are generally all through by the first of May. I castrate lambs at two to four days old ; dock all at about one week to ten days old, and wean at four months. I shear at about the middle of May, and sack the fleeces 'loose' in regular wool sacks. I have now 475 head of all ages—all full-blood Merinos. In fair weather, I always feed liberally with salt and sulphur (one part sulphur to two parts salt), except to ewes in pregnancy. I shear but once a year, and fleece averages for entire flock from 11 to 12 lbs.

"Respectfully yours, C. F. MILLS."

We extend our compliments to Mr. Mills for the concise, clear and full account of his way of handling sheep. We have not the pleasure of a personal acquaintance, but his letter indicates that he understands his business, and will doubtless succeed.

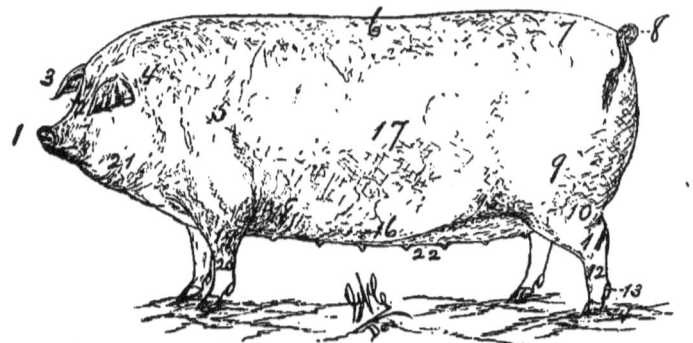

1, Nose, or Snout; 2, Face, or Dish; 3, Ears; 4, Neck; 5, Shoulder; 6, Back; 7, Rump: 8, Tail; 9, Ham; 10, Lower Thigh, Leg or Twist; 11, Hock, or Heel; 12, Shank, or Hind Cannon; 13, Onglons, or False Hoofs; 14, Hoof, or Foot; 15, Flank; 16, Belly; 17, Side or Ribs; 18, Girth; 19, Fore-arm; 20, Knee; 21, Cheek, or Jowl; 22, Nipples, or Dugs.

PART FOURTH.

SWINE.

LARGE BREEDS.

		PAGE
BERKSHIRES . . . . Chapter	LIX	294
POLAND-CHINAS . . . . "	LX	298
DUROC-JERSEYS . . . . "	LXI	301
CHESTER-WHITES . . . . "	LXII	395
TODD'S IMPROVED CHESTER-WHITES . . "	LXIII	307
GOTHLANDS . . . . "	LXIV	309

MIDDLE BREEDS.

CURTIS VICTORIAS . . . . Chapter	LXV	310
DAVIS VICTORIAS . . . . "	LXVI	312
CHESHIRES . . . . "	LXVII	314

SMALL BREEDS.

SMALL YORKSHIRES . . . . Chapter LXVIII	317
ESSEX . . . . " LXIX	320
NEAPOLITANS . . . . " LXX	322
ENGLISH OR BLACK SUFFOLKS . . . . " LXXI	323
AMERICAN OR WHITE SUFFOLKS . . . . " LXXII	324

HINTS ON SELECTION, CARE AND MANAGEMENT.

CHAPTER LXXIII. 325

Chapter LIX.

BERKSHIRES.

As indicated by the name, this variety of swine originated in the county or shire of Berk, England. The old original Berkshire was a large, raw-boned, coarse hog, with lop ears; was black and white in color, with occasional red or sandy spots.

Improvement of the breed was begun about the year 1780, by crossing with the Chinese hog; but it was not until Lord Barrington's time (1820 30) that the breed was brought to any degree of perfection. (It is stated by some authors, that the Neapolitan hog was the main source of Berkshire improvement; this, however, is firmly denied by others, and we have nowhere been able to find safe authority for the use of the Neapolitan at all in this connection.) The methods pursued by Lord Barrington can only be surmised, but it is certain that he added much to the merits of the Berkshire breed, and achieved a reputation fully proved by the fact that nearly all of the English Berkshires trace their ancestry to his herd.

Probably the first importation to the United States was made by John Brentnall, of New Jersey, in 1823. Some years later, about 1832, Sidney Hayes, an English farmer residing near Albany, N. Y., brought over a few head. Since that time numbers have been imported, and the improvement made by American breeders has been so marked as to cause competent judges to decide in favor of the American-bred hog. Professor James Long, in his admirable work, "The Book of the Pig," speaking of breeding for exhibition, says:

"In America the Berkshire pig is much more extensively bred than with us, and there is in that country not only a very much larger number of breeders of pigs of an exhibition type, but there is a Berkshire Pig Association, which is supported by a large body of members, although English breeders, to whom the Americans originally came for the foundations of their herds, have hitherto lacked sufficient spirit and energy to carry anything of the kind to a successful issue."

Although an English variety of swine, we prefer to accept the standard of American breeders as outlined in the following

DESCRIPTION OF AMERICAN BERKSHIRE.

Color black, with white feet, small white line in face, and a white spot at tip of tail. (Occasionally there is a small splashing of white on arm, and sometimes spots occur on other portions of the body, but their

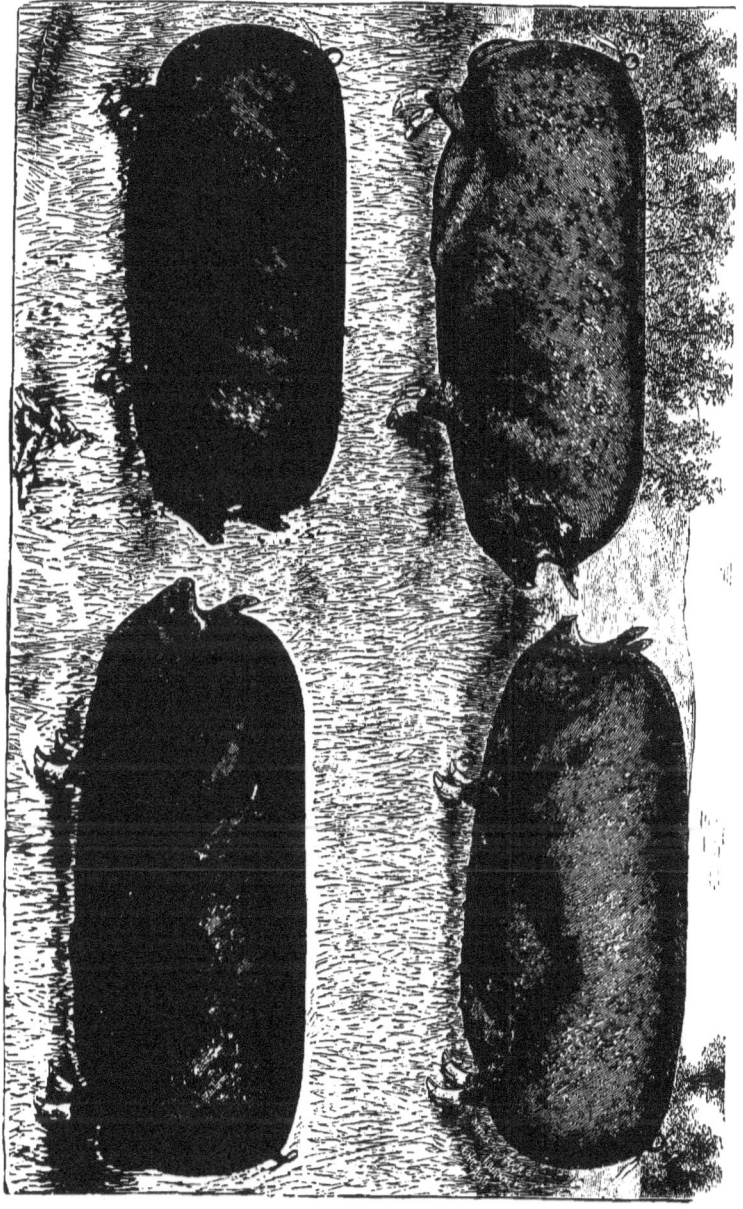

presence is regarded with disfavor, and they are entirely excluded by breeders of the more fashionable strains.) The face is short, fine, well dished and broad between the eyes; ears erect or inclining forward, stiff at base, but so thin and delicate as to shake and tremble with every movement of the animal; jowl heavy; neck short and thick; shoulders deep and full; back broad and straight, or slightly arched; long ribs well sprung, giving roundness of barrel, and short ribs long and spreading, giving breadth and fullness of loin. The hips are long, heavy, round and deep, bearing their flesh well down to the hock; tail fine, small and set well up to the sacral curve; legs short, straight, fine-boned and set wide apart; body medium to long; hair fine, rather thin in fashionable strains, and skin elastic and pliable.

The following Scale of Points has been adopted by the American Berkshire Association (John G. Springer, of Springfield, Ill., secretary), and is now in general use:

Color	4	Forward	47
Face and Snout	7	Sides	6
Eye	2	Flank	5
Ear	4	Loin	9
Jowl	4	Ham	10
Neck	4	Tail	2
Hair	3	Legs	5
Skin	4	Symmetry	6
Shoulder	7	Condition	
Back	8	Style	5
Forward	47	Perfection	100

Secretary Springer writes under date December 21, 1892:

"* *Twelve volumes of the American Berkshire Record have been published.
* *Volume XIII., for which entries are being made, will be closed in a short time.*
* *The last number recorded at this writing is 28780.

"Among swine the Berkshire has continued to hold its place in high esteem, and is to-day, as has been the case for years, the standard for comparison of other breeds. The Berkshire in America has in the last few years made great progress in excellence, so that it is thought that we now have here the best in the world, and to prove this our breeders are quite anxious to come in competition with English breeders at the World's Columbian Exposition.*"

CHARACTERISTICS.

The Berkshires possess great muscular power and extraordinary activity. This latter feature is, indeed, very generally considered a serious objection, inasmuch as too great activity is not conducive to an economical production of fat. The sows are noted for their prolificacy, and the pigs when dropped are strong and lively. They may be fattened for market at any age desired, and when continuously and properly fed attain great size and weight. The average live weight of well kept shoats placed on the market at nine to twelve months old should be from 240 to 300 pounds. When mature, a weight of from 500 to 650 pounds is not uncommon. Berkshire boars when used in crossing—or in grading up common stock—transmit with considerable certainty all the valuable qualities of their breed. The objections urged against them may be summed up as follows : (1) They are too nervous and excitable, requiring very careful handling to secure best results ; (2) their bone is too small, rendering them more liable to mishaps—such as hip-shot and broken legs—than are the larger-boned breeds. Where Berkshires are carefully handled and properly fed, we know of no better variety, but in the hands of the ordinary farmer, where attention is denied or partially withheld, they cannot be accorded first, nor in our opinion, even second place.

The illustration, kindly furnished for our use by the *Western Agriculturist and Live Stock Journal*, of Quincy, Ill., is a fair representation of the breed.

Chapter LX.

POLAND-CHINAS.

The Poland-China breed is one distinctively American in origin and type, originating chiefly in Warren and Butler counties, Ohio, where the type was soon fixed by the enterprising breeders of that section. It became known as a breed locally under various names—such as the "Warren County Hog" and the "Big Spotted"—about 1835 to 1840; but the now firmly established name, "Poland-China," was first officially adopted by the National Swine Breeders' Convention, held at Indianapolis, Ind., in 1872.

The Big Chinas—large white hogs with sandy spots—were taken to Warren county in 1816; the Berkshires were introduced about 1830: the Irish Graziers—white hogs with sandy eye-spots—about 1839; and the Byfields—which are said to resemble the Chinas in form—about the same time. From a judicious blending of these different breeds upon a basis of the best "native" hogs, supposed to have descended largely from original Poland stock, brought in by early settlers from Germany, we have the present Poland-China breed.

Improvement of the breed has been largely the result of private individual enterprise and skill, Mr. A. C. Moore, now of Canton, Ill., and Mr. D. M. Magie, of Oxford, Ohio, being especially deserving of notice in this connection. So much, indeed, have their labors been appreciated, that persistent attempts have been made by respective friends of these two gentlemen to name the breed "Moore" or "Magie," instead of Poland-China; fortunately, however, the name is too firmly settled to admit of change for reasons of a personal nature, and the friends of these prominent breeders must be content with simple credit for their recognized efficient work.

DESCRIPTION.

Color black and white spotted, sometimes black, sometimes white predominating; size large, mature hogs weighing from 600 to 750 pounds, and shoats at eight or nine months weighing upwards of 250 pounds. The nose is medium, face neatly dished, head small in proportion to body, with thin, drooping ("lop") ears and full, heavy jowl. The neck is short, back straight, shoulders deep, girth large, ribs well arched, loins full and wide, hams very heavy and legs short, with good-sized, strong bone. In some specimens the hair is decidedly curly, but in a

POLAND-CHINAS.
Bred and owned by A. C. Moore & Sons, Canton, Ill.

majority of cases the coat is straight or at most slightly wavy, covering a skin of similar color and medium thickness.

The following Scale of Points may be used in connection with the description given:

Nose	4	Forward	51
Head	4	Back	6
Width between eyes	4	Ribs	9
Ears	5	Loins	7
Jowl	3	Hams	12
Neck	4	Hair	4
Shoulders	9	Width of body	5
Girth around heart	9	Legs	6
Depth of body	9		
Forward	51	Perfection	100

The scale has been subject to a number of changes, but the above, we believe, has been more generally accepted than other arrangements

CHARACTERISTICS.

The Poland-China has a stronger following among Western farmers than has any other breed of swine, and we think justly so; they are large, mature reasonably early, and long before maturity may be turned into pork at the highest market price. They are uniformly quiet, even lazy, and never lose flesh by reason of excitability. They have strong, firm bone, permitting a heavy load of fat, and rendering them less liable to mishaps when placed with fattening steers. On the whole the Western farmer can hardly find a better hog.

In the South they have not done so well; reports from central and southern Texas indicate that the Poland-China is out of his element when taken below the central part of the state, and in this respect, must admit the superiority of his red-haired brother, the Duroc-Jersey. Our illustration is an accurate picture of a magnificent trio, bred by the well-known and thoroughly reliable firm, A. C. Moore & Sons, Canton, Ill.

Chapter LXI.

DUROC-JERSEYS.

In the following history of their origin, we are largely indebted to the report of Col. F. D. Curtis, Vol. I. of the American Duroc-Jersey Record, compiled by the able secretary of the Association, Chas. H. Holmes, now of Beatrice, Nebraska.

At the first meeting of the National Swine Breeders' Association at Indianapolis, Indiana, 1872, a committee was appointed on "Jersey Red Swine," from whose report, as adopted by the convention, we clip the following:

"The positive origin of this family of swine is unknown. They have been bred in portions of New Jersey for upwards of 50 years, and with many farmers are considered to be a valuable variety. They are of large size, and capable of making a heavy growth, 500 and 600 pounds weight being common. Mr. David Pettit, Salem, Salem county, N. J., has known of these hogs for 30 years, and Mr. D. M. Brown, of Windsor, for 50 years. They are now extensively bred in the middle and southern portions of New Jersey. In neighborhoods they were bred quite uniform, being of a dark red color; while in other sections they were more sandy, and often patched with white. They are probably descended from the old importations of Berkshires, as there is no record of the Tamworth—the red hog of England—ever having been brought to this country; nor is it likely, as the Tamworths were not considered valuable swine, and were confined to a limited breeding."

The name "Jersey-Red" was first used about 1870 by the late Joseph R. Lyman, at that time agricultural editor of the *New York Tribune;* and a Mr. Lippincott, of New Jersey, was probably the first breeder to advertise under the name thus given.

In the meantime, another strain of red hogs was finding favor in New York under the name "Duroc;" they were so called by Isaac Frink, a farmer living near Milton, Saratoga county, N. Y. Mr. Frink secured a pair of pigs in 1823 from Mr. Kelsey—the then owner of the famous stallion Duroc—who stated that the pigs were "imported;" as to what was meant by the expression used, we can only infer, but it is probable that if "imported" from England, a name would have been imported with them; and since Mr. Kelsey called them simply "Red Pigs," we are justified in believing them brought from a distance— probably Queens county, N. Y., where Mr. Kelsey formerly resided— but not imported from Europe. Mr. Frink could as well have named them "Kelsey" as Duroc, but the fame of the horse so overshadowed that of his owner as to doubtless warrant Mr. Frink's choice of a name.

These two families of swine, under separate names, were undoubtedly of the same origin; and this, probably, is found in the old red type of Berkshire, as pictured by Low, in his "Domestic Animals of Great Britain."

That the two names represented one hog had been long recognized; and, after several attempts to effect an organization, the Duroc or Jersey-Red Swine Club met, in first annual session, at the Grand Pacific Hotel, Chicago, November 15, 1883. During this meeting, there were some remarks about the propriety of leaving out the word "or" in the name of the Club, which finally resulted in changing the name to "Duroc-Jersey Swine Breeders' Association," as now known.

Improvement of the breed has been very great, especially within the past decade. The old Jersey Red or Duroc was a coarse, heavy, raw-boned, lop-eared and "lank-sided" animal, whose greatest merit lay in his growth and feeding qualities; while his modern brother, as will be seen from the next topic, is among the best of economic breeds of swine.

DESCRIPTION AND CHARACTERISTICS.

Color cherry or sandy red, without admixture of other tints; nose medium to short; face slightly dished, wide between eyes; ears medium, drooping, and jowl large, full and well rounded. The neck is short; shoulders broad and deep, bounding a chest of great capacity; back broad, and neatly moulded to long, deep ribs; hams very heavy, with low, full twist; legs medium in length, with strong, firm bone; tail well up but rather thick; hair soft, straight and shining—the whole combined with an action not nervous, but vigorous and sprightly. To those who are familiar with the Poland-Chinas, we might briefly state that the Duroc-Jersey resembles them very closely in nearly all points except color. In size the Duroc-Jersey ranks among the largest of modern breeds, individuals weighing at maturity 400 to 700 pounds, and marketing at eight or nine months an average weight of from 175 to 250 pounds, dressed.

They are quiet, ravenous feeders, good grass hogs, and bear forcing for market as well as any.

In the South they have no superior, at least among the large breeds, as they never sun-scald, and adapt themselves readily to climatic conditions under which even the hardy Poland-China will not thrive.

The cross of the Duroc-Jersey on the Essex we regard as of more value for pork than the pure bloods of either breed, as they combine the size and forcing qualities of the former with the remarkable fattening powers of the latter in a very happy manner.

DUROC-JERSEYS.
Property of C. H. Holmes, Beatrice, Neb.

The following Scale of Points for judging Duroc-Jersey swine, to be used in connection with description already given, has been formally adopted by the Association :

Color	5	Forward	55
Head	10	Sides	10
Ears	5	Belly	5
Cheeks (Jowl)	5	Hams	10
Neck	5	Legs	5
Shoulders	5	Tail	5
Chest	10	Hair	5
Back	10	Action	5
Forward	55	Perfection	100

Our illustration gives an excellent idea of this now popular breed of swine.

Chapter LXII.

CHESTER-WHITES.

The breed derives its name from the place of its origin—Chester county, Pennsylvania. In 1818, a sea captain—James Jeffries by name —brought over from Bedfordshire, England, a pair of superior white pigs, showing bluish spots in skin—since known as "Bedford" hogs— and placed them on his farm near West Chester, Pa. These pigs and their progeny, in connection with the Big Chinas, brought to Delaware county, Pa., about the same time, were used by the farmers of Chester county, in grading on a foundation stock of large, coarse white hogs— probably descendants of the old English Large Yorkshire—supposed to have been imported about 1811, until after many years of careful selection and judicious inbreeding the Chester-White breed was brought before the American Farmer, and turned over to him for further improvement.

The modern Chester-White is well known throughout the Eastern and many Western states, and has, at one time and another, found a place in most of the mixed-bred herds in the Mississippi Valley. The writer well remembers the time when a black hog was looked upon with more or less disfavor by a great majority of Western farmers; and the Chester was at that time *the* hog sought for to improve and maintain the herd. One of the most prolific and valuable brood sows we have ever known was of this breed, a sow that for beauty and utility combined would be hard to surpass; her owner, however, not fancying the white color, persisted in using a black boar, and declared that the magnificent litters she brought owed their great excellence to the sire.

Improvement of the Chester has been very constant. Our Western farmers are, almost to a man, good judges and good handlers of swine; and those who have not been carried away during the last fifteen or twenty years by the popular tide in favor of black hogs have used their abilities to advantage in perfecting the Chester-White breed.

DESCRIPTION AND CHARACTERISTICS.

Color white—as the name indicates—with hair of medium length, mostly straight, neatly parted on the median line, and in the best specimens, showing a handsome curl or rosette just over the loins. The head is of medium length, broad between the eyes; ears thin, drooping, pointing well forward, and showing a decided bend or "lop" near the point; neck short and thick; jowl large; body long and deep; back broad, hams large and rounded; legs short and squarely placed; tail small, with brush of soft hair, and back and belly lines almost parallel.

In size, the Chester-Whites rank with the largest, weighing at maturity 600 or 700 pounds, and marketing at eight or nine months a dressed weight of 175 to 250 pounds. They do not claim early maturity, but no hog can surpass them, in favorable climate, for capacity to transform corn into fat pork in shortest time and at least expense. They are quiet, even lazy, and make excellent animals to follow steers in the feeding pens. The brood sows produce large litters, and are excellent mothers, the only objection we have ever heard on this point being that they are apt to be cross at pigging time, which is, perhaps, well founded. In the South they have no place; the white breeds of swine cannot stand the severe summer sun of this latitude without danger of sun-scald,

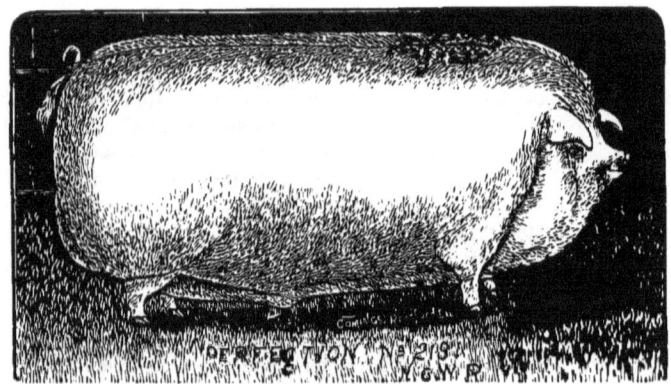

CHESTER-WHITE BOAR.
Property of N. G. ALEXANDER, Delavan, Ill.

mange, or other troubles; and while there are many breeders—and partisan ones too—of each of the modern white breeds in the South, justice toward all interests demands the above statement.

The following Scale of Points for judging Chester-White swine has been adopted by the National Chester-White Breeders' Association, and should be used in connection with the description already given:

Color	3	Forward	48
Head	5	Sides	6
Ears	2	Loin	7
Jowl	2	Belly	4
Neck	3	Flank	3
Brisket	4	Ham	10
Shoulders	6	Tail	2
Girth at heart	10	Limbs	7
Back	7	Coat	3
Ribs	7	Action	5
	—	Symmetry	5
Forward	48		—
		Perfection	100

Chapter LXIII.

TODD'S IMPROVED CHESTER-WHITES.

This breed has lately forced itself into recognition among the farmers of Ohio and other Western states, and we can do no less than grant its claim to the title of "breed," since it is already proved by the marked similarity of its pure-bred offspring. We are not personally familiar with the breed, but give the following account of its origin, and a description, based on letters from breeders, and the history as outlined by S. H. Todd in Volume I., Record of Todd's Improved Chester-White Swine, which appeared in 1885:

TODD'S IMPROVED CHESTER BOAR, DANDY, 917.
Owned by C. W. Baker, Delaware, Ohio.

"Kneeland Todd took a boar of the breed known as 'Norfolk Thin Rind'—black belted with white—and a white sow pig of the Connecticut—so-called 'Grass breed,' to Ohio in 1834. Isaac Hoskins had moved to Wakeman, Ohio, from New Bedford, Mass., the previous year—1833—taking with him at that time, a boar of the 'Byfield' breed—large white, rather leggy and slow to mature—and a sow of the 'Auterdale' breed—probably identical with the 'Grass breed' above mentioned. These two gentlemen bred carefully and with good judgment, and finally bred the best animals of each herd together. At this juncture—1848—the twin brother of Kneeland Todd bought a boar from Mr. Mead. of Norfolk, Ohio, of what Mr. Mead called the 'Large Grass breed', and this boar was used on the Todd-Hoskins stock with great success. About 1862, the same gentleman purchased a white boar with fine curly hair, called 'Normandy,' said to be of French origin. This proved to be a valuable addition, and the combination animal thus produced became quite well known as the 'Todd Hog.'

"Mr. S. H. Todd—son of the originator of the Todd Hog—in 1867 began crossing these animals with pure Chester-Whites, using in all some six or seven crosses, and finally producing what is now known as Todd's Improved Chester-White."

DESCRIPTION AND CHARACTERISTICS.

Color white, with occasionally bluish spots on skin; hair fine and thick; head small; face slightly dished; ears fine, thin and drooping; jowl full; neck short and well arched; shoulder heavy; back straight, with broad loin; ribs well sprung, dropping to deep sides and low flank; hams deep and rounded; tail small, and legs fine boned and straight.

The following Scale of Points was adopted by the Record Association at the annual meeting, January, 1885; C. W. Baker, Delaware, Ohio, is the present secretary:

Head	7	Forward	53
Ear	2	Loin	7
Jowl	4	Belly	5
Neck	3	Flank	3
Brisket	3	Ham	10
Shoulder	6	Limbs	6
Girth around heart	9	Tail	2
Back	6	Coat	3
Side	7	Color	3
Ribs	6	Symmetry	8
Forward	53	Perfection	100

TODD'S IMPROVED CHESTER SOW, SWEEPSTAKES, 1454.
Owned by N. H. TILLMAN, Arcanum, Ohio.

Our illustrations, both of Chester-Whites and Todd's Improved Chesters, can hardly be said to do justice to their respective breeds, but will serve to illustrate whatever of difference there may be between them. Many, indeed, are of opinion that there should be but one breed of Chester-White swine, and maintain that the two breeds here given separate chapters will soon be combined under a compromise standard of registration.

Whether such may prove to be the result or not, has no effect on the present status of the two breeds; they are given a separate class at fairs and exhibitions, and if the combination is not made very soon, there will remain small probability of a union at any time.

Chapter LXIV.

GOTHLANDS.

This breed, new in America, originated in Gothland, Sweden, and is said to be of remarkably pure descent, improved by care and selection, with few, if any, out-crosses.

The first importation to America was made in 1880 by S. V. Anderson, who brought over a few head as an experiment. Since that time they have found considerable favor—mainly in Iowa and Illinois, and a Registry Asssociation was organized in 1888, with Mr. Grant W. Spear, of Aurora, Ill., secretary. We are indebted to Messrs. White & Conover, of Lynnville, Iowa., for the following detailed

DESCRIPTION AND CHARACTERISTICS.

"They have a medium sized head, rather short nose, small ear, slightly drooping, or leaning forward ; broad between ears, and with stout, heavy jaw. Top and under lines good; girth large, length good, loin broad, flank deep, with heavy ham and shoulder, ham extremely good ; legs rather short, strong and well set ; hair rather fine and very thick ; skin smooth and flexible ; flesh nicely marbled and of excellent quality, with small per cent. of shrinkage in dressing. Most of them are spotted black and white, but some you will find nearly black, while others are nearly white, according to the fancy of the breeder. If fed mostly on nitrogenous foods they will grow to a very large size ; or if early maturity is desired, by good feeding with plenty of corn and skimmed milk, they may be brought to maturity much sooner, often weighing 350 to 400 pounds at one year of age. They are not coarse, but a hog of medium size ; neither are they as round and chubby as the Yorkshire, but have a much larger per cent. of lean meat and muscle. As to their health, they have proved themselves to be exceedingly healthy and rugged ; they endure our winters nicely, as they are a native of a cold climate. They are a quiet, docile animal, about like the Poland-China, which breed they resemble in their general make-up and disposition more than any other of our native breeds, but are stronger and more vigorous. They make excellent mothers.

"They are an excellent hog to ship, having as they do a short, strong leg, strong heavy loin, and rather short back. Crippled and broken-down hogs are very scarce. They are a good hog to follow cattle, as they are not easily disabled."

A letter received from Mr. Spear, dated Dec. 22, 1892, states :

"* * The Gothland Breeding Association has gone out of business, as the cost of importing new swine was so much for the value received that the breeding was dropped."

This is unfortunate, and but illustrates the fact that it takes not only time but money to introduce any new breed, however meritorious, and obtain for it established recognition.

Chapter LXV.

VICTORIAS.

(Originated by F. D. Curtis.)

There are, unfortunately, two distinct and separate breeds of swine, each called "Victoria." Col. F. D. Curtis, of Charlton, N. Y.,—in whose recent death, May 28, 1891, the world has lost a man of truly great worth, not only in his private life, but as a breeder of live stock, and also as a constant instructor through the columns of our best agricultural and live stock periodicals—some twenty-five years ago began a system of crossing with several varieties of English swine, in the hope of dropping the objectionable characteristics, and combining the good points of each in a separate breed. In this he has been successful, so far as fixedness of type is concerned, his breed receiving the following recognition and complimentary notice from the National Swine Breeders' Convention, 1872:

"The family of pigs known as Victorias originated with Col. Frank D. Curtis, Kirby Homestead, Charlton, Saratoga Co., N. Y. They were made by crossing the Byfield hog with the native, in which there was a strain of Grazier. Subsequent crosses were made with the Yorkshire and Suffolk, the result being a purely white hog of medium size. The name has no significance, unless it is intended as a compliment to the English Queen. These pigs, if pure bred, should all have a direct descent from a sow called Queen Victoria, which may be said to be the mother of the family. She was pronounced by good judges to be almost perfect, and was the winner of a number of first prizes."

DESCRIPTION AND CHARACTERISTICS.

We may best explain their peculiarities by another reference to the above report, signed by the chairman of the committee, Chas. E. Leland:

"The color is pure white, with a good coat of soft, fine hair; the head thin, fine and closely set on the shoulders; the face slightly dishing; the snout short; the ears erect, small and very light or thin; the shoulders bulging and deep; legs short and fine; the back broad, straight and level, and the body long. The hams round and swelling and high at the base of the tail, with plates or folds between the thighs; the tail fine and free from wrinkles, or rolls; feathers or rosettes on the back are common; the skin is thin, soft and elastic; the flesh fine-grained and firm, with small bone, and thick side pork. The pigs easily keep in condition, and can be made ready for slaughter at any age."

And now a word as to the unfortunate naming of these two distinctly different breeds. We have no interest in either breed, and shall try to give an impartial review of the case from both sides. To this end we have placed them under separate headings, distinguishing each breed by the name of its originator. Would it not be the part of wisdom—since both parties seem so enamored of the present name—to call the breed just described the CURTIS VICTORIAS, and the other the DAVIS VICTORIAS, each in honor of its founder? The breeds are certainly different, and must be disassociated in the public mind. We make the suggestion in good faith, and earnestly hope that breeders concerned will accept at least something equivalent.

Chapter LXVI.

VICTORIAS.

(Originated by George F. Davis.)

A new breed produced within the last decade, by a judicious blending of the blood of four different breeds—Poland-China, Chester-White, Berkshire and American or White Suffolk. Previous to 1882, breeders of the Davis Victorias were compelled to show their animals as grades at fairs and Fat Stock Shows; but at the annual meeting of the Illinois State Board, in the year mentioned, they were given a class by themselves, and were admitted on an equal footing with other swine, as forming a pure and distinct breed. At the Illinois State Fair in 1882,

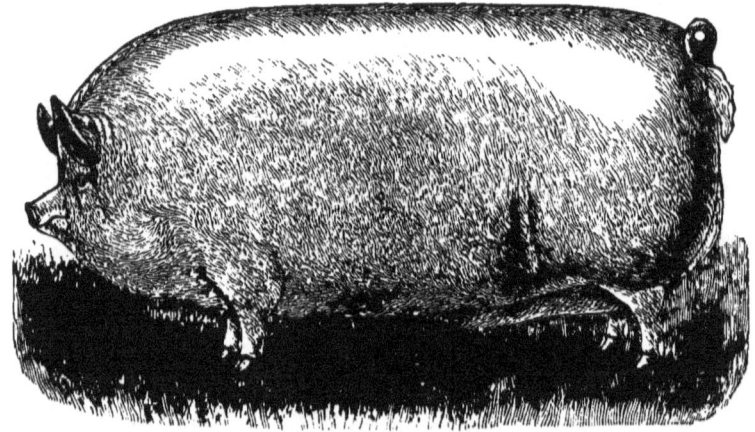

DAVIS VICTORIA BOAR, DANDY.
At seven months; winner of sweepstakes over all breeds shown at the World's Industrial and Cotton Exposition, New Orleans, La.; property of Geo. F. Davis, Dyer, Ind.

Mr. G. F. Davis, of Dyer, Ind., the originator of the breed, exhibited a small herd in competition with Chester-Whites, winning first and second prizes on boars, second on sows under one year old, and in the breeders' ring the herd premium of $25 for the best boar and four sows. In 1885, Mr. Davis exhibited his herd at the World's Industrial and Cotton Exposition, New Orleans, La., his seven months old "Dandy" (see illustration) winning the grand sweepstakes over all breeds shown. Why

Mr. Davis adopted the name "Victoria" we cannot see; possibly he was unaware of the existence of the Curtis Victorias, already described. Certainly Mr. Curtis has a prior claim to its use, but the point must be settled by breeders, and we predict will be settled to the satisfaction of all concerned.

DESCRIPTION AND CHARACTERISTICS.

Color white; size medium to large, weighing at 10 to 12 months 300 to 400 pounds; head small and finely dished, not so short as the White Suffolk or Small Yorkshire, with erect or only slightly drooping ears, and heavy, firm jowl; back straight and broad; shoulders deep and square; hams full and low, and legs short, with fine but firm bone.

The following Scale of Points was adopted by the Victoria Swine Breeders' Association, at the Chicago meeting, June, 1887:

Color	2	Forward	49
Head	3	Loin	12
Ears	2	Flank	2
Jowl	1	Ham	12
Neck	3	Tail	2
Shoulders	7	Legs	3
Girth around heart	6	Feet	3
Back	12	Hair	3
Sides	6	Action	4
Ribs	7	Symmetry	10
Forward	49	Perfection	100

Their breeders claim for them an unusual economy in production of flesh. The sows produce large litters and are good mothers; they stand board floors remarkably well, and it is claimed that they are not so susceptible to mange, scurf, sun-scald and similar troubles, which have made buyers—especially in the South—fight shy of white hogs in general. There is ample room for both of the Victoria breeds, and we are glad to notice their rapid advancement in public favor wherever introduced.

Chapter LXVII.

CHESHIRES.

At our request, Mr. R. D. Button, a leading breeder of Cheshires, Cottons, N. Y., very carefully prepared an outline of history and characteristics of the breed, and the article so nearly expresses our own opinion that, with some minor changes, and with Mr. Button's permission, we publish in full:

"Jefferson county, N. Y., is without doubt, the birthplace of this breed of swine, and to A. C. Clark is universally conceded the honor of having given them a name and character. The sires he used were Yorkshires, belonging to that family of English hogs known as the 'Large White' breed. Breeders are not all agreed as to what dams were used, many believing that the first dam was a large white sow imported from Cheshire, Eng., to Albany, N. Y. She was taken to Jefferson county by Mr. A. C. Clark, and used as the leading factor in making up his herd. Mr. Clark was a breeder with sound judgment and good sense, and he early perceived the docility and motherly qualities of this dam and her progeny, and by judicious crosses and careful selections he in time produced a herd of swine that were uniform in size and characteristics. His herd was shown at many of the leading fairs of New York, and nothwithstanding the fierce rivalries of other breeders Mr. Clark carried away many of the honors for large white breeds.

"There are breeders who profess to believe that the imported sow was a myth, and assert that Mr. Clark used only the best white sows of his neighborhood, and when he found a better sow than his, he bought and used her, if she proved a satisfactory breeder. We are, however, of the belief that the Albany sow was a truth and verity, and found that belief on repeated statements of Ezra J. Clark (son-in-law of A. C. Clark, and afterward owner of his herd), with whom we were intimately associated for a number of years in breeding, selling and exhibiting Cheshire swine. Mr. Ezra J. Clark always maintained that A. C. Clark bought and used the Albany sow as his prime factor, and all reports of buying and using only native sows had their origin in the fertile brains of rival breeders and exhibitors. Between 1850 and 1865 Mr. Clark was a leading breeder and exhibitor in New York, and fought both wordy and legal battles for his favorites. Business complications arising, he sold his interest and good-will to Ezra J. Clark, who associated with him Mr. McLean, and afterward Daniel Green, under the firm name Clark & Green. In 1870 this firm made an exhibit at the leading western fairs, ending with the great St. Louis Fair, where they won the $500 offered by the pork packers for the best herd for packers' uses. This breed had been widely disseminated during these exhibitions, but the low price for pork during the following years was so discouraging that many sold or butchered their stock, and engaged in more remunerative pursuits. The old Clark herd was still retained in its purity, although greatly reduced in numbers.

"About 1875 several parties in Madison Co., N. Y., were engaged in breeding Cheshires; and, with different ideas of what a Cheshire should be, bred for early maturity, and a shorter body and head. About 1882 a few of the prominent breeders began to talk of forming a register, and in January, 1883, a call was issued for breeders to meet at Syracuse, N. Y. But little was accomplished, however, owing to jealousies between different sections and breeders. Several subsequent meetings were held, and by mutual concessions, it was agreed to adopt the following

DESCRIPTION AND CHARACTERISTICS.

"Head short to medium in length, short in proportion to length of body; face somewhat dished and wide between the eyes; ears small, erect, in old animals often pointing slightly forwards; neck short; shoulders broad and full, hips broad; body long, broad and deep; hams broad, nearly straight with back, and running well down towards hock; legs small and slim, set well apart, and supporting the body on the toes; tail small and slim; hair fine, medium in thickness and quantity; color white, a few blue spots in skin not to disqualify, but objectionable. When grown and well fattened, should dress from 400 to 600 lbs.

CHESHIRE BOAR.
Property of E. W. Davis, Oneida, N. Y.

Scale of Points: To be used with description given above:

Head	8	Forward	56
Face	8	Hams	10
Ears	5	Legs	10
Neck	5	Tail	5
Shoulders	10	Hair	5
Hips	10	Color	4
Body	10	General appearance	10
Forward	56	Perfection	100

"Cheshires are now given a separate class at most of the large fairs, and are regularly shown at the various exhibitions in New York, New Jersey, Pennsylvania and other States."

Another opinion reaches our hands as to the origin of Cheshire swine; and coming, as it does, from the pen of Mr. E. W. Davis, of Oneida, N. Y., secretary of the Cheshire Swine Breeders' Association, we have taken the liberty to make the following extract:

"The hog known as Cheshire was first bred by A. C. Clark, of Jefferson Co., N. Y. He commenced with an imported Large Yorkshire boar, and bred upon the best common sows he could find. These common sows were all white, and were grade Suffolk, Small

Yorkshire, etc.; selections were carefully made from these, and after a time, another Large Yorkshire boar from imported stock was used. There was a story that a sow was imported from Cheshire, England, but that is wholly a myth. I have investigated the matter carefully, and those who ought to know if there was ever any such an importation know nothing of it, and unhesitatingly say, there was never any such importation."

The above shows plainly a difference of opinion as to the reputed "Cheshire" or "Albany" sow. As it is simply a matter of belief with both parties—no definite proof being available on either side—we prefer to give the opinions as we receive them, without further comment than to say that both gentlemen are known to be careful, reliable breeders, thoroughly impressed with the superior merits of their favorite swine. In the South, Cheshires are scarcely known at all, and would doubtless fall heir to the same troubles which have thrown other white breeds into disfavor with Southern farmers.

The illustrations of Daisy 2nd and Vulcan—which were engraved after accurate sketches from life—give a good idea of the appearance of the breed. Mr. Davis writes:

"They are not fancy pictures, but are the work of one of the best artists, and I instructed him to reproduce the animals exactly."

CHESHIRE SOW.
Property of E. W. Davis, Oneida, N. Y.

Chapter LXVIII.

SMALL YORKSHIRES.

This breed, which is quite well known in the United States, may be traced directly to the old York and Cumberland breeds of England; indeed, it may be well claimed by their breeders that the Small York is of line-pure descent. Probably no other breed of modern times, save, perhaps, the Essex, is more nearly thoroughbred in fact, or has less admixture of other blood. The breed is peculiar to Yorkshire, England, and has been known as such for many years.

Introduction into the United States was first accomplished about the year 1860; but it is only within the last few years that the Small Yorks have attracted much attention on this side of the Atlantic. A record has been established (Geo. W. Harris, of New York city, is the present secretary), and the breed is quite prominently advertised in most of our agricultural and live stock publications.

DESCRIPTION AND CHARACTERISTICS.

Color pure white, with pinkish skin, occasionally darker spotted under the hair; size small to medium—weighing, when mature, from 375 to 450 pounds. The body is short, rounded and deep; head short; face sharply dished; jowl and neck heavy; short, fine legs, and thick, rounded quarters. They are hardy, and well covered with hair—hence not so liable to mange and sun-scald as are many of the white breeds; they are quiet, excellent range or grazing hogs, and are remarkably prepotent—the pigs from York boars being uniformly white, and possessing the early maturing qualities of the breed in marked degree. In the South, the Small Yorks do as well as any of the white breeds, but cannot compete with their colored rivals in hardiness.

The following Scale of Points has been adopted by the American Small Yorkshire Club:

HEAD	Small........................... 2 Nose, Shortness of .... 5 Dish of Face .... 3 Width between the Ears .... 3 Ears—Small, thin and Erect...... 2		15—HEAD.
TRUNK	Top line straight from Shoulder to Tail ...... 5 Bottom or Belly line.............. 3 Length .... 10 Depth .... 5 Width, even from *Shoulder* to *Ham* .... 5 Breadth of Loin .... 5 Flank, deep and full 2		35—TRUNK.
	Forward		50

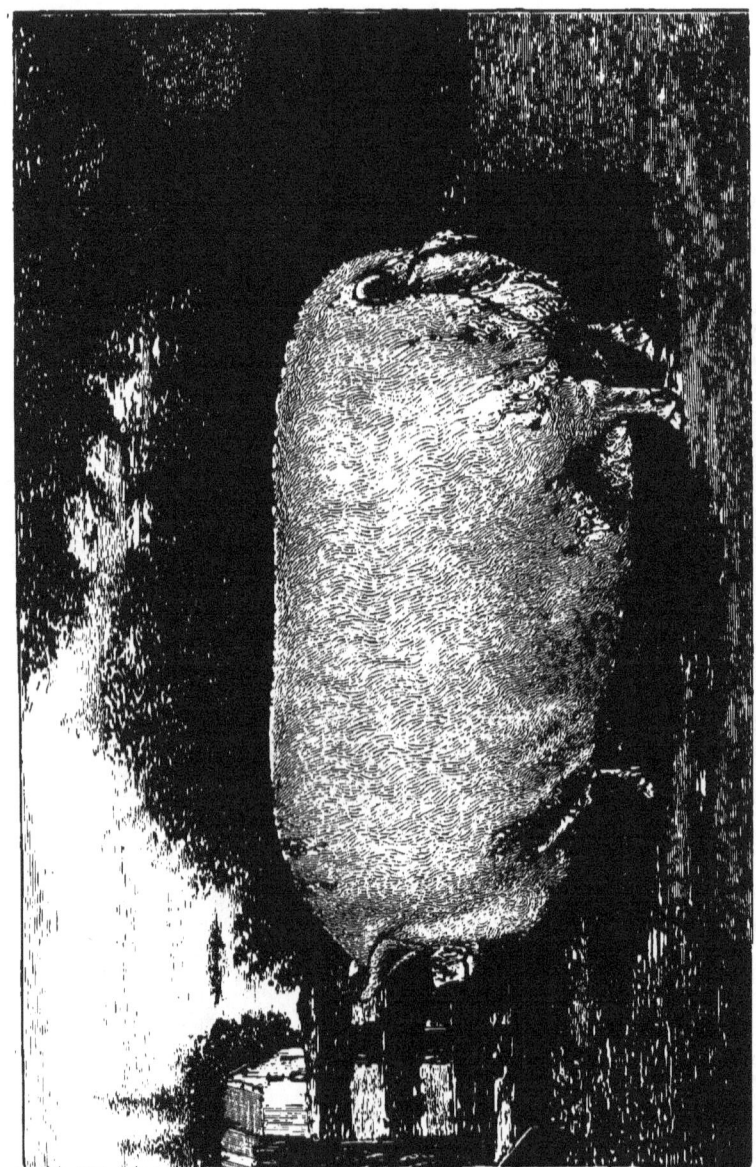

SMALL YORKSHIRE BOAR, SUCCESS 2nd.
Property of W. C. Norton, Agent "Ridge Farm Herd," Aldenville, Pa.

SMALL YORKSHIRES.

	Forward 50		
HAMS	Length, vertical 10		
	Breadth, front to rear 5		25—HAMS.
	Thickness 10		
SHOULDERS . .	Breadth, front to rear 3		5—SHOULDERS.
	Thickness 2		
LEGS	Short 5		10—LEGS.
	Straight, feet set up 5		
SKIN	Not *too* thin, nor ridgy nor coarse 2		5—SKIN.
	Free from eruption and discolored spots 3		
HAIR	Full coat and *fine* 5		5—HAIR.

Perfection 100

Our illustration is a good likeness of the noted prize-winning boar Success 2nd, property of W. C. Norton, agent "Ridge Farm Herd," Aldenville, Pa.

Chapter LXIX.

ESSEX.

This breed takes its name from the county or shire of Essex, England, where it originated. The old Essexshire hog was large, gaunt and "slab-sided," with a color varying for each individual animal. About 1830 Lord Western imported from Italy a boar and sow of the breed of Naples. According to Professor Long, he failed in his attempts to breed these black Neapolitans pure, and finally began crossing on the native breed. From Long's Book of the Pig we quote:

"The result was highly satisfactory, and the new variety was commonly successful at every agricultural show at which they were exhibited."

Lord Western bred them a number of years, but they at last began to lose somewhat their vigorous thrift and hardy constitution. At this juncture a tenant of his lordship—Mr. Fisher Hobbes—turned his attention to their breeding, still further improved them, fixed the type, and called them the "Improved Essex."

In America the Essex has become well known, particularly so at the South, Col. Richard Peters, of Atlanta, Ga., being one of the first importers, and, with Mr. Harris, of Rochester, N. Y., steadily pushing the Essex breed with all energy. In a letter to the Author, 1888, Col. Peters says:

"I commenced breeding from the English stock in the year 1856, and have kept them pure, with some of the original blood in their veins, having obtained, with much difficulty, an occasional pure-bred to avoid close in-and-in breeding."

DESCRIPTION AND CHARACTERISTICS.

The modern American-bred Essex is a small to medium-sized hog, weighing from 250 to 400 pounds at maturity; black, or more properly, ash-black in color—with fine head, short nose, beautifully dished face, erect thin ears, heavy jowl, short neck, close, "chunked" body, and short, firm boned legs. They fatten easily, range well, are not troubled with mange or sun-scald, and dress as large a proportion of live weight as any known breed. Where the large hogs thrive, and corn is cheap, as in the Western United States, we doubt much if the Essex can ever compare profitably with the Poland-China or Duroc-Jersey; but in the South, where, unfortunately, Cotton is still King, we have not found his equal. We have heard some objections to the Essex because he "gets too fat;" we can only suggest, in answer to this, that we beg to be excused from close acquaintance with a hog that gets too lean; tendency to fatten quickly means giving a greater return for food invested. In an experiment conducted under the direction of the Author, 1884, it was found that it took the following weights of food to produce 100 pounds of gain—live weight—with representatives of four different breeds:

Essex . . . . 285 pounds to produce 100 pounds gain.
Duroc-Jersey 296   "   "   "   "
Poland-China 300   "   "   "   "
Berkshire 485   "   "   "   "

The Duroc-Jerseys were not quite pure-bred, having a strain of Poland-China in their veins; the Berkshires were placed at a disadvantage by reason of a slight indisposition, so that really they should be thrown out of the experiment altogether, but the Essex—thoroughbreds—showed the high assimilating power of the breed in a very substantial manner. For the Southern farmer, we cannot recommend a better hog than the Essex, unless the Duroc-Jerseys shall, as they promise, still

ESSEX SOW.
Property of FRANK WILSON, Jackson, Mich.

further improve. An American-Essex Breeders' Association has been organized, F. M. Srout, of McLean, Ill., secretary, and the following Scale of Points has been adopted:

Color	2	Forward	49
Head	3	Loin	12
Ears	2	Flank	2
Jowl	1	Ham	12
Neck	3	Tail	2
Shoulders	7	Legs	3
Girth around heart	6	Feet	3
Back	12	Hair	3
Sides	6	Symmetry	10
Ribs	7	Action	4
Forward	49	Perfection	100

Chapter LXX.

NEAPOLITANS.

The Neapolitan, although not bred at present in the United States (unless, perhaps, a few may be found in the vicinity of New York), deserves a place among the breeds now known in America, from the fact —if for no other reason—of its having taken so important a part in the foundation of the Essex breed. The Neapolitan is a native of Italy, and is supposed to be descended from eastern stock, brought in by the early Italian voyagers. Youatt (Youatt on " The Pig") says of the Neapolitans that they are "black, or rather brown, with no bristles, and consequently delicate when first introduced into our northern climate." They resemble the modern Essex somewhat, but are almost destitute of hair, and the head and front parts are lighter and more bony. From the report of the National Swine Breeders' Convention, November 20, 1872, we clip the following detailed

DESCRIPTION OF THE NEAPOLITAN.

"Head small, forehead bony and flat; face slightly dishing; snout rather long and very slender; ears small, thin, standing forward nearly horizontal, and quite lively; jowl very full; neck short, broad and heavy above; trunk long, cylindrical and well-ribbed back; back flat and ribs arching even in low flesh; belly horizontal on the lower line; hind quarters higher than the fore, but not very much so; legs very fine, the bones and joints being smaller than those of any other breed; hams and shoulders well developed and meaty; tail fine, curled, flat at the extremity and fringed with hair on each side: general color, slatish or bluish-plum color, with cast of coppery red; skin soft and fine, nearly free from hair, which, when found upon the sides of the head and behind the forelegs, is black, soft and rather long; flesh firm and elastic to the touch."

They are considered too delicate for American farmers, and will probably never be extensively introduced, unless the breed should undergo an almost complete transformation.

Chapter LXXI.

ENGLISH, OR BLACK SUFFOLK.

In America, there is such a common impression that the Suffolk is a white hog, that it is necessary to treat of the two breeds under different heads. We have never seen a specimen of the pure Black Suffolk, but we give a description based upon that given by the best English authors of modern times. The origin of the breed is at best doubtful; probably the Neapolitans formed much of the basis of modern Suffolk excellence, and indeed some are of opinion that the Essex, Black Dorset and Black Suffolk are merely different strains of the same breed. According to descriptions and portraits, it would seem that the Dorset very closely resembles the Essex, but not so with the Black Suffolk, as will be seen from the following

DESCRIPTION AND CHARACTERISTICS.

The head is short; snout turned up, not quite so much as in the Small Yorks, but yet showing much of similarity to that well-known breed. The body is deep, with well-sprung ribs dropping to flattened sides, and short, small-boned legs from bulging quarters. Their characteristics may be summed up as follows: Early maturity, medium size, great aptitude to fatten, high dressing qualities, and a black color which withstands the effects of summer heat.

We are not aware that any of the Black or English Suffolks are bred in the United States. The breed might find some favor here, but their white namesakes have become so well known and so widely disseminated, that it would be well nigh impossible at this late day to change the nomenclature of the breed.

Chapter LXXII.

AMERICAN, OR WHITE SUFFOLK.

This is an undoubted descendant of the English York and Cumberland breeds, resembling the Small Yorkshire of to-day so closely in all points except size—Suffolks being somewhat larger—as to preclude any necessity for futher description. Many writers class the Suffolk and Cheshire together as representatives of the "Middle White" breed of England. We believe, however, that Professor Long, in his "Book of the Pig," comes nearer the truth, when he states that the Suffolk as a white hog is only recognized in America, whereas in England—its supposed home—it has been absorbed into what he calls the "English Small White Breed," of which the Small Yorkshire is the representative in America.

If we were to state any point of difference, other than noted above, between Suffolks and Small Yorks, it would be to compare faces. Yorkshire breeders have shortened-in the face, and made a trifle sharper "dish" than is the case with the Suffolk. The latter is about the best type of the old Chinese hog that we now have, and displays such a tendency to extreme fat—"chuffiness" as to amount, with many, to a decided objection. From the report of the National Swine Breeders' Convention, 1872, we quote the following detailed

DESCRIPTION OF AMERICAN SUFFOLK.

"Head small, very short; cheeks prominent and full; face dished; snout small and very short; jowl fine; ears short, small, thin, upright, soft and silky; neck very short and thick, the head appearing almost as if set on front of shoulders, no arching of crest; chest wide and deep—elbows standing out; brisket wide but not deep; shoulders thick, rather upright, rounding outwards from top to elbow; crops wide and full; long ribs, well arched out from back; good length between shoulders and hams; flank well filled out, and coming well down at ham; back broad, level, straight from crest to tail, not falling off or down at tail; hams wide and full, well rounded out, twist very wide and full all the way down; legs small and very short, standing wide apart—in sows, just keeping belly from the ground; bone fine, feet small, hoofs rather spreading; tail small, long and tapering; skin thin, of a pinkish shade, free from color; hair fine and silky, not too thick; color of hair pale yellowish white, perfectly free from any spots or other color; size, small to medium."

Chapter LXXIII.

HINTS ON SELECTION, CARE AND MANAGEMENT OF SWINE.

The breeding and handling of swine is something of far more importance than is generally supposed by a great majority of our farmers—those who should be, really, best informed on the subject. The amount of pork that is consumed yearly in the United States is enormous, and gives something of an idea of the magnitude of the swine industry. Many seem to think that the breeding of swine requires only a little of the skill and foresight which is recognized as being of prime necessity in the handling of any of the other races of domestic animals; but to such as have tried it we need not say the idea is a mistaken one. True it is, that not so much of close attention and tender petting and care to keep them from the rugged blasts of winter, and the fierce, scalding heat of summer, is always given; but it may be stated as an axiom, that good care pays as well with hogs as it does with other races of live stock. There is something fascinating about the feeding and handing of a yard full of swine—a sort of pleasurable excitement in day by day watching their growth, and noting their greedy appetites. Someway, the farmer always feels that an animal is gaining when it eats, and a hog that won't eat is not the one that makes the profit for his owner.

We may state it as an indisputable fact that no other animal sustains such a close relation to the farmer's profit and loss account as does the hog, and the reason is obvious; there is always more or less waste—generally more—about a farm-house, that cannot be utilized in any other way than by feeding it to hogs. It matters not how careful the farmer's wife may be, she cannot prevent this constant waste from the table, and the pig-pen is the natural and legitimate avenue through which it can be turned to account. Every gallon of house-slop has a certain definite value, and, although it is impossible to rate its worth in dollars and cents, on account of the fact that there is great difference in richness of the portions thrown from different tables, yet we may say, in a general way, that every four to seven gallons of such waste is equivalent to one pound of pork when properly fed in connection with grain or other food stuffs.

Perhaps the most common mistake made by the average farmer, is to adopt one of two extremes—either feed entirely on dry corn, all the animals will eat, or allow them to range freely on what is supposed to be good grass, and expect them to grow fat and contented without other food. In the first place, no hog can stand full feeding on dry corn alone for many weeks in succession; he may not become diseased, so far as appearance and action are concerned, but the fevered condition due to feeding corn exclusively is sure to be there, and only time is required to bring it out. Do not think that we would underrate the value of corn in fattening hogs—we are too well aware of its importance in swine feeding to make any statements that are not pretty strongly based on a good foundation—but we do question whether, as generally fed, there is not more loss than gain in its use. It is a mistake to suppose that when corn is cheap it can be fed at a profit, regardless of other conditions; the hog demands a variety, and will not give greatest return for time and food invested, unless this variety is given. More than this, the hog requires bulky food, not highly concentrated, and to provide this, something besides corn is necessary.

Concerning the second practice, we may say: In a large section of the country hogs are allowed to range on grass, and are fed corn to "harden the flesh," and prepare the animal for market; such treatment is little better than the other extreme, for it is no longer a disputed point, that hogs full-fed on proper diet will make a much greater relative return for food consumed than if the same food is given, but in smaller quantity. We cannot protest too strongly against the custom of allowing hogs to run wild the first year (stock-hogs), and feeding heavily for a short time just before placing on the market; it is a waste in two directions: (1) loss of time, and consequent loss of interest on investment; and (2) a very great loss by reason of the constant exertion required to secure whatever sustenance they may from the grass at their command; all exertion is work, and all work has a natural tendency to decrease the production of fat. It is urged in favor of this system that while the hog is running at large he is growing, and that if fed for early market, this growth will be lost. Those who argue on this line forget that the object in raising stock of any kind is to realize the greatest profit in the shortest possible space of time. There is only one reason (perhaps two) that should cause a farmer to carry over a stock of hogs to fatten the succeeding winter, and that is, market; we have always been of opinion that farmers are primarily to blame for the low prices at which their pork is sold. If they would get out of the old ruts and pay off their debts in some other way than by sacrificing a crop at the lowest point of the market to do it, they would soon be in condition to bid defiance to the periodical depressions that affect the market. Every farmer should study the market as closely as he studies the weather, and when there is good promise of better prices in the future, it may be profitable to hold.

Another thing which is in favor of early and high feeding, is the fact that buyers pay more per pound for shoats—say eight to ten months old, and this class of hogs is always in demand when old and "short-fed" hogs can hardly be sold at any price. To the practice of growing and selling the hog crop between tax dates—defrauding Uncle Sam out of his dues—we cannot forbear calling attention. The plan may be of doubtful propriety, but so long as taxes are rendered at a certain date each year, the farmer can avoid taxes on his entire fat hog crop as legitimately as can the banker by collecting all the greenbacks possible to have on hand the first day of January. The sows are bred about the middle to the last of September of each year, bringing their litters about the middle to the last of January following, and the pigs are fattened and sold at an age—anywhere from eight to eleven months, and out of the way before the next annual date for the rendition of taxes. It may shock some of the literal upholders of law to know that many farmers are actually doing this very thing, but such is the fact; the hog is to the farmer what the greenback is to the money lender, and who shall dispute his equal right to use him in an equally legitimate way.

While speaking of the proper food for hogs, we may notice some very interesting experiments that have been carried on—first by Professor Sanborn, of Missouri, and afterward by Professor Henry, of Wisconsin—regarding the relative effects of fat and carbohydrates as compared with albuminoids in the production of flesh and fat in the body. According to these experiments, and they are certainly accurate, it is found that a diet made up largely of protein (albuminoids) causes a very much larger proportion of lean meat: while a diet composed mainly of the starchy elements (carbohydrates) and fat, gives a very large proportion of fat, which is scattered through the body in bunches. To sum up, in the words of Professor Henry, the experiments show that when there is an excessive proportion of carbohydrates in the food, or a corresponding deficiency of protein:

"1st. That there is an excessive development of fat not only on the outside of the muscles and beneath the skin, but also among the muscles.

"2nd. That the muscles of the body fail to develop to their normal size, especially some of the most important ones, as those along the back.

"3d. That an abnormally small amount of hair and thin skin results.

"4th. That while the brain, heart and lungs do not seem to gain in weight, the spleen, liver and kidneys are unusually small.

"5th. The amount of blood in the body is greatly reduced from the normal.

"6th. The strength of the bones may be reduced one-half."

The practical value of these results to the farmer has been disputed, but they certainly teach a very important scientific truth. The farmer wants to know the exact ration that will give the greatest gain in live weight—be it muscle or fat—in proportion to food consumed, always keeping the animal in healthy condition; and it may be noted that, until buyers can be educated up to the point of appreciating the superior value of lean pork over fat, it will hardly pay to put any extra expense into hog feeding to obtain this large proportion of lean meat. The health of the animal is of prime importance, and we may be pardoned for saying that herein lies the great value to the farmer of the lesson drawn from Professor Henry's experiments. It is a fact, as stated above, that corn is not a good food-stuff for exclusive feeding, and the experiments by the Professor seem to show the reason. Corn is deficient in protein, and is not, therefore, a good food, unless supplemented by something richer in this element. The remarks by Mr. T. G. Terry, before the Indiana Swine Breeders' Association, Indianapolis, Ind., January, 1888, illustrate very aptly the exact place filled by the results of these experiments, and we quote his statements in full as reported in the *Breeders' Gazette* of February 1st, 1888:

"I have made a good many experiments in feeding, commencing back in 1869, and have tried different plans, and last fall I made the most successful experiment in feeding for lean for my own pork. When I killed one of the pigs (a cross-bred Cheshire-Poland-China), it happened to be just the time Professor Henry's experiments were published, and I will say that taking the center cut of the ham it did not have fat enough to fry it. The pig was six months old, and dressed 135 lbs. I fed it on oats, bran and shorts, and nothing else (no milk), and the verdict of those who ate the pork was that it was the nicest and juiciest ever put into their mouths. I am feeding all my pigs intended for family pork in that way. It may cost more, but for our own eating we can afford it."

This last statement contains the milk of the cocoanut. It may cost more, undoubtedly does cost more, to feed protein than to feed starch; the thinking, reasoning farmer will, therefore, feed just such proportion of this valuable ingredient as will bring highest returns in gross weight, and no more—since the buyer will pay no more for lean meat than for fat; but when it comes to feeding for the home barrel, we can afford to put a little extra expense into the feed in order to produce an extra amount of that richest of all meats, lean pork.

We had no idea of writing an essay on the feeding of swine. The reader can obtain more valuable information from the statements of actual methods pursued by such men as are represented in the letters given below, and we must beg pardon for thus wandering so far from our intention in the preceding discussion. We may, however, state briefly a few points, as an aid in the selection of breeding stock, and trust the reader will find something of interest, if not of profit, in their perusal.

The boar is by all odds the most important, if not the largest, half of the herd, and his selection should be made with the greatest care. We do not propose to give any advice as to breed from which he should be selected; there are a good many breeds, and from the preceding chapters under Part Fourth, the reader may obtain that which will aid in choosing a breed best suiting his own peculiar conditions. But it may be stated, that a boar should combine the best of the dominant characteristics of the breed to which he belongs, He should be close, compact, shorter than the model, rather than longer, and should be sprightly, active and vigorous—even bold—in appearance. If breeding to secure any particular result, the boar should be selected with reference to the particular characteristics desired; if breeding to sows too long and straight in the face—a very common fault—he should have an unusually short and sharply dished face; if bred to sows inclined to be peaked and narrow across the back, he should have especial width and fullness in these parts; if mated with sows that are inclined to lay on fat in bunches, he should be selected from a strain or breed that is noted for interlarding its fat and lean; in brief, select the boar with reference, always, to correcting whatever evils may exist in your herd, and you will obtain satisfactory results.

The sow is selected with a view to modifying the impress of the male on their combined offspring. She controls almost entirely the number of pigs in a litter, and exercises a very important influence on their strength and stamina at the time they are ushered into the world. The sow should always be selected from a family noted for its prolificacy; it is a well known fact that the quality of bearing either large or small litters is one which runs in families, and when a sow is selected for profitable breeding she should, by all means, be taken from one of these large bearing strains. The sow should be almost the opposite of the boar in many ways—instead of being short and close-coupled, she should be long and rangy in her make up, especially wide and deep at the pelvis, and with at least twelve well developed, prominent nipples. As a rule, better pigs, larger litters and greater profits will be obtained from sows fully matured in all respects. Those who practice breeding young sows —turning them off for the market after one, or at most two litters—cannot compete with equally skillful breeders who breed only from matured sows. The sow should not be selected before she has reached an age of at least four or five months; about this time changes occur which might lead to quite a different choice from selections made when the pigs were only a few weeks old. Health and constitution are two prime factors in profitable pork raising, and to secure these, both sow and boar must have a large girth back of the fore legs, and be deep and wide in the chest. Clean skin; thin, soft, glossy hair; fine, delicate ears; short, neatly-dished face; short neck, and fine-boned, trimly made legs, are sure indications, in either boar or sow, that the animal will be an easy keeper; while the reverse—long head, straight nose, and narrow or flat-sided body—almost always denote a large appetite, and not always an equivalent return. A mean between these two types will usually be found more profitable, and there are many breeds now known that fill this middle ground to perfection.

In the following letters will be found a good many solid facts. "Nothing succeeds like success," and the breeders who have thus given us the benefit of their experience are all men who have made a success of the business of raising hogs. We advise a careful perusal.

Berkshires.

HAW HILL, SPRINGFIELD, ILL., August 10, 1888.

* * * *

"Whether pigs are to be reared and sold for breeding purposes, or to be grown and fattened for market, our general rule is to breed the sows as nearly as practicable during the second week in November; the pigs will then come about the 1st of March following.

"In this latitude, with the breed we handle, nine months is long enough to allow for the growing and fattening of a hog; this brings the fattened hogs into market about the first of December. The first of March is also a good time to have pigs come that are to be reared and sold as breeders. Both they and those intended for pork have the summer on grass. All are thus more cheaply raised, are more healthy, make better pork product and better breeding stock. We prefer a good boar from two to five years of age, to one only eight to twelve months old, though the latter may give every promise of making a very superior animal when fully matured. A young boar, however, from an early spring litter, if properly taken care of through the summer, may be used with full-grown sows in November, or better, a month later. The pigs will hardly be inferior in size and vigor to those sired by an older boar, particularly if the sows bred to the old boar were young or not well matured. In fact, we keep two boars all the time, often three, and when we get one that is particularly to our liking we use him year after year, though not, except rarely, on his own get. At the time the boars are to be used in the fall, we wish them to be in good, healthy condition—the young boar growing, and the old one laying on flesh as fast as his restricted allowance of feed will permit, for he should not be fed all the rich food he can eat, like a fattening hog, nor as much as a young and growing boar. After he has commenced service he is fed more liberally, depending upon the amount of service required of him; and so also with the young boar—his rations are increased, though only as needed to keep him in a good, vigorous condition.

"The condition of the sows at the time they are served is also a matter of importance. Having summered on grass, and being only moderately fat, they are taken up in October and put on a diet of more or less grain, depending on the weather. They take, as it were, a new start in growth if young, or in laying on flesh if old. When they do this, and come in season, it is the right time to breed them. They are more certain to hold if served at this time than later, or after they become fat. One good service is all that is needed. The sow is placed in a pen or yard by herself until fully over her heat. She is then put with others that have been bred. It is best not to keep more than four or five in the same yard; two or three only would be still better, though it is more trouble to have so many small lots to feed, and more expensive making so many shelters. Some regard is also had to dividing them according to size.

"The time of service is noted down, and time when due to farrow—counting sixteen weeks from date of service—is also noted. From the 18th to the 21st day the sow is noticed carefully, to see if she comes in heat again. If she does she is served, and the new date recorded. About the middle of February, or two weeks before the pigs are due, each sow is put in a comfortable pen by herself, and well bedded. Here she is gentled by the feeder, to whom she soon becomes accustomed. Her feed during this time is such as will tend to keep the bowels open. Much use of dry corn is avoided. When she makes her bed, preparatory to farrowing, care is taken that she does not have too much straw or litter to work with. Better have a warm or well-sheltered pen and less bedding for there is much danger of the pigs being over-laid when the bedding is too plentiful or coarse. The pigs usually come strong, and soon find their way to the teats. If they are weak and helpless, it seems hardly worth while spending time with them. Half of a litter may thus be lost, and sometimes all, but if any survive they are apt to do better and make us more money, considering time and trouble saved, than to have saved all. We are inclined to think the career of the runt pig, as a runt, begins before it is born, and comes from not being as well nourished as his fellows before entering life on his own account. The early backset thus given a pig may doubtless be overcome, in a measure at least, by special care and liberal feeding afterwards. In cases of scarcity of stock the extra attention given runt pigs, or those weakly at birth, may be made to pay well.

"After the pigs are farrowed, the sow is given all the warm drink she will take. This is made by scalding wheat bran and ship stuff with hot water, and then adding cold water and skimmed milk, if the latter is at hand, until reduced to the right temperature. If given her cold at this time of year, she will go to her bed chilled and uncomfortable, but if warm and palatable she will lie down and be quiet, while the little pigs will suck, sleep and grow strong. It is surprising how fast a few good fillings with milk and a few good sleeps will send them along.

"The feed of the sow is but little increased during the first week or ten days. By the time the pigs are three or four weeks old, if they have done well, they will have become a real burden to the sow, and she will begin to fall off in flesh rapidly unless in the meantime her rations have been gradually increased in richness as well as in quantity. When four weeks old the young pigs are offered feed in a trough by themselves, where it cannot be reached by the sow. They soon learn to eat, and with this help they grow still faster. When they are eight or ten weeks old the sow is taken from them, or they from the sow, as is most convenient at the time. Before weaning, however, they are all carefully marked, and the marks recorded, so that the parentage of each may always be known. About two weeks before weaning the males that are intended for pork-making are castrated. In case any of these are not fully recovered or doing well, they are left with the sow a few days or a week longer than the others.

"A few weeks after weaning, all the young boars that are to be sold for breeding purposes are separated from the others, and placed out of sight, as well as they can be, of other pigs or hogs. They are kept until sold on grass so far as practicable, in the orchard or small pasture, and fed on almost anything that happens to be available, only they are given very little corn. We prefer oats, rye, vegetables, purslane and wind-fallen apples. When we buy feed, it is usually wheat bran, ship stuff and oil meal [linseed] for making into swill with skimmed milk.

"The sow pigs are kept and fed in much the same way, as are also the barrows and all intended for fattening for pork, except that these last are put on more of a corn diet early in the fall. As soon as new corn is large enough, some is cut each day and thrown to the pigs, stalk and ear together, on the ground, while they are still in the pastures. Later, the feeding stock is separated from the breeding stock. We try to keep the latter in good growing condition during summer and fall, but from the 1st of September to the 1st of December the others are fed with a view to fattening as well as making growth. We aim to have them weigh from 225 to 250 pounds at nine months old, and to have them sold before winter sets in. The most of the breeders are also sold by this time, though some of the young sows are always reserved to be bred in the fall and then sold during the winter as sows due to farrow in the spring.

"In this hurried recital of our methods, little has been said of the kinds and quantities of feed given, simply because what can and should be used in our climate or locality cannot perhaps be had in another. The pig is as omnivorous a feeder as is man, and can about as readily adapt himself to the circumstances of feed and surroundings as can his keeper. For similar reasons nothing has been said of the construction of pens and shelters. Here hogs do well with open sheds facing the south. With a good and dry floor, thereby insuring to the hog a dry bed, he will not suffer much in winter if reasonably well fed. If warmer quarters are provided, less feed may be required; but it is hard to draw the line between, or explain in a few words, the dangers or risks of warm and poorly ventilated hog-houses, as compared with the advantages and safety of less expensive and more airy quarters.   PHIL THRIFTON."

The writer of the above needs no introduction to the reading public. The "Haw Hill" breeder is a Berkshire man all over, and one who has done much to advance the breed in popular favor. His methods are clearly outlined, and will furnish an excellent guide for breeders of any class of swine.

Duroc-Jerseys.

PINEWOOD, TENN., August 6, 1888.

* * * *

"We couple our sows early in November, which brings the farrowing time to the latter part of February or first of March. Pigs farrowed at this time will be ten weeks old by the middle of May, at which age they will have been weaned and ready for shipment, enabling us to get them off to their new homes before the hot weather of spring comes on. If bred for pork, we prefer that the farrowing should be a couple of weeks later, as the grass will by that time be a little farther advanced, thus enabling the sows to suckle better. After the sows are bred we separate them from the herd, and keep them in lots or pastures in which there is plenty of good water. We feed them so as to keep in thrifty condition, using the best variety of food that we can command. We usually feed corn, oats and cut sorghum. Sorghum we value very highly; it supplies the place of grass, as it is very sweet and juicy, and tends to keep the sows from becoming feverish, as they frequently do if fed on dry food all the time. We keep the vermin off by greasing the sows with any waste grease, in which we put a little coal oil. We keep within their reach a mixture of

Wood ashes	1 bushel.
Charcoal	1 bushel.
Salt	½ bushel.
Sulphur	5 pounds.

"A couple of weeks before farrowing time we remove the sow to a lot in which is a movable house 8 x 10, open on one side, which faces the south, the roof sloping toward the north. Into this house we throw a lot of hay out of which the sow makes her bed. The sow should be noticed a week before farrowing, and if her bowels are not open she should be fed warm bran slops, which will generally open her bowels and prevent that feverish condition that is so often seen at farrowing time, and which causes so many sows to eat their pigs, or kill them by being restless, and lying on them. At farrowing time it is best to leave the sow to herself, as frequently sows are excited by the presence of some well-wisher, and in their efforts to drive off the intruder, kill the little pigs. After the farrowing is all over, and while the sow is quiet, remove any dead pigs and the afterbirth, as sometimes sows are caused to kill and eat their pigs by getting a taste of those that may be left dead in the bed. For the first day or so warm bran slops will be sufficient food to give her, after which the feed may be gradually increased until the pigs are two weeks old, by which time she should have all she will eat of as great a variety of feed as can be given her. When the pigs are a little over two weeks old they will begin to eat a little slop, which should be given them in troughs about three inches deep; warm kitchen slops will be most acceptable to them, after which cornmeal, made into a thin mush and well cooked, is much relished by them. At a month old we give them meal raw, mixed in kitchen slops or cold water, in which a little salt is put; we sometimes give corn soaked in water for 24 hours, again dry corn, changing the feed to keep the appetite sharp. Care has to be exercised in feeding, as sometimes heavy feeding causes indigestion and scours, which sets the pigs back several weeks, if it does not kill them. At the age of 10 weeks the pigs are weaned and such as are suitable we ship or reserve for breeders; the others we castrate and spay, and place with the herd that is being handled for pork. Sometimes the pigs when a few days old are troubled by their tails and ears becoming sore. If not attended to promptly the tails frequently come off near the body. At the first appearance of the sores we wash the tails and ears with castile soap and anoint them with lard, in which a little carbolic acid and sulphur have been incorporated. Occasionally sows are observed to lie on their bellies and refuse to let the pigs suck; this is because the pigs bite the teats with their sharp, briery tusks; remove them with a pair of nippers, and the trouble will be removed and the pigs will be none the worse for the operation. Whether pigs are being bred for breeders or for pork the sows should be kept separate from the pork hogs, nor should many sows be allowed to carry their pigs in the same lot, for the reason that the oldest and strongest pigs will whip the smaller ones and appropriate their share of the milk as well as their own. Pigs that are destined to be killed for pork we place in the clover fields, and give them daily a feed of dry corn to keep them gentle and to push them forward. Pigs farrowed in March should, if properly handled, average 200 to 250 pounds by the middle of November. Those that come later are carried through the winter and killed the following winter or fattened and sold in June.

"S. L. GRAHAM & SON."

The Messrs. Graham have our thanks for their methods in detail. The antiseptic mixture (wood ashes, charcoal, salt and sulphur) which they use is of much more importance than many suppose; hogs fed liberally on green stuff, and given free access to simple preventives of this kind, are the last ones to succumb to attacks of cholera and other dread diseases to which the hog tribe is subject. The plan of changing food at frequent intervals, to keep the appetite sharp, should be emphasized; too many expect a hog to thrive on one particular kind of diet, and think all that is necessary is to give them plenty of it.

Small Yorkshires and Berkshires.

"BERMUDA PARK PLACE, GRISWOLDVILLE, GA., Aug. 14, 1888.

* * * *

"We have had some experience both at the North and in the South in breeding, and find that this section—Middle Georgia—offers the same advantages for hog raising that is found at the North. It is true that some kinds of feed, such as corn, are more expensive, but as a compensation, so much is not needed. The pastures or fields furnish more or less sustenance at all seasons of the year, and are peculiarly rich in the fall, just before the fattening season; this lightens the expense of corn feeding.

"We have made a specialty of Berkshires and Small Yorkshires. Other breeds would doubtless do as well. In the Berkshire, we have size and weight; in the Yorkshire a compact form and quick growth. They make a good cross for fattening purposes. We keep such numbers only as the farm will support. We have the sour milk from a dairy, and can manage five hogs and pigs to each cow in milk. This gives us the coarse slops for the larger hogs, and pure milk for the pigs, which are fed separately. We feed little grain in the summer, only enough to keep the stock growing.

"We breed for two purposes—for sale as breeders and for use on the plantation. We do not breed or dress for the shows. We have registered hogs that will go into the tub this winter. It is cheaper and easier to raise and fatten a thoroughbred Yorkshire than any grade known to us. In order to secure health we have the hog lots on a hill side, with pens and sheds at the upper end, and an abundance of pure spring water at the other. We never pen our hogs except for fattening. We never clean them except to wash pigs infected with scab or some skin disease. Hogs clean themselves in the wallow as chickens do in the dust. It is safe to keep 50 or 100 hogs and pigs together, but beyond that remember the danger of disease is increased. The males are changed every year or two. A good plan is for neighbors to exchange males frequently, thus insuring both health and vigor.   N. G. BUFF."

Mr. Buff is a breeder who has had success with white hogs in the South, but he is located in a section that will compare favorably—as he says—with more northern localities in this respect. In other and less favored spots—as to water, pasture and elevation—the reports are pretty uniformly against white hogs in general, unless handled with great care.

INDEX.

Illustrations in Bold Faced Type.   *Quotations in Italics.*

	PAGE
Abbess (Polled Durham cow)	**203**
Abdallah	66, 70
Aberdeen-Angus	196-200
Acme (Am. Holderness bull)	**145**
Adelaide (Am. Holderness cow)	**147**
Advanced Register, Conditions for admission to	118, 120
Albany sow	314, 316
Alderney	125
Alexander's Abdallahs, The	66, 70
Alhambra	62
Allen, Lewis F.	*135, 136, 170, 220*
Allerton	72, 73, 74, 108
Almanzor	48
Almonts, The	66
American Eclipse	48-49
American Holderness	144-147
American Merinos	238-254
American Saddle Horses	58-60
American Star	62, 68, 71, 106
American (or White) Suffolk	324
American Thoroughbred, Origin of	47-48
American Trotter, The	*80, 82*
American Trotters	61-89
Andrew Jackson	66
Anglesea Cattle	180
Anna (German Coach mare)	**43**
Ansel	108
Ap Guilm (North Wales Black bull)	**181**
Aquierre Family of Merinos	240, 244
Arion	79
Atwood Merinos	241-243
Atwood Register	*241-242*
Atwood, Stephen, Certificate of	241, 242
Auterdale Breed (Swine)	307
Axtell	73, 74
Ayrshire Group	**137**
Ayrshires	135-139

	PAGE
Baldstockings, The	66
Banquet	56
Bard, The (American Thoroughbred)	**50, 51, 52,** 54
Baron (Hampshire ram)	**268**
Baron Valiant (Aberdeen-Angus bull)	**197**
Bars First	90
Bartlett's Childers	48
Barnum, P. T.	*140*
Bashaws, The	64, 66
Beautiful Bay	64
Bedford Swine	305
Beef Breeds	115
Beef, Selection for	225
Belgian Draft	19-21
Belle Hamlin	70
Belle Vara	77
Bellfounder, Imported	62, 66, 71
Berkshire Group	**295**
Berkshires	294-299
Betsy Malone	54
Betsy Trotwood	68
Bicycle Sulky	63, 80
Big Chinas (Swine)	298
Big Spotted (Swine)	298
Billy Boyce	101
Bishop's Hambletonian	68
Bisson's Belle, Butter Record of	128, 129
Black Faced Heath Breed (Sheep)	257
Blackhawks, The	66
Black Suffolk	323
Black-Top Ewes.	**251**
Black-Top Merinos	249-251
Black-Top Register	*250*
Blaze	48, 61
Blue Bull	66, 82
Blue Bulls, The	66
Blue Ribbon of the Turf (Curzon)	*50*

335

336 INDEX.

	PAGE
Blue Sign	80
Boars, Care of	328, 329
Bolingbroke	158
Bond's First Consul	64
Bonner, Robert	*71*
Bos gaurus	211
Bos Indicus	210
Bos Primigenius	184
Bos taurus	210
Boulonnais	19
Bowman, J. H. & W. R., Methods of	*112*
Brahmin Cattle	210, 214
Brahmin Group	**213**
Breaking Colts	110, 112, 113
Brienz, Butter record of	150
Brinker's Drennon	58
Brunette (Belgian mare)	**21**
Brittany Bull	**152**
Brittany Cow	**153**
Brittanies	152-153
Brown, Prof. Wm., Report of	*170, 172*
Brown Swiss	148-151
Brown Swiss Cow	**151**
Buchour (Brahmins)	210
Buckden (English Shire stallion)	**28**
Buck-Kneed	**105**
"Bull-dog Trotter" (Allerton)	73
Bulls, Care of	226, 228-231
Bulrush	64
Butter fat, Test for	120, 130, 172
Butter Records:	
Ayrshires	139
Brown Swiss	150
Guernseys	132
Holstein-Friesians	122, 123
Jerseys	128, 130, 132
Button, R. D., Letter from	*314, 315*
Byerly Turk	48
Byfield (Swine)	298
Cabell's Lexington	58
Cade	61
Calf-Kneed	**105**
Calves, Care of	225-233
Calving	226, 227, 228, 230-232
Campbell, Jno. R. Jr., Methods of	*288, 289*
Cannock Heath Sheep	264
Canadian Pony	96
Cart Horse	22, 27
Cashmere Goats	211
Cattle, Selection, Care and Management of	223-233

	PAGE
Cattle, Summary of Part Second	115
Cawdor, Earl of	*180*
Champions, The	66
Cheshires	314-316
Chester-Whites	305-306
Cheviot Ram	**258**
Cheviots	257-259
Chicago Horseman	*54*
Chinese Swine	294, 324
Clark Chief	68
Clays, The	64, 66
Cleveland Bays	34-36
Clingstone 2nd (Atwood ram)	**242**
Clothilde (Holstein-Friesian cow)	**119, 122**
Clydesdales	22-26
Clydesdale Stud-Book	*22*
Coffin-joint lameness	110
Coleman's Eureka	58
Colts, Care of	111-113
Comet	158
Conklin's Abdallah	71
Contracted feet	109
Copperbottom	58
Copperbottoms, The	66
Corns	109
Cotswold ewes	**275**
Cotswolds	274-277
Cow, Parts of, Named	**114**
Cows, Care of	225-233
Cricket	80
Curb	109
Curtis, Col. F. D., Death of	310
Curtis Victorias	310-311
Cuyler	68
Cyclone (Hampshire ram)	**267**
Dairy Breeds	115
Daisy 2nd (Cheshire sow)	**316**
Dandy (Davis Victoria boar)	**372**
Dandy (Todd's Improved Chester boar)	**370**
Daniel Lambert	66
Daniel Lamberts, The	66
Darley Arabian	10, 48, 61
Davis, E. W., Letter from	*315, 316*
Davis Victorias	312-313
Dehorning	163, 166, 192, 198, 229
Delaine Ewes	**253**
Delaine Merinos	250-254
Delaine Wool	250, 252
Delmarch	108

	PAGE
Demi-Sang	37
Demuth	56, 57
Denmark	58
Development of the Trotter	100–108
Devon Bull	**169**
Devons	167–172
Dexter	68, 74, 101
Dexter Strain of Kerries	156
Dickinson ewes	**247**
Dickinson Merinos	246–249
Dictator (American Trotter)	**65**, 68
Dictators, The	66
Dillon, Levi, Letter from	*176*
Diomed, Imported	62
Dipping	289
Direct	80, 101
Dobroy First	90
Docking horses	46
Docking sheep	291
Dolly Varden (Hereford cow)	**189**
Donovan	52
Dorset Sheep	255
Dorset Swine	323
Draft Breeds	9
Draft, Selection for	99
Drake Carter	56, 57
Duchess Family of Shorthorns	160
Duchess of Smithfield (Ayrshire cow)	**138**
Du Hays	*10*
Durhams	157
Duroc	50, 62, 106, 301
Duroc-Jersey Group	**303**
Duroc-Jersey Record	*301*
Duroc-Jerseys	301–304
Duroc Swine	301
Dutch-Belted Cattle	140–143
Dutch Belted Cattle Herd-Book	*140*
Dutch-Friesians	106, 119
Dutch mares	27, 90
Early lambs	288, 289
Eclipse	48, 49, 62
Edgemark	79
Edith (Devon cow)	**171**
Edward Everetts, The	66
Edward The Great (Dutch-Belted bull)	**141**
Elaine	72
Elaine of Abelour (Aberdeen-Angus cow)	**199**
Electioneer	70, 71, 72, 73, 79, 82, 88, 104, 107

	PAGE
Electioneers, The	66, 104
Elkwood	52
Elmo (Brown Swiss bull)	**149**
Else (German Coach mare)	**43**
Emperor of Norfolk (American Thoroughbred)	52, **53**, 54
Engineer	61
English Shires	27–30
English Style Riding	58
English (or Black) Suffolk	323
English Thoroughbred, Degeneracy of	49, 56
Esbly (French Coach Stallion)	**38**
Escurial Family of Merinos	238, 243
Escutcheon	121, 122, 224
Essex	320–321
Essex Sow	**321**
Ethan Allen	64
Ethan Allens, The	66
Ewes, Care of	287–291
Exmoor Ponies	93
Farceur (French Draft stallion)	**17**
Fearnaughts, The	66
Feather	26, 30
Feeding for fat or lean	327, 328
Fellowcraft	56, 57
Fides	56
Fields, Wm. M. & Bro., Methods of	*111, 112*
Fireaways, the	44, 62
Firenzi	52, 56
Flanders Draft Horse	10, 15, 22
Flora	70
Flora Temple	68
Flukes	134
Flying Childers	48, 49, 61
Flying Jib	80, 82
Forest Breed (Cattle)	154, 167, 180, 184
Foundation Stock, Saddle Horses	58
Founder	109
Francoui (French Coach stallion)	**39**
Freeland (Oxford ram)	**272**
French Canadians	63
French Coach	37–39
French Draft	15, 18
French Merinos	237
Front Leverage in Trotting Action	**103**
Frost, J. M., Letter from	*214*
Frou Frou	78, 79

INDEX

	PAGE
Gaits, Saddle	58, 60
Gallipoli	10
Galloway King (Galloway bull)	**193**
Galloway robes	194
Galloways	191-195
Garibaldi (Belgian Draft stallion)	**20**
General Knox	64, 106
General Purpose Breeds (Cattle)	115
George M. Patchen	66
George Wilkes	73, 74, 82
Geraldine	56
German Coach Horses	42-43
German Merinos	238
Gestations in cows, Period of	210, 230
Gestation in mares, Period of	96
Gestation in sheep, Period of	291
Gestation in swine, Period of	330, 332
Gilderoy (Clydesdale stallion)	**23**
Gimcrack	62
Godolphin Barb (Arabian)	10, 48, 61
Gold-dust	64
Goldsmith Maid	70, 101
Gordon, Jno. I., Secy, Letter from	*270*
Goth (English Shire stallion)	**29**
Gothlands	309
Grand Bashaw	64, 66
Grass Breed (Swine)	307
Graves, C. A., Methods of	*112, 113*
Green's Bashaw	66
Green Mountain Maid	70, 71
Green Mountain Morgan, Hale's	64
Gaudaloupe Family of Merinos	243
Guernseys	131-134
Guy (Pacer)	80, 82
Guy (Trotter)	70, 71, 77, 78
Guy Wilkes	71
Hackneys	44-46
Hal Pointer	80
Hambletonian, Bishop's	68
Hambletonian, Rysdyk's	62, 64, 66, 68, 70, 72, 73, 74, 77, 104, 105, 106
Hambletonians, The	66
H-a-m-i-l-t-o-n-i-a-n	68
Hamlin's Almont	70
Hammond, Edwin, Certificate of	244
Hampshire ewes	**269**
Hampshires	267-270
Hanoverian Coach Horse	42
Haphazard	62
Happy Medium	68, 76, 82, 104
Happy Mediums, The	66

	PAGE
Harold	70, 106
Heat, Recurrence of in mares	113
Heavy Carriage Breeds	9
Hedgeford, Imported	58
Helm, H. T.	*63*
Henry Clay	66
Henry, Prof. W. A., Report of	*327*
Herefords	185-190
Herod Line of Horses	48
Hiatogas, The	66
History of the Oldenburg Horse (Hoffmeister)	*40*
Hog, Parts of, Named	**292**
Holderness	144
Holstein-Friesian Breeders' Controversy	120-121
Holstein-Friesians	116-124
Horned Dorset Group	**256**
Horned Dorsets (Sheep)	255-256
Horse Breeder, The	*44, 46*
Horse, Parts of, Named	**8**
Horses, Selection, Care and Management of	99-113
Horses, Summary of Part First	9
Hubback	158
In-breeding defined	158
Indian Buffalo (Bos gaurus)	211
Indian Pony Group	**97**
Indian Ponies	96-98
Infantado Family of Merinos	238, 243
Iroquois	50
Irish Grazier Swine	298
Irish Longhorns	173
Jay Eye See (American Trotter)	63, 65, 66, **69**, 70, 87, 101
Jersey Bull	**127**
Jersey Group	**129**
Jersey Reds	301
Jerseys	125, 130
Johnston	80, 101
Joker (American Merino ram)	**239**
Jolie 2nd, (Guernsey cow)	**134**
Joseph (Percheron stallion)	**11**
Journal Royal Agrl. Society	*264*
Justin Morgan	64
Kanucks	63
Kentucky Prince	71
Kerries	154, 156
Kerry Cows	**155**

INDEX. 339

	PAGE
Kildeer	56
King Herod	48
Kirsch	57
Kite track	63, 80
Knoxes, The	66, 106
Kyloes	215
Kremlin	72, 73, 79, 80
Lady Aldine (Dutch Belted cow)	**143**
Lakenfield Cattle	140
Lambs, Care of	288-291
Laminitis	109
Lamplighter	56
Landessohn (Oldenburg Coach stallion)	**41**
Landseer's Fancy, Butter record of	128
Large Breeds (Swine)	293
La Tosca	57
Leading Sires, 1892	82
Leamington	50, 57
Lebed First	90
Leicester ewe	**279**
Leicester Group	**280**
Leicesters	278-281
Leiston (Suffolk Punch stallion)	**32**
Leverage in Wild Animals, Ratios of	107, 108
Lexington	50, 57
Lincoln Group (Sheep)	**284**
Lincoln Horse	22, 27
Lincolns (Sheep)	282-285
Lindsey Arabian	64
Line Trotters	105
Little Albert	77, 78
Little Brown Jug	101
Little Minch	52
Lobasco	77, 73, 79
Lochlyoch mares	22
Longhorns	173, 175
Longhorn steers	**174**
Long Island Blackhawk	66
Long, Prof. Jas.	*294, 320, 324*
Long-wooled Breeds	235
Lord Clinton	77, 78
Lord Kingsbury (Hackney stallion)	**45**
Lord Derby (Cleveland Bay stallion)	**36**
Lord Preston (Lincoln ram)	**283**
Lorena (Polled Durham cow)	**203**
Louis (Percheron stallion)	**13**
Low, Prof. David	*27, 34, 48, 49, 93, 135, 168, 215, 220, 236, 255, 257, 260*

	PAGE
Lubezney First	90
Magie Swine	298
Magna Charta	64
Main (Advanced) Register, Conditions for admission to	118-120
Mambrino	61, 66, 73
Mambrino, American	66, 73
Mambrino Chief	66, 68, 71, 73
Mambrino Patchen	68
Mambrino Paymaster	66
Mambrinos, The	66
Manager	80
Manzanita	71, 79
Marion 5th of Castlemilk (Galloway cow)	**195**
Marius (Shorthorn bull)	**159**
Mares, Brood, Care of	110-113
Marshall	*163*
Marske	48
Martha Wilkes	76, 77
Mary Marshall	108
Mascot (Pacer)	80, **81**, 82
Massena, Butter record of	128
Matchem	61
Matilda 4th, Butter record of	128
Maud S.	63, 66, 68, 70, 76, 77, 101, 106, 108
Maxey Cobb	68, 74
Mayflower	71
McDowell, Jas.	*248*
Medley, Imported	62
Merinos	236-254
Merritt, Consul	*285*
Messenger-Duroc	62, 72
Messenger-Durocs, The	66
Messenger, Imported	61, 62, 64, 66, 68
Mexican Pony Group	**95**
Mexican Ponies	94-96
Midas (Guernsey bull)	**133**
Middle Breeds (Swine)	293
Middle White Breed (Swine)	324
Middle-wooled Breeds	235
Midnight	70
Milk Mirror	121, 122, 224
Milk Wedge	224
Miller, J. H.	*202*
Mills, C. F., Methods of	*291*
Miss Hervey	62
Miss Russell	70
Mohawks, The	66
Montarco Family Merinos	240, 243

	PAGE
Montgomery, W. B., Letter from.	*152, 153*
Moore Swine	298
Moquette	79
Morfe Common Sheep	264
Morgan, Justin	64, 66
Morgans, The	66
Morrills, The	66
Muir, L. P., Secy., Letter from	*194*
Muotta (Brown Swiss cow)	**149**
Mustangs	94
Nancy Hanks (American trotter)	**75**, 76, 101, 104
Native Full Bloods	19
National Live Stock Journal	*156, 186*
National Stockman	*252*
Navicular Disease	110
Neapolitans	322
Negretti Family of Merinos	238, 240, 243
Nelson	72, 74
Netherland Prince (Holstein-Friesian bull)	**117**
Nettie Norton	50
Norlaine	72, 79
Norfolk	54
Norfolk Reds (Cattle)	163
Norfolk Thin Rind	307
Normans	15
Normandie Bull	**177**
Normandie Cow	**178**
Normandies	176-179
North Devons	167
North Wales Black Cattle	180-183
Norton, C. W. & Sons, Methods of	*230, 231*
Norton, Oak G., Death of	231, 232
Norval	72
Nutwood	82
Oldenburg Coach Horses	40-41
Oldenburg-German Coach Horse Controversy	42
Onward	82
Orloff Trotters	90
Oval tracks (Regulation)	80
Oxfordshires	271-273
Pacers, 2:10 list of	80
Pacing Blood	58, 66, 68, 80, 82
Packard, Hon. S. B.	*184*
Palo Alto	72, 73

	PAGE
Pancoast	68
Parole	50
Part First, Summary of	9
Part Second, Summary of	115
Part Third, Summary of	235
Part Fourth, Summary of	293
Patron	68
Patton Stock	158
Paular Merinos	243-246
Paulina (Red Polled cow)	**165**
Pauline Paul, Butter record of	123
Pearl	64
Pedigrees:	
Electioneer	88
Emperor of Norfolk	54
Jay Eye See	87
Mascot	89
Maud S.	85
Nancy Hanks	84
Phallas	86
The Bard	52
Pembrokes	184
Perchero-Norman Controversy	12, 15
Percherons	10-14
Percheron Stud Book	*10*
Perfection (Chester-White boar)	**306**
Peter's Halcorn	58
Peters, Richard, Letter from	*214, 320*
Phallas (American Trotter)	50, 51, 56, 60, **67**, 68, 86
Phœnix	158
Pocahontas	101
Piertetje 2nd, Milk record of	123
Pigs, Care of	330, 334
Pilot	63, 64
Pilot Jr.	63, 66, 70, 71
Pilots, The	66
Points for rejection, Horses	100
Poland-China Group	**299**
Poland-Chinas	298-300
Polkan First	90
Polled-Angus	196
Polled Durhams	201-203
Pony Breeds	9
Potomac Mare	54
Prather, S. E., Secy., Letter from	*263*
Prince Albert	58
Prince Charlie (Shorthorn bull)	**161**
Prince Bismark (Paular ram)	**244**
Princeps	70
Princess	68

	PAGE
Princess Family Shorthorns	160
Prioress	50
Racine	57
Rambouillet Sheep	237
Rams, Care of	288-291
Rarus	71, 101
Ratios of Front Leverage	102, 104, 105
Ratios of Rear Leverage	104-108
Raveloe	57
Ray, Jno. P., Letter from	*243-246*
Rear Leverage in Trotting Action	**107**
Red Letter Registry (Devons)	172
Red Polled Cattle	163-166
Red Polled Group	**164**
Red Wilkes	82
Regulus	61
Reversion, Case of	191, 192
Rich Family Merinos	245
Ringbone	109, 110
Rivers, Wm., Letter from	*281*
Robert J.	80
Robinson Family Merinos	239, 245
Royal Georges, The	66
Royalty (Cleveland Bay stallion)	**35**
Roy Wilkes	80
Running Breeds	9
Running Horses	47
Running Records by Distance	56
Rysdyk's Hambletonian	62, 64, 66, 68, 70, 72, 73, 74, 77, 104, 105, 106
Sable	71
Sable Wilkes	71
Saddle Gaits	58, 60
Saddle Horses	58-60
Saddle Horse Stud Book, rules for entry	*58*
Salvator	56, 57
Sam Booker	58
Sampson	48, 61
Sanborn, H. B., Methods of	*110*
Sanders, J. H.	*10*
Saxon Merinos	238
Scandanavian Horses	34, 90, 91
Select (Guernsey cow)	**131**
Selection for Beef	225
Selection for Draft	99
Selection for Milk	224
Selection for Speed	99-108
Shattuck, L. E., Methods of	*289-290*

	PAGE
Shearing	289, 290, 291
Sheep, Parts of, Named	**234**
Sheep, Selection, Care and Management of	286-291
Sheep, Summary of Part Third	235
Sherman	64
Shetland-pony Stud Book, Rules for entry	*92*
Shetland Pony Group	**91**
Shetlands	90-92
Shorthorns	157-162
Short-wooled Breeds	235
Shropshire Group	**265**
Shropshire Record	*264*
Shropshires	264-266
Signal's Lily Flagg, Butter record of	128, 130
Silesian Merinos	238
Silkwood	80
Simmenthal Cattle	207-209
Simmenthal Group	**209**
Singlefoot	60
Sir Charles (Hereford bull)	**187**
Sir Hugh (Ayrshire bull)	**135**
Sir Peter	62
Sleepy Tom	101
Small Breeds (Swine)	293
Small Yorkshires	317-319
Smetanxa	10, 90
Smiths, Powell and Lamb, Methods of	*225, 226*
Smuggler	101
Snap	48
Solid Color Defined	126
Sources of Saddle-Horse Blood	58
Sources of Trotting Blood	61-64
Southdown Group	**261**
Southdowns	260-263
Sows, Care of	330-334
Spanish Cattle	220
Spavin	109
Spear, Grant W., Secy., Letter from	*309*
Speed Improvement, Cause of	80
Speed, Selection for	99-108
Spiletta	48
Splint	109
Springbok	50
Springer, Jno. G., Secy., Letter from	*296*
Stallion Crown by Records	72, 73, 74, 79
Stallions, Care of	110-113
Stamboul	72, 73
Standard (Cotswold ram)	**276**

	PAGE		PAGE
Standard-Bred defined	82, 83	Thriflon, Phil., Methods of	330, 332
Star Eagle (American Saddle stallion)	59	Todd's Improved Chester-White Record	307
Star Gaited	106	Todd's Improved Chester-Whites	307-308
St. Clair	66, 71	Tom Hal	66
Stericker, R. P., Methods of	111	Tom Ochiltree	50
Stewart, Henry	236, 240	**Tinwald Chieftain** (Clydesdale Stallion)	**25**
St. Julien	70, 78, 101	Trinkett	70
St. Lawrence	63	Tristan	56
Stone, J. L.	264	Trotting Breeds	9
Stubbs, C. E., Secy., Letter from	40	Trotting Records, 1888	68-72
Stump-The-Dealer	58	Trotting Records, 1892	72-80
Success 2nd (Small Yorkshire boar)	**318**	Trotting Records for age, 1888	71-72
Suffolks, Black (Swine)	323	Trotting Records for age, 1892	78-80
Suffolk Color (Horses)	31	True Briton	64
Suffolk Punch	30-33	Turf	61
Suffolk Reds (Cattle)	163	Turf, Field and Farm	52, 56
Suffolks, White (Swine)	324		
Sunol	71, 76, 79, 101, 100, 108	Van Meter's Waxy	58
Suprenaut (French Draft stallion)	**16**	Varnon's Roebuck	58
Sussex Cattle	204-206	Velocity	64
Sussex Group	**205**	Vermont Blackhawk	64, 66, 74
Sweeny	109	**Victoria** (North Wales Black cow)	**182**
Sweepstakes (Todd's Improved Chester Sow)	**308**	Victorias, Curtis	310, 311
Swine, Feeding of	326-328	Victorias, Davis	312, 313
Swine, Selection, Care and Management of	325, 334	Vinette	80
Swine, Summary of Part Fourth	293	Volunteer	70
		Volunteers, The	66
		Von Schluembach, Letter from	207
Tammany (American Thoroughbred stallion)	**55**	**Vulcan** (Cheshire boar)	**315**
Tamworth Swine	301	Warren County Swine	298
Tarentine Sheep	236	Warren, J. B., Letter from	180
Tea Tray	56	Water Ox (Indian Buffalo)	211
Telegraph	71	Waxana	71
Ten Broeck	50, 56, 57	Waxy	71
Terra Cotta	52	Welsh Ponies	93
Terry, T. G.	328	**West Highland Bull**	**216**
Texas	58	**West Highland Cow and Calf**	**218**
Texas Cattle	220, 222	West Highlands	215-219
Texas Steer	**221**	White & Conover, Letter from	309
The Bard (American Thoroughbred)	50, **51**, 52	White, Mrs. Harriet Davis	212
The Trotting Gait	100-108	White Suffolk (Swine)	324
Thibet Shawl Goats	211	White Turk	48
Thompson, S. D., Secy., Letter from	14	Wildair Breed	64
Thoroughbred Blood in Trotter	73	Wildflower	71
Thoroughbred defined	47	Wild Forest Breed	154, 167, 180, 184
Thoroughbreds	47-57	Wilkses, The	66
Thoroughpin	109	Williams, Consul	176
		Williams, C. W.	74
		Windfall (Guernsey cow)	**134**

	PAGE		PAGE
Winslow Wilkes	80	Yorkville Belle	56
Woodbury	64	*Youatt, William*	27, 48, 236, 278, 322
Woodford Mambrino	70	Young Bashaw	64, 66
Wood, Jas., Letter from	207, 208		
Wood's Hambletonians, The	66	Zebu Cattle	210
W. Wood	80		

www.ingramcontent.com/pod-product-compliance
Lightning Source LLC
Chambersburg PA
CBHW031852220426
43663CB00006B/585